A Vision for Girls

A Vision for Girls

Gender, Education, and the Bryn Mawr School

Andrea Hamilton

With a foreword by Helen Lefkowitz Horowitz

The Johns Hopkins University Press
Baltimore and London

The Johns Hopkins University Press

2715 North Charles Street

Baltimore, Maryland 21218-4363

www.press.jhu.edu

Library of Congress Cataloging-in-Publication Data

Hamilton, Andrea, 1966–

  A vision for girls : gender, education, and the Bryn Mawr School /
Andrea Hamilton ; with a foreword by Helen Lefkowitz Horowitz.

    p. cm.

Includes bibliographical references and index.

  ISBN 0-8018-7880-2 (hardcover : alk. paper)

  1. Bryn Mawr School—History.   I. Title.

  LD7251.H324 2004

  371.822′09752′6—dc22   2003018306

A catalog record for this book is available from the British Library.

George Keller, Consulting Editor

This work is not an official or sanctioned history of The Bryn Mawr School. The opinions expressed in this work are those of the author only and do not represent the opinions of The Bryn Mawr School, its trustees, administrators, faculty, alumnae, or students.

Contents

Foreword

"Ought Women to Learn the Alphabet?" asked the New England reformer Thomas Wentworth Higginson, rhetorically, in the middle of the nineteenth century. To him, as to us today, to ask the question is to answer it. Of course, women are to be educated. Higginson, a strong supporter of female education, hoped by the very absurdity of the question to refute all critics. In a fundamental way, however, the question has had a much longer history than Higginson might have imagined. To educate American girls and women in ways beyond the traditional has been a dangerous experiment that has challenged basic notions of female nature and has seemed to threaten the social order. Each new advance has been met by efforts to contain the threat that education posed, and visionary efforts to educate some girls and women have been linked to regressive efforts to deny that education to others.

One such bold venture in female education—the Bryn Mawr School of Baltimore, Maryland—is the subject of Andrea Hamilton's lively and well-researched book. Impelled by important and fascinating founders, school heads, and teachers and by extraordinarily rich archival records, Hamilton undertook a difficult project. She sought to tell the story of the Bryn Mawr School in terms of local and national educational history and broad socioeconomic trends. She determined not to shy away from controversy, from moments of exclusion and conflict. She wanted to weave her story into the larger conversation about girls' education, past and present. Lacking scholarly histories of independent schools for girls to serve as models, she had to carve her own path through the wealth of archival, local historical, and educational materials.

The Bryn Mawr School was unique in its origins. Founded in 1885 in a Southern city whose established white families carried the expectation that its female members should be ornamental as well as useful, the girls' school offered from the outset a rigorous education designed to meet the highest standards of college entrance. The five young Baltimore founders—M. Carey Thomas,

Mary Garrett, Mamie Gwinn, Julia Rogers, and Bessie King—had determination, prestige, and economic means. They created the school at the same time that the Pennsylvania college sharing its name opened, with Thomas as its founding dean. The two Bryn Mawrs based their curricula and pedagogy on a commitment to women's intellectual sameness with men. They saw education as opening opportunity for new lives rather than preparing young women for existing social or domestic roles. The Bryn Mawr School insisted from the outset that students must prepare for the highest standard for college entrance and, to dramatize this aim, made them pass the Bryn Mawr College entrance examination as a requirement of graduation. The college served as a primary source of teachers and school heads, including the brilliant Edith Hamilton, who served as headmistress from 1896 to 1922. Mary Garrett funded scholarships for the school's graduates to attend Bryn Mawr College. Yet this remarkable educational opportunity was not meant for all girls. The school imposed religious and racial restrictions on both its teaching staff and its student body.

Could such a school succeed? Hamilton traces the Bryn Mawr School's difficult passage from its innovative pedagogical and socially narrow beginnings to the present. The arc of the narrative moves from the founders' vision to that of a school adapted to its specific community, responsive to its special forces, and thus able to attract a paying student body and philanthropic gifts. Hamilton chronicles the difficult internal struggle waged by teachers, parents (including fathers), and alumnae to wrest control from remnants of the founding committee. Under new leadership, the school shifted its mission to join the country-day school movement in the first half of the twentieth century and moved from an urban site to a suburban-style campus. Partially reversing itself in the second half of the century, the school sought to hold on to its elite base, attract African American students, and foster engagement with the wider world of political and social issues and causes. In both moments the Bryn Mawr School redefined itself and marketed itself anew to students, parents, and donors.

In Hamilton's telling, the story of the Bryn Mawr School moves beyond its local particulars to illumine much about the history of American education and life. In this account she gives us no simple story of progress. Rather, we confront opportunity and restriction, possibilities and constraints, abstract ideals and local realities. The importance of Hamilton's contribution is that she never loses sight of the complexity of the school and its relation to society. Her history of the Bryn Mawr School helps us understand aspects of the unique position held by American women in national social, intellectual, and cultural life. At the same time it reminds us of the shadows cast by discrimination and of the complicated way that race, religion, and class thread their way through educational institutions. By placing the Bryn Mawr School in the larger frame of girls' education, this book shows the challenges that educational change has posed to notions of female nature and to a social order riven by deep divisions.

Helen Lefkowitz Horowitz

Preface

When I was a graduate student in American history at Tulane University, my advisor, Wilfred McClay, told me about a girls' school that he thought had a fascinating and historically significant past. I listened and saw the possibilities. A history of the Bryn Mawr School, founded in 1885 in Baltimore, Maryland, could explore issues of relevance to scholars, to educators, and to anyone more generally interested in girls' education today.

Historians of education and of women have documented the history of public education, which included girls from the beginning, and of innovations in women's education, including the development of female academies in the antebellum period and women's increasing presence in the realm of higher education in the postbellum period. And, in recent decades, debates about the merits of single-sex education for girls have proliferated both in scholarly venues and in the popular media. But scholarly studies of schools for girls (as opposed to colleges for women) are scarce. The Bryn Mawr School had a rich tradition of educating young women, association with famous personages, and relatively unexplored archives. If I could write a history of the Bryn Mawr School—not an insiders' institutional history that detailed all aspects of the school, but a history that connected key elements of the school's development to the history of women and education—I could make a contribution to our understanding of girls' education in the United States.

I made my first visit to the Bryn Mawr School in the spring of 1995, and everything I encountered during my days at the school convinced me that I had chosen the right topic. The people at Bryn Mawr were warm and helpful. I met with administrators and teachers, visited classes, and ate in the school cafeteria. The school archivist loaned me a key to the library so that I could come and go as I pleased. In the Bryn Mawr School's archives, I discovered early correspondence between the school's founders and headmistresses and teachers and uncatalogued boxes of school brochures, yearbooks, and publications, as well as scrapbooks, newspaper clippings, and magazine articles pertaining to the school and its history.

As is often the case, the nature of the sources was idiosyncratic. Although the correspondence between founder M. Carey Thomas and Headmistress Edith Hamilton was extensive, information about the school's other headmistresses and their administrations at the Bryn Mawr School was unfortunately scarce. Many letters and documents in the archives were undated or unsigned. When I felt reasonably certain that I could derive the approximate date or author from an incompletely referenced source, I used the source and noted it as "unreferenced" or "unsigned" in the endnotes. In chapter 3, for example, I reconstructed a correspondence between Headmistress Amy Kelly (who was on sabbatical in Europe) and school administrators Elizabeth Thomas and Margaret Hamilton (residing in Baltimore) from the early 1930s. Although many of the letters had no signatures, the sequence of dates and issues discussed in the correspondence made their authorship apparent. Rosamund Randall Beirne's account of the Bryn Mawr School's history, although not an academic study, occasionally helped me reconstruct details.[1] (For the record, neither Edith nor Margaret Hamilton is any relation to me.)

School records of enrollments, student histories, and curriculum for many decades was incomplete and, sometimes, nonexistent, or at least not available to me. I was given access to the minutes of Bryn Mawr board meetings for some years but not for others. It is my understanding that some sensitive papers (such as records of the turmoil at Bryn Mawr as the school debated desegregation in the 1950s and early 1960s) had been removed from the archives before I arrived. Conflicts over the contents of my manuscript prevented me from conducting interviews with members of the Bryn Mawr School community as I would have liked. Nevertheless, the school's archives offered the possibility of a rich reflection on the development of the institution within the larger contexts of educational and women's history.

I left Baltimore impressed with the Bryn Mawr School that I had met, both in person and in the archives. My hope is that my book reflects that admiration and that it grants the school new prominence as a historically significant institution in the education of girls. I have tried to convey the Bryn Mawr School's history in a manner accessible and helpful to a broad audience interested in the history of education and of women.

All historians have thanks to give to those who helped them translate their evidence and ideas onto paper, but my appreciation is particularly heartfelt because, without the help of many, this book would never have been published. The story of the Bryn Mawr School's changing attitudes toward this book has been chronicled in the *Baltimore Sun*, the *Chronicle of Higher Education*, and elsewhere, but I leave it to others to interpret the school's actions.[2] My thanks to Mike Bowler of the *Baltimore Sun* for listening to my story and taking it seriously and to Jennifer Ruark at the *Chronicle of Higher Education* for spreading the story to a broader academic audience. I appreciate their insight, sensitivity, and keen perception of the issues at stake. Laura Kalman, professor of history at the University of California, Santa Barbara, organized a letter of petition to the Bryn Mawr School urging the institution to drop its objections to the publication of my manuscript. I am grateful to the more than 140 historians and archivists who signed the letter, and I remain in awe of Professor Kalman's active conviction in academic freedom that led her to mobilize scholars for an unknown person like me. Finally, I appreciate those members of the Bryn Mawr School community who supported me and reminded their institution of its tradition of encouraging intellectual freedom.

Wilfred McClay has been a wonderful teacher and adviser. He fought for me and this book, and he continued to believe in my potential even when it looked like this book would never be published. He is a true friend.

When the dust settled, I still faced the task of turning a draft manuscript into one ready for publication. Thanks to the Johns Hopkins University Press for editorial guidance.

My husband, Scott Wendorf, has worked as hard as I have to make this book a reality, and he means everything to me.

A Vision for Girls

Introduction

> Given two bridge-builders, a man and a woman, given a certain bridge to
> be built, and given as always the unchangeable laws of mechanics . . . it is
> simply inconceivable that the preliminary instruction given to the two
> bridge-builders should differ in quantity, quality, or method of presenta-
> tion because while the bridge is building one will wear knickerbockers
> and the other a rainy-day skirt.
>
> — M. CAREY THOMAS,
> "EDUCATION FOR WOMEN AND FOR MEN"

For M. Carey Thomas, the pioneering educator of the late nineteenth and early
twentieth centuries, the human mind had no gender. Women and men had fulfilled different social roles throughout the ages, but they ought, in her view, to
have identical educational opportunities. From Thomas's perspective, education
designed for women's supposed propensities lacked rigor and meaningful content and limited women intellectually and in later life. Thomas would devote
her career and her life at Bryn Mawr College to proving her exceptional ideas
about the nature of women and the education they deserved. Although Thomas
is best known for her work at Bryn Mawr College, her association with another
educational institution—the subject of this study—illustrates the depths of her
commitment to changing the shape of female education.

Infused with a sense of mission and experimentation, Thomas and four
friends established the Bryn Mawr School, a private college-preparatory school
for girls in Baltimore, Maryland, in the 1880s. The school, which still thrives
today, would give them an arena for implementing their ideas about the relationship between education and the roles of women in society. Because of the
school's exceptional commitment to challenging how most Americans concep-

tualized the role of gender in the education of girls, the history of the Bryn Mawr School is particularly interesting to those concerned with the history of women's education. For the founders, the issue was simple: girls deserved an education just like that of boys in quality, quantity, and scope. Any concessions to supposed female propensities were anathema.

Gender lay at the heart of the Bryn Mawr School, its goals, and its hopes for its students from its conception. From the very beginnings of our nation, we have thought about education in gendered terms, and educators, politicians, and families have debated and formulated educational policy and choices in light of it. The expectation that girls and boys would develop into women and men who would fill different roles in society has in large part shaped their education. In public schools, the arena in which the vast majority of our children have been and continue to be educated, girls and boys have sat side by side and received largely the same instruction. Until recently, however, the general expectation—of the schools, their students and their families, and the larger society—was that boys would assume roles in the public realm, while girls' primary identities would be derived from their roles in the domestic sphere, with employment opportunities limited primarily to such suitably "female" occupations as teaching, nursing, social work, or clerical work. Such expectations have shaped the nature and outcomes of education for girls and boys.

And so, in Baltimore in the 1880s, it is not surprising that a group of young women committed to changing the status of women in late-nineteenth-century America focused on education as the arena for their reform efforts. M. Carey Thomas (who would become president of Bryn Mawr College and one of the great educational leaders of the late nineteenth and early twentieth centuries) and Mary Elizabeth Garrett (heir to the Baltimore and Ohio Railroad fortune and a dedicated philanthropist and reformer) and their supporters astutely linked their desire to change the status of women to a new conception of how and why girls should be educated. The Bryn Mawr School reflected their exceptional vision for how a new kind of girls' education might help transform how people thought about women and their place in society.

The founders of the Bryn Mawr School planned a model institution intended in part to inspire women in other cities to establish similar schools for girls. The early Bryn Mawr established standards for academic achievement, as well as for improvements of female health, unprecedented in the history of girls' education. From its outset, the school offered education identical to that of the best boys' schools, and its mission was to secure for its students access to the best of the colleges and universities opening to women in the late nineteenth century. The founders designed the school specifically as a feeder institution to Bryn Mawr College, for which it was named. Under Thomas's direction, Bryn Mawr College had modeled itself on the most rigorous institutions for men, in contrast to other women's colleges, such as Vassar and Wellesley, which initially took shape along the lines of older seminaries offering education linked to notions of women's special nature. Thomas had similarly ambitious plans for the girls' school.[1] The Bryn Mawr School stands as the first exclusively college-preparatory school for girls in the United States, committed to preparing its students for the highest level of education available.

Like all institutions, the Bryn Mawr School has a particular past that can teach us much about the individuals, ideals, events, and times that created it and much about the nature of institutions and the realities they face. While the founders dreamed of what they could accomplish through education, girls and their families often had their own ideas about the kind of education they wanted and needed. Popular expectations and demands inevitably influenced the school from its earliest days, and, as the decades passed, changing times exerted their influence, too. Throughout the twentieth century, the Bryn Mawr School struggled to be true to its founding mission. But the school also responded to its community of support and came to reflect the ideals and aspirations of its students and their families. The school became a product of the visions of its founders and of a host of administrators, teachers, parents, and students who nourished and sustained it. Its history highlights how individuals redefined and adapted their school and the education it offered to changing circumstances. Indeed, as the school adapted to changing times and expectations, it reflected not only its historical roots but also changing conceptions about women and their education in modern America.

The history of the Bryn Mawr School reflects changing expectations for women in the late nineteenth and twentieth centuries and the evolution of the education deemed most appropriate for girls. This book is organized chronologically. Chapter 1 explores the people and ideas behind the school's founding, particularly what I call the founders' "vision," the school's mission to create a new model for the education of girls. The difficulties of translating the founders' high ideals into a working institution are discussed in chapter 2; this problem, faced by all schools, was more intense because of the particular vision and personalities of its early leaders. Edith Hamilton, who served as the Bryn Mawr School's headmistress for more than two decades before she became famous for her studies of classical mythology, figures prominently during this period of the school's history.

Although founders Thomas and Garrett and Headmistress Hamilton struggled to implement the founder's educational vision and establish the institution in Baltimore in the 1890s and the first two decades of the twentieth centuries, later administrators faced continuing challenges in adapting the school to the needs of the Baltimore community, recruiting sufficient students, and ensuring the institution's financial viability. Chapter 3 traces how the growth of Baltimore suburbs and the popularity of the new country-day model of education, as well as the Great Depression, forced the Bryn Mawr School to adapt its founding vision to the demands of its environment in the 1920s, 1930s, and 1940s. Chapter 4 focuses on the school's embrace of the "country-day" model of education in the context of the mid-twentieth century.

The final two chapters explore the substantial changes at the school in the latter decades of the twentieth century. Chapter 5 addresses the effect of the civil rights movement on Bryn Mawr and the school's ongoing attempts to diversify and bring the "real world" to its students in the 1980s and early 1990s. In chapter 6 the focus is specifically on the Bryn Mawr School as a single-sex institution. Although always for "girls only," in the 1980s the school consciously revisited and reasserted its relationship to gender and society. This final chapter examines the relationship between the school's history and the literature on female "difference," as promoted by the work of scholars such as Carol Gilligan, and the heightened interest in single-sex education in recent years.

The history of the Bryn Mawr School is both unique and reflective—the story of a single institution and yet also a study of much larger educational phenomena. Understanding the fabric of women's past experiences, as well as identifying the best educational environments for girls (and boys, too), demands that we enhance our understanding of the development of single-sex schools. The history of the Bryn Mawr School—one particularly significant institution—contributes to that larger goal. The history of the Bryn Mawr School illustrates the continually changing visions of education for girls in America.

CHAPTER ONE

The Bryn Mawr Vision
Imagining a Model School

> When [the founders of the Bryn Mawr School] grew up in Baltimore and
> indeed even when the Bryn Mawr School opened in 1885, no school in
> Baltimore which admitted girls prepared for any college, and no
> Baltimore girl, as far as they knew, had ever gone to college. No girls'
> school included Latin, Greek, or laboratory science in its school course.
> — M. CAREY THOMAS,
> "A BRIEF ACCOUNT OF THE FOUNDING AND
> EARLY YEARS OF THE BRYN MAWR SCHOOL," 1931

Setting the Stage, I: Women's Education in Nineteenth-Century America

The story of the Bryn Mawr School began when several affluent women evaluated the status of their sex in the late nineteenth century and decided to revolutionize that status through a new approach to women's education. They linked their desire to change the position of women to a new conception of how and why girls should be educated. In the founding of a model school for girls, they hoped to transform the lives not only of a few schoolgirls but of women nationally.

Debates and experiments in "How?" and "For what?" to educate women had a venerable tradition in American history. In the early republic, many elite Americans concluded that providing young women with some form of education was crucial to the survival of the emerging nation precisely because, more than anyone else in society, mothers were entrusted with raising children. In the fragile new United States, the duty of child rearing took on heightened significance when "republican mothers" were viewed as training future citizens. These citizens would sustain the new nation and its republican form of government, which was, indeed, dependent on the virtue of its inhabitants. Thus combined, anxiety about the viability of the new nation and a growing cultural recognition of mothers' influence over their children provided new imperatives for society to concern itself with the education of its female citizens.[1]

Powerful and related arguments for society's vested interest in female education evolved simultaneously. In addition to the secular impulses of Republican Motherhood, religious impulses, particularly in response to the Second Great Awakening of the late eighteenth and early nineteenth centuries, stressed the importance of women's influence in society, this time as good Christians who nurtured their families, communities, and, indeed, the entire nation. Educating godly women as godly wives, mothers, and teachers could be the means of spreading Christian virtue across the country. By the early nineteenth century, as a rapidly increasing number of cities and states established common schools to prepare children of both sexes for life in the expanding, industrializing nation, they required a growing supply of teachers. Women—who were believed to be "natural" teachers for children (an outgrowth of their "natural" roles as mothers), who had the potential to civilize and raise the moral level of the country, and who could, not incidentally, be employed for lower wages than their male counterparts (as their incomes were considered only supplemental to family resources)—seemed the ideal candidates to staff the new schools. And if women were to be teachers, they needed improved education themselves.[2]

Secular and religious ideas, along with a healthy dose of pragmatism, combined to provide new witness to the advantages—even social necessity—of educating women in the early nineteenth century. In response to this receptive climate in the pre–Civil War period, new female academies and seminaries (the latter term adopted by schools such as Mt. Holyoke to connote their seriousness of purpose, particularly in teacher training) multiplied, first in the Northeast and subsequently in the South and West. These female educational institutions, which became the dominant mechanism for women's education beyond common schools, varied greatly in their quality and scope. Serving the daughters of the upper classes and particularly the emerging middle classes, some concentrated primarily on cultivating traditional female "accomplishments," while others made strides in offering advanced education and serious teacher preparation. As critics and reformers alike observed, the vast majority were plagued with problems such as meager funding, poorly trained teachers, haphazard courses of study, and generally low academic standards. Nevertheless, these female academies and seminaries rapidly became important places for teacher training and also employment for single, educated women.[3]

Traditionally, the female academy movement is associated with three influential figures. Emma Willard, Catharine Beecher, and Mary Lyon, with distinctly different personalities and ideals, concurred on the pivotal importance of improving women's educational opportunities. Emma Willard is best known for the high-quality female academy she established in Troy, New York, in 1821, which offered some of the most rigorous education then available to several generations of young women. (Her Troy Seminary evolved into the present Emma Willard School, a prestigious girls' college-preparatory school that, like the Bryn Mawr School, is today a prominent member of the National Coalition of Girls' Schools.) Drawing on the tradition of Republican Motherhood, Willard sought state funding for female education incorporating some of the elements of the male collegiate liberal arts curriculum. She argued that the well-being of the nation required educated mothers and, by extension, teachers.

Catharine Beecher, the eldest daughter of the prominent Beecher family, founded female seminaries in Hartford and Cincinnati, but her greatest influence lay in her widely disseminated writings, which included *A Treatise on Domestic Economy* (1841), *The Duty of American Women to Their Country* (1845), and *The American Woman's Home* (1869), authored with her sister Harriet Beecher Stowe. These books expounded upon the duties and virtues of female domesticity, and they highlighted the necessity of female education and the value of teacher training for women. Beecher championed female teachers as the key to simultaneously educating, civilizing, and Christianizing the growing United States.[4]

Mary Lyon and her Holyoke Seminary, which opened in South Hadley, Massachusetts, in 1837, epitomized a very different vision of education for young women and ultimately had the most direct impact on the shaping of women's colleges later in the century. Dedicated to training young women from modest backgrounds (in contrast to the fashionable clientele patronizing Beecher's seminaries and many of the other academies), Lyon developed a system of education devoted to empowering women to serve society as Christian teachers with missionary spirit. With its system of highly routinized schedules, shared domestic work, close teacher-student mentoring, and religious intensity, Mount Holyoke became a model for many other female seminaries—often established by its graduates, at least 70 percent of whom became teachers. After the Civil War, the earliest women's colleges looked to Mount Holyoke for guidance; indeed, the school trained many of their future educators, including Vassar's and Wellesley's first heads.[5]

Despite their differences, Willard, Beecher, and Lyon shared with other pioneers of women's education common grounding in two distinct areas: belief in female difference or women's special nature stemming from their roles in the domestic realm and promotion of the social expediency or usefulness of educating women so they might use their unique traits to the benefit of society. Clearly, they defined themselves and their arguments within the terms of the middle-class separate spheres ideology accepted by most Americans—female and male—of their day. These women made no claims to the inherent rights of women to an education and few appeals to the essential similarities of the sexes, claims and appeals that later reformers, such as Elizabeth Cady Stanton in the mid-nineteenth century and the founders of the Bryn Mawr School in the late nineteenth century, would eventually bring to the debate. Their arguments for the enhancement of women's education never challenged the primacy of men in the public world. Willard, for example, specified that women's fathers, brothers, and husbands were their "natural guardians" and "rulers" and concluded that, because women's natural roles were in the home, "public speaking forms no part of female education." Likewise, Beecher denounced "purely intellectual" education for women, opposed the opening of male institutions of higher learning to women, criticized women's participation in the business world, and denounced the movement for women's suffrage.

As many historians have noted, middle-class women successfully expanded the boundaries of the female sphere, redefining it to allow women enhanced opportunities for education, experience, and employment beyond the strict confines of home. And yet that very rhetoric that endowed women with a sense of mission and a rationale for acting on their special natures simultaneously reinforced deeply rooted beliefs in women's difference, which had been used to exclude women from education and activity in the public realm in the first place. Ironically, this use of the notion of female "difference" to achieve new opportunities for women proved one of the key elements of women's education that would, decades later, galvanize the founders of the Bryn Mawr School to promote a new kind of education for girls.[6]

Advances in female education were not confined to the North and Midwest in the early nineteenth century. In the antebellum South, educating girls was an established tradition among elite families. Female seminaries and "colleges," many of which incorporated strong academic standards with the traditional emphases on feminine accomplishments, flourished in the Old South. As in other regions, separate spheres ideology, as well as religious impulses, motivated the establishment of many schools. Unlike many northern and midwestern academies, however, southern female academies never intended to prepare their students for employment. As Christie Ann Farnham argued in *The Education of the Southern Belle*, education for elite white women was seen as a means of enhancing their gentility and emphasizing their position within the social order. In this context, female education reinforced the status quo in the Old South. Southern academies offered many young women quality education that mirrored the rigor of much male education. But the South's defeat in the Civil War—and the subsequent romantization of the southern lady—caused female education in the South to lag behind the advances in women's education apparent in other regions in the postbellum period.[7]

Both the female academy movement and the general expansion of public common schools (which spread literacy and rudimentary education to increasing numbers of girls and boys across the country) increased women's access to education in the first half of the nineteenth century. The post–Civil War period saw dramatic expansions in female education, particularly at the more advanced levels. Indeed, many interrelated innovations and trends—among them the development of the public high school, the establishment of the first true colleges for women, the growth of coeducation in higher education, and increasing employment opportunities for women, both in the rising number of educational institutions and in the professions gradually opening to women—transformed the educational landscape. In this environment, the prominence of female seminaries faded as new institutions evolved to fit the perceived educational needs of women. And society's understanding of the relationships among women, education, and female roles in society would face complex challenges in the face of new and broader opportunities available to women.

Female academies and seminaries had once offered the most advanced education available to women, but the late nineteenth century saw the development of the high school as an institution distinct from either the common schools below it or the colleges and universities above it. In contrast to older forms of education beyond the common school, which had generally been single sex, coeducation dominated American public high schools. Some older eastern and southern cities maintained sex-segregated school systems and high schools (among them Baltimore, Boston, New York, Philadelphia, Charleston, and New Orleans), but coeducation was overwhelmingly the norm: only 12 of 628 cities surveyed by the U.S. Commission of Education in 1889 had public single-sex schools.[8]

As David Tyack and Elizabeth Hansot argue in their history of coeducation in American public schools, "middle-class parents of girls were among the high schools' most ardent supporters, and girls from such families could arguably be seen as the mainstay of the institution." At a time when only a very small percentage of Americans received formal education beyond the common school—in 1890, only 3.5 percent of American seventeen-year-olds had graduated from secondary schools (and only 14% of those were preparing for higher education)—girls disproportionately dominated the high school. Indeed, the U.S. Commission of Education reported that, in the nation's ten largest cities, three-fourths of the high school students were girls. Across the country overall, 57 percent of high school students and 65 percent of high school graduates were girls. Significantly, girls not only attended high school in greater numbers, they also outperformed boys—earning higher grades and winning more competitions, as well as maintaining better attendance and graduation records.[9]

Did girls' success in high schools mark a real change in attitudes toward female education and its relationship to women's places in society? Apparently, not many individuals perceived girls' achievements in this way; their constant arguments to the contrary are evidence that they did not want to think that the new institutions offering women more advanced education were altering traditional female roles significantly. Recognition of education's potential to prepare women for employment that might prove necessary at some point in their lives continued to grow and, as in the older female seminaries, the relationship between women's education and teacher training remained particularly strong. High schools frequently rationalized their mission in terms of familiar arguments of the social expediency of educating girls as essential to creating a teaching force for the nation's schools. Indeed, many high schools did train large numbers of their students to this end: in Saint Louis in 1900, for example, more than 46 percent of female high-school seniors were in the normal course of study. Furthermore, high schools (in addition to common schools) became major employers of women: in 1890, women made up 58 percent of high school teachers. Some public high schools did prepare some of their graduates for further education, particularly in teacher-training normal schools at state colleges and universities. Although many parents and students alike appreciated the potential for teaching as respectable employment for single women, they were apparently equally comfortable with the notion of high schools simply as good places for training girls for what they assumed to be their most desirable and expected future roles: those of traditional wives and mothers.[10]

In her history of higher education for women, Barbara Solomon estimates that, from 1870 to 1900, the number of women in higher education increased about eight times, from around 11,000 to 85,000. Concurrently, female students as a percentage of the total student population in colleges and universities rose from about 21 percent to 35 percent. The range of institutions opening to women was broad—encompassing public and private, coeducational and single-sex settings—although, significantly, women did not necessarily enjoy the same status as their male counterparts within many schools. Some state universities began accepting women by midcentury (e.g., Iowa in 1855; Wisconsin in 1867; Kansas, Indiana, and Minnesota in 1869), while many southern states alternatively opened separate institutions for women (such as Mississippi State College for Women in 1885). An increasing variety of private institutions were coeducational, from small religious colleges modeled after Oberlin (which had admitted women at its founding in 1833) to newly founded research universities such as Cornell University (1868), Boston University (1873), and the University of Chicago (1892). New colleges devoted exclusively to training women included Vassar (1865), Wellesley and Smith (1875), and Bryn Mawr (1884). "Coordinate" colleges, which experimented with creating female divisions within or related to established male universities—such as Radcliffe-Harvard, Barnard-Columbia, and the southern Sophie Newcomb–Tulane University—offered an alternative pattern to either coeducation or strict segregation of female students and their institutions.[11]

As at the precollegiate level, coeducation was clearly becoming the norm in higher education: in 1890, 43 percent of institutions of higher education were coeducational versus 20 percent for women only, a trend that would accelerate in the twentieth century.[12] Despite the predominance of coeducation (at both the precollegiate and collegiate levels), the women's colleges established in the late nineteenth century would exert an influence greater than their numbers might suggest. Particularly the northeastern women's colleges—the "Seven Sisters" of Vassar, Wellesley, Smith, Mount Holyoke, Radcliffe, Barnard, and Bryn Mawr Colleges—became truly national institutions, training highly influential generations of women and serving as models for female education in many settings and locations. Opportunities for higher education for women in the South lagged behind other regions, largely because devotion to ideals of southern womanhood, as well as poverty, flourished in the wake of the defeat of the Confederacy. Only a few of the southern female "colleges" in the late nineteenth century maintained academic standards sufficient to claim the title fairly.[13]

Within the expanding landscape of higher education for women in the late nineteenth century, the development of the northeastern women's colleges proved the most direct catalyst for the establishment of new kinds of schools for girls like the Bryn Mawr School. The new women's colleges faced the reality that very few young women had adequate academic preparation to undertake true college-level work. Vassar (the first to open in 1865) and Wellesley (which followed in 1875) were forced to run preparatory departments for the ill-prepared students they had to accept in order to fill their classrooms. When first dean and then president of Bryn Mawr College M. Carey Thomas insisted that her school for women would maintain the highest standards of any colleges open to women (or, for that matter, men), she faced essentially the same dilemma: how to maintain strict admissions standards and create a rigorous higher education for women when girls' precollegiate education was inadequate?

Private girls' schools, which had traditionally educated the daughters of the well-to-do who were most likely to be interested in further education, often devoted significant time to female "accomplishments," sometimes at the expense of thorough academic training. Public high schools—which educated a much broader segment of the population, many of whom did not plan to pursue higher education, at least not at the more exclusive private colleges and universities—seemed more committed to normal school training for girls than to college preparation, at least in the nineteenth century. And so new institutions evolved to prepare girls for the higher education newly open to them. Indeed, private girls' schools (both new ones and older institutions adapting to the changing demands of the day) would train a significant majority of the students at the nation's most prestigious women's colleges in the late nineteenth and early twentieth centuries. At Bryn Mawr College, for example, 73 percent of students in the classes of 1889–93 had been trained at private schools (in contrast to only 7% trained at public high schools and the remainder either privately tutored or transferring from other colleges). In the classes of 1894–98, 78 percent of Bryn Mawr College students were graduates of private schools, with 17 percent graduates of high schools.[14]

In the late nineteenth century, more girls and young women were attending high schools, colleges, and universities than ever before. But obviously not everybody—neither educators nor families nor students—agreed on how and why women should be educated. In this time of rapid growth and change in the educational opportunities open to female students, the stage was set for new kinds of schools to explore the possibilities.

Setting the Stage, II: Five Women in Baltimore

In an environment still shaped by Victorian ideals about the inherently different natures of women and men and yet also characterized by a growing range of new opportunities for women and concurrent ambiguity about how, why, and for what women should be educated, some individuals would seize the opportunity to rethink traditional attitudes—toward women, their education, and their role in society. In these uncertain decades of the late nineteenth century, five women in Baltimore gathered and began exploring how they might reshape women's education—and through it, women's lives and opportunities far beyond their limited years of formal schooling. An environment receptive to many changing notions about women and the exact nature of their place in society allowed this group of individuals and the institution they founded to pioneer a new way. Together these women would ponder critical questions and challenge a host of prevailing assumptions about the nature of women and the kind of education they deserved. They would devise a blueprint for a new kind of school that would offer opportunities to girls that they themselves had never known and that they believed no other girls had experienced. These five women would envision a model school they hoped would challenge and change prevailing perceptions about the ideal education for girls. The cogency and uniqueness of that vision would give rise to the Bryn Mawr School, an institution they dreamed would help revolutionize, on a national scale, the landscape of women's education and transform prevailing perceptions of what it meant to be a woman in American society.

Baltimore in the last quarter of the nineteenth century was, in many ways, typical of the modern urban landscape. The city was mired in the problems common to many American cities experiencing rapid industrialization and growth: dire poverty and overcrowding, poor sanitation and living conditions, frequent epidemics and high mortality rates, a dearth of crucial city services, rule by political "bosses" and machines, and a maldistribution of wealth. The harsh world of Baltimore's poor, particularly its immigrant and African American communities, contrasted starkly with the privileged existence of its wealthy elite. Baltimore's pressing urban problems would continue for decades, but by the late nineteenth century, some individuals were taking a more active interest in the conditions of their city. Evidencing an impulse that marked the beginnings of an urban progressivism that would grow in the early decades of the twentieth century, some socially prominent men—joined by a smaller number of women—began laying plans for enhancing their city. Their diverse efforts would include reforming Baltimore government, extending city services for the poor, improving sanitation, establishing better public schools, increasing decent housing, and generally beautifying the urban landscape.[15]

In addition to—or sometimes instead of—focusing on the dire urban problems plaguing the city, some Baltimoreans centered their efforts on enhancing the city's cultural life. Perceiving their city as culturally inferior to leading northern cities, they pledged to enhance the intellectual and artistic life of Baltimore until it rivaled the best in the nation. Their efforts resulted in an impressive amount of institution building, ranging from new schools and libraries to a music institute, symphony orchestra, and art gallery. Notably, among the aspirations of Baltimoreans was the establishment of a truly great educational institution that would both educate its citizens and bring prestige to the city. The drive to create such a research university resulted in the Johns Hopkins University, established in 1876.[16] With the support of a core group of Baltimore citizens, the new university flourished, undeniably elevating the intellectual life of the city as its supporters had hoped. But Johns Hopkins University offered an education for men only.

That fact concerned some Baltimore residents—though certainly not enough to convince the university to admit women. With the support of a core group of Baltimoreans, large numbers of them women, the Baltimore Annual Conference of the Methodist Episcopal Church opened the Woman's College of Baltimore City (later Goucher College) in 1888. From the beginning, the Woman's College committed to maintain college-level standards, but given the dearth of institutions (in Baltimore or in the South from which it hoped to draw) adequately preparing girls for higher education, the Woman's College compromised. Like other women's colleges (including Vassar and Wellesley) before it, the Woman's College of Baltimore opened a preparatory department. In 1888–89, 43 percent of the college's students were classified as "special" students, exempted from entrance examinations and taking only a few courses, primarily in art, music, or education. For this reason, the Woman's College did not satisfy everyone as a remedy to the state of women's education in Baltimore. As Dr. Lilian Welsh, longtime professor of physiology and hygiene and head of the department of physical education, remarked in 1912, "Until shortly before this time Miss [M. Carey] Thomas had no particular liking for Goucher College. Her standards for the education of women were high and unless a college offering advanced opportunities for women measured up to her ideals, she treated it with scant courtesy."[17]

The quality of female education in Baltimore and far beyond prompted five single young women to imagine the possibilities of a new kind of educational institution for girls, an innovative school that would stretch the limits of what was currently thought possible for girls by providing them with a rigorous college-preparatory course of study equal to that expected of boys preparing for the country's best universities. Despite varied educational backgrounds, Martha Carey Thomas, Mary Elizabeth Garrett, Mary Mackall Gwinn, Elizabeth Tabor King, and Julia Rebecca Rogers shared a commitment to the life of the mind, the promise of education, and the rights of women to pursue both. Summoning the courage to challenge currently acceptable actions and education for women (and undoubtedly bolstered by their combination of social position, family support, and substantial financial resources, which gave them significantly more freedom to act upon their unconventional ideas than less-privileged women would have enjoyed), these young friends pooled their energy and imagination to envision a new kind of school that might revolutionize how the education of girls was viewed not only in Baltimore but across the country.

M. Carey Thomas would eventually achieve by far the most fame of the group as president of Bryn Mawr College and an outspoken leader in the world of education. Growing up the eldest daughter of a large Quaker family—in a home infused with evangelical sentiment, immersed in a world of benevolent activities, and committed to education for children of both sexes—Thomas enjoyed educational opportunities far beyond those of most men, let alone women, of her day. After graduating first from a Quaker girls' boarding school and then from the newly opened coeducational Cornell University, Thomas returned home to Baltimore to pursue her dream of graduate study at the recently established Johns Hopkins University. Despite the fact that Hopkins was intended for men only, the university—clearly influenced by Thomas's father, who was a university trustee and a friend of President Daniel Coit Gilman—permitted

Thomas to begin graduate study in 1877. Although Thomas would be allowed to study with university professors, take examinations, and become a degree candidate, her gender barred her from attending any seminars with male students. When Thomas entered the university, attempting a difficult course of study in philology and Greek, it was without the support or companionship of fellow students.

These circumstances surrounding what was at the time an anomalous undertaking at Hopkins left her generally discouraged and confused, isolated and uncomfortable in the all-male environment at Hopkins and ill at ease residing with her family. They were extremely supportive of her educational pursuits but embraced an evangelical mindset at odds with Thomas's own growing skepticism. Increasingly, Thomas found the solace and support she craved through the friendship of other young women. Eventually, Thomas, accompanied by her friend Mamie Gwinn, pursued graduate work first in Leipzig, Germany, and then in Zurich, Switzerland, where, in 1882, she received her doctoral degree, *summa cum laude*. She returned to the United States determined to put her education to use—she hoped at the newly forming Quaker women's college Bryn Mawr (where, again with the help of male relatives sitting on the school's board, she would become dean and then president).[18]

While Thomas had academic training and connections to the larger world of higher education, Mary Garrett provided the finances to underwrite the friends' educational venture. Garrett was the daughter of Baltimore and Ohio Railroad President John Work Garrett, one of the wealthiest and most powerful men of his day. John Garrett was part of the same group of leading businessmen as Johns Hopkins—benefactor of the university that bears his name—and enjoyed strong connections to the political bosses of Maryland and to the Democratic party. In contrast to Thomas's middle-class Quaker background, Mary Garrett's lifestyle was typical of the nation's wealthiest families, modeled on the European aristocracy, and characterized by lavish homes and country estates, rounds of elaborate social events, and extensive travel abroad. Upon his death in 1884, John Work Garrett left a fortune of 5.6 million dollars (the largest estate of his generation of extremely wealthy Baltimore men), and Mary inherited one-third of it.[19]

Mary Garrett shared Thomas's passion for learning and her commitment to acting upon it. Although Garrett herself had not attended college, travel had exposed her widely to European art and culture. At the time she became acquainted with Thomas, she was studying for the Harvard examination, which, while it would not lead to admission to the university for a woman, would attest to her educational achievements. Garrett clearly had intelligence and determination.

Of his favorite child, John Garrett said, "If the boys were only like Mary, what a satisfaction it would be to me. I have often wished in these last few years that Mary was a boy. I know she could carry on my work after I am gone."[20] But Mary was not a boy, and that meant that her opportunities to use her intellect and enthusiasm were limited. Although fighting illness and depression throughout much of her life—which doctors by the 1890s attributed to her unmarried state—Garrett devoted her energy and her money to a range of causes, from woman's suffrage to enhancing the educational opportunities for girls and women. Notably, Garrett's financial support enabled the Johns Hopkins University to establish its medical school and ensured that the medical school would admit female students. Along with Thomas, Garrett—independent and wealthy in her own right after her father's death in 1884—would play the most critical role in launching and sustaining their ambitious education project in Baltimore. While Thomas's primary focus never strayed from her work at Bryn Mawr College, Mary Garrett—infused with a sense of responsibility to use her fortune to further worthy causes—poured all her energy into their new school.[21]

Although they ultimately played a less formative role in the establishment and particularly the early management of their joint venture, three other young women shared in the friendship and plans taking shape in the early 1880s. Mary "Mamie" Gwinn also came from a prominent family. Her grandfather had been a U.S. senator and ambassador, and her father, a Johns Hopkins University trustee like both Thomas's and Garrett's, was Maryland's attorney general. Gwinn was educated extensively at home, including broad exposure to music, theater, and the arts, and her intellectual attainments equaled those of Thomas. Gwinn accompanied Thomas abroad in her pursuit of a doctorate degree and resided with her at Bryn Mawr College during the formative years of the model school, and her influence on both Thomas and their girls' school was substantial. Gwinn eventually earned a Ph.D. at Bryn Mawr College in 1888 and taught at the college until the early twentieth century. Julia Rogers (Mary Garrett's close companion) and Elizabeth "Bessie" King (Thomas's cousin and childhood friend, whose Quaker father served on the boards of Hopkins, Haverford College, and eventually Bryn Mawr College)—although neither would play a prominent role in the model school beyond its earliest years—completed the circle of friends.[22]

Designating themselves the "Friday Evening," these five single women created a club devoted to shared literary endeavors (such as a novel to which they all contributed) and the pursuit of culture. Their biweekly meetings provided a forum for wide-ranging discussions, creating, according to Thomas's biographer Helen Horowitz, "an occasion for these talented women, in their early twenties and living with their families, to meet and talk seriously about life, religion, vocation, and, not incidentally, marriage." Together they explored the possibilities, dilemmas, and ramifications of options they would face as young women: education and participation in the professions, self-support and independence, and free love and marriage, including the sacrifices women inevitably made if they chose to marry and have children. As women with education (whether formal or informal) and leisure (without significant familial or domestic responsibilities), they explored the questions confronting other similarly situated single women, who faced uncertainty as to what, exactly, to do with their education and how to fill their lives in a society in which marriage and motherhood were accepted as women's ultimate destiny.[23]

In seeking the answers to their questions, they turned to each other as their primary source of support and encouragement, forming deep and long-lasting attachments. During the years of the Friday Evening meetings, Mary Garrett and Julia Rogers lived and traveled together, and Mamie Gwinn accompanied Carey Thomas (as she was known to family and friends) abroad during her years of graduate study in Germany and Switzerland. During Thomas's years at Bryn Mawr College, first Mamie Gwinn and then, after Gwinn's marriage, Mary Garrett resided with Thomas at the college "Deanery." Although the founders of the Bryn Mawr School would clearly reject many of the tenets of nineteenth-century womanhood and separate spheres ideology—decrying the notion that their opportunities in the world should be limited by their gender—they nonetheless derived their primary sense of identification and emotional support from relationships with other women.

Inevitably, the question of the exact nature of the friends' intimate relationships with one another arises. First Thomas and Gwinn and then Thomas and Garrett not only lived together but constructed their lives together. Their tangled relationships—characterized by Gwinn's and Garrett's jealousies of each other's relationship with Thomas and by Thomas's horror at Gwinn's eventual marriage—sometimes mirror a classic lovers' triangle. Were their relationships—obviously emotionally intimate—also physically so? Can they be construed as sexual (lesbian in the modern sense), or were they rooted more in emotional than in physical closeness? In her biography of M. Carey Thomas, Helen Horowitz explores the difficulty of interpreting the exact nature of Thomas's relationships with both Gwinn and Garrett. Horowitz argues that Thomas loved both women passionately (as opposed to the more sentimental female friendships of an earlier generation) and that she became aware of new studies of homosexuality by her middle age—significantly after the days of the young women's Friday Evening friendships and the founding of their school. According to Horowitz, "Both before and after she learned about female sexuality and lesbianism, Carey Thomas believed her attachments to Mamie and Mary were right and fitting, that love of a woman for a woman was better than any love for a man."[24] This belief of Thomas's, more than speculations about their level of physical intimacy, illuminates these women's shared emotional lives.

Out of their friendships would evolve a shared commitment to doing something useful and meaningful, for themselves specifically and for the cause of women generally. In a world characterized by severely limited opportunities for women to use their education and assert their rights to independence and self-determination, the friends of the Friday Evenings would move beyond merely discussing their plight as women to embark on projects addressing their specific concerns. Not surprisingly, given that their friendship had been rooted in shared intellectual and cultural pursuits, they would focus on education as the central starting point of their endeavors. Undoubtedly influencing them as well was the fact that M. Carey Thomas (who was in the midst of launching her own impressive career in the field of women's education at Bryn Mawr College) was using the world of education to live out many of the friends' hopes and dreams for women by pursuing a prestigious career promising intellectual challenge, financial independence, and a forum for acting upon their convictions that women deserved serious education and expanded opportunities. Specifically, the five women would embark on two ambitious projects in Baltimore: funding a new medical school for Johns Hopkins University on the express condition that it would admit women and establishing a school for girls whose commitment to rigorous intellectual training would be unprecedented. They would succeed in both undertakings.[25]

For five single young women living in the 1880s to launch such ambitious plans obviously took exceptionally large doses of imagination, confidence, and determination. In addition to these personal qualities, the women had a combination of family support, prestigious social connections, and personal wealth that made it possible to realize their goals. All five women came from well-known and well-respected Baltimore families (although Garrett's and Gwinn's family pedigrees eclipsed the others in terms of social prestige). Thomas and Gwinn frequently relied on their fathers' support and advice in planning their endeavors, and the friends readily used their fathers' influence at Johns Hopkins to gain publicity and attract students and teachers to their school. Mary Garrett's personal fortune enabled the women to establish a school according to their own design, without regard to the wishes of either male supporters, who normally would have been required to finance their institution, or of parents, who might normally have demanded a larger say in their daughters' school. Essentially, financial independence gave the founders the freedom to implement their own vision of the ideal education for girls. As Carey Thomas wrote Mary Garrett in 1884, "I am so glad, Mary, to think that you will have money some-day. There is so much good to do, and what some of us do in another way you can do in that way, and after all it is rarer than the other ways and does not exclude them."[26]

The friends planned to use Garrett's money to correct the educational deficit they perceived in Baltimore: the lack of rigorous college-preparatory education for girls.[27] Thomas herself had been educated at boarding school, and she decried the lack of high-quality local education she considered appropriate for herself and her younger sisters. Like several cities, Baltimore operated a public high school for girls, but the founders made no reference to it. (Although coeducation dominated public education in the United States, some eastern and southern cities operated separate-sex schools as a long-established tradition—reluctant to mix middle-class girls with boys of working-class or immigrant backgrounds, in competition with private single-sex schools, and in an effort to maintain the support of affluent families who preferred single-sex education.) Baltimore also boasted numerous private schools. When Johns Hopkins University opened in 1876, Baltimore reportedly supported sixteen private schools for boys and thirty-four private schools for girls, thirty-one private coeducational schools, and thirty-four parochial schools. In her biography of Headmistress Edith Hamilton, Bryn Mawr School alumnae Doris Reid claimed that, when the Bryn Mawr School opened in 1885, Baltimore had twenty-nine private schools for girls. Despite what seemed like an impressive number of girls' schools, Reid noted that those schools were mainly small ventures headed by impoverished ladies, and none of them offered serious college preparation.[28]

The friends planned that their new school would provide a starkly contrasting vision, an institution with goals explicitly rejecting those of most other public or private schools open to girls. First, by providing serious academic training for Baltimore schoolgirls, the founders expressly sought to promote college attendance among Baltimore women. Most specifically, they wanted to provide a steady stream of motivated and well-trained students for the new Bryn Mawr College, whose entrance requirements, academic standards, and intellectual rigor M. Carey Thomas planned would surpass those of all institutions of higher education then open to women. Hence, the model Baltimore girls' school would be christened "The Bryn Mawr School," after Bryn Mawr College, and would serve as a "feeder" school for that institution. The school would not only prepare girls for college but also provide its top graduates each year with full scholarships to Bryn Mawr College (including tuition, room, and board).[29]

While they dreamed of how their school could specifically affect women of Baltimore, the five founders saw their endeavor in more sweeping proportions from the very beginning: they hoped the Bryn Mawr School would be more than a local project, with its influence isolated to a handful of Baltimore girls; instead, the Bryn Mawr School would influence the education of girls on a grand scale. The school would be of real importance in ensuring that Bryn Mawr College could maintain its rigorous admissions standards. Most importantly, the school could serve as a model for the education of girls, serving to instruct and inspire women across the country. By establishing a school for like-minded women in other cities to emulate, the founders believed that their local school could potentially enhance both the quality of girls' education and the number and caliber of women attending colleges and universities. Their "experiment," as Thomas later referred to the establishment of Bryn Mawr, would not only create a local school for girls dedicated to upholding the highest expectations for its students but also, according to Mary Garrett, "prove the possibility of the existence of such schools and so be indirectly the means of the creation of similar ones in other places."[30]

The founders emphasized the connections between changes in female education and changes in women's later lives. Particularly for Thomas, transforming the content and quality of girls' education was not just an end in itself but a means to different kinds of lives for women. A Bryn Mawr School education would be a significant step in the larger task of preparing young women to pioneer new roles, including professional careers, self-support, and independence—goals very different from those espoused by traditional female education. While increasing numbers of individuals and institutions were accepting the value of advanced education for girls and women, the Bryn Mawr School was rare in making such an explicit link between the education it offered and its goals for changing the lives of women. It is thus no coincidence that the establishment of the Bryn Mawr School coincided with the gradual opening of more such opportunities to educated women.

Female college graduates in the late nineteenth and early twentieth centuries enjoyed a wider range of options than had previous generations. Many of the women pursuing these educational and professional opportunities did not marry: between 1889 and 1908, approximately 43 percent of Wellesley College graduates and 55 percent of Bryn Mawr College graduates remained single. Instead of marriage, which typically required middle-class and affluent women to relinquish employment outside the home, many female college graduates chose to pursue professional opportunities newly opening to women.[31]

By far the most women continued to enter the field of teaching, but opportunities for women in higher education expanded greatly. The women's colleges of the late nineteenth century produced new generations of educated women and provided professional opportunities for their talented graduates. While most Bryn Mawr College graduates from the classes of 1889–93 chose precollegiate teaching (37%), the next most popular career was college teaching (17%). In 1870, women had made up 12 percent of the faculty in American institutions of higher education; by 1880, they were 36 percent of the faculty. Although frequently confined to women's colleges and female divisions of coeducational institutions and although their proportions among faculty would drop to about 20 percent in the late nineteenth and early twentieth centuries, these increases—particularly given women's severely limited access to higher education before the Civil War—were dramatic.[32]

Other professions proved slower in opening to women. Only 3 percent of Bryn Mawr College graduates of 1889–93 pursued careers in medicine and law. Nonetheless, the gains were concrete and offered new promise to educated young women. Slightly fewer than twenty-five hundred female physicians practiced in the United States in 1880, but by 1910 the number had grown to at least nine thousand. Women also found some law schools open to them by the 1870s and 1880s, although the legal profession as a whole proved more resistant than the medical field to women's participation. Highlighting this contrast is the statistic that, by 1900, 5.6 percent of physicians and surgeons in the United States were female, whereas women were only 0.4 percent of lawyers and judges. Women faced continuing obstacles in access to the professions, from limited hospital and residency programs open to women, to barred access to state bars and law firms, to hiring practices at coeducational colleges and universities that favored male professors in most departments. But women like M. Carey Thomas recognized the tremendous significance of women's gains in the professions and fought to increase their opportunities. Although the connections between the establishment of a single girls' school in Baltimore and women's increasing participation in the professions at large might seem tenuous, the founders of the Bryn Mawr School saw the two phenomena as clearly linked. They saw changing conceptions of girls' education and changing women's adult lives as part of a common endeavor.[33]

The five founders, who now called themselves the "Committee," looked far beyond Baltimore to garner support for their undertaking. Although education for women was more widely available by the 1880s—even Baltimore was in the midst of planning the opening of its own college for women—Baltimore as a whole did not seem particularly enthusiastic about the Committee's plans for the education of its daughters. M. Carey Thomas recalled that, upon learning of the founders' plans for their new Bryn Mawr School, the president of Johns Hopkins University, Daniel Coit Gilman, "urged the Committee not to carry out their plan of appointing women college graduates as teachers because he said 'that he had observed that women were so different from men that they had not the same need of education as men and for them a college education was oftener a liability than an asset.'" Whether or not Thomas accurately quoted Gilman in her 1931 "Brief Account of the Founding and Early Years of the Bryn Mawr School," her recollections reflected the prevailing attitudes that the founders believed themselves to be battling. M. Carey Thomas's niece, Millicent Carey McIntosh (a graduate of both the Bryn Mawr School and Bryn Mawr College, later president of Barnard College, and influential longtime member of the Bryn Mawr School's governing board), recalled that, in 1885, her mother (Thomas's younger sister) was so embarrassed at being a student at Bryn Mawr College "that when she saw her friends on the streets of Baltimore she would cross over to the other side so that she wouldn't have to speak to them."[34]

Anticipating and encountering the opposition or indifference of many Baltimoreans, the founders turned to the ever-increasing network of educated women pursuing careers in the education of other women. As a figure of grow-ing importance in the world of women's education, M. Carey Thomas used her connections to this network—centered particularly around the recently estab-lished women's colleges in the Northeast and including a few coeducational uni-versities—to help staff and promote the Bryn Mawr School. She contacted her friend Marion Talbot (a graduate of Boston University—which she attended after being denied admission to Harvard—who studied at MIT, taught at Wellesley College, and eventually became dean of women and assistant profes-sor of sociology at the new University of Chicago in 1892) for help in identify-ing potential candidates to head the Bryn Mawr School. Talbot, although offering no specific recommendations, applauded Thomas's efforts, noting that, given the dearth of private college-preparatory schools for girls, "the step which you are taking is important and will have an effect throughout the country I am confident."[35]

Talbot's letter praising the founders' plans at the Bryn Mawr School was just one of dozens that poured in from women across the nation—many in response to inquiries from Thomas, others requests for information about the proposed school and potential teaching positions, and still others just sending best wishes for the opening of a school believed to be an important step in the advancement of women's education. Helen M. Barrett of Rochester, for instance, declaring herself "much interested in the work of preparatory schools for girls," wrote to Julia Rogers that the Bryn Mawr School would fill "a great educational need of the present time" and confided her dream of establishing such a school in her hometown. One woman wrote that "the proposed plans for your school for girls, preparatory for college, seem to me exceptionally fine," while another classified the Bryn Mawr School's opening as "one of the onward steps in the higher education of women." Louisa Richardson, a professor at Carleton Col-lege, declined an offer to teach Latin at the Bryn Mawr School, but assured the Committee of her interest in their venture. She praised the proposal to require all students to study classical languages, noting her own conviction and experi-ence that it was certainly "possible for girls to learn to read Latin for leisure."[36]

When the Bryn Mawr School finally opened, the founders advertised their school far beyond Baltimore (even though the school had no boarding depart-ment and thus was not soliciting students from other cities). Announcements of the school's opening appeared in newspapers in Pennsylvania, New York, Con-necticut, Maine, Rhode Island, and elsewhere. In 1893, the school was even featured (and won a blue ribbon in the educational division) as an innovative model for girls' education in an exhibition in the Woman's Building of the World's Columbian Exposition in Chicago. But what, exactly, made the Bryn Mawr School and its educational vision so exceptional?[37]

The Grand Experiment: The Critical Components of the Model School

In a time when the predominant arguments for rationalizing female education (and often women's suffrage and expanded public, political, and professional influence) were grounded in belief in the differences between the sexes, the Bryn Mawr School founders rejected any elements of education they saw as supporting what they considered this basically false premise. From their perspective (and experience), education catering specifically to supposed female propensities was, first, based upon false assumptions about women's intellectual abilities and capacity to function independently in the public world and, second, inevitably inferior in content and quality to the education granted young men. And so the Bryn Mawr School was deliberately designed to help transform both the conceptualization of and the common practices of female education.

An obvious question is why, if the founders believed in the intellectual similarities of women and men and the education they thus deserved, did they choose to found a school for girls only rather than a coeducational institution in which girls and boys might be educated identically side by side? Why, indeed, support single-sex education to promote the similarities between the sexes? M. Carey Thomas, despite leading a woman's college herself, spoke in favor of coeducation. In 1920, she argued that "only by having the schools and universities coeducational can we assure the girls of the world of receiving a thoroughly good education. There is not enough money in the world to duplicate schools and universities for women, and if we could duplicate them, they would soon become less good."[38]

The regional and class preferences of Baltimore families who chose private education certainly would have supported the establishment of a single-sex rather than coeducational school. Although coeducation (particularly in public education) was overwhelmingly the norm in most parts of the United States, many established cities (especially in the East and South) had strong traditions of favoring single-sex education. As Boston Superintendent John D. Philbrick noted in 1880, the "civilized upper classes everywhere" preferred separate-sex schools: "It is precisely among those classes that the education of the sexes always has been, and continues to be, most exclusively unmixed."[39] Too, the founders' support of a girls' school may have stemmed from fear that coeducational institutions would inevitably slight girls, whereas female-only institutions could devote all their resources to their female students. Girls' schools could encourage the highest of standards for female students and simultaneously provide places of employment for educated women and offer independent women as role models for students.

The Committee founded the Bryn Mawr School in 1885 and incorporated it in 1890, according to an 1896 school catalogue, "to provide for girls the same advantages that had for some time existed in the best secondary schools for boys."[40] Those "advantages" that the founders hoped to provide for girls would be much more than a series of "additions"—such as extra courses or activities—to the traditional offerings of existing girls' schools. The founders were thinking in much broader terms about a kind of school whose whole culture would challenge traditional assumptions about girls and about how and why they should be educated.

The defining principle of the Bryn Mawr School was that it would be *exclusively* college preparatory. The school's opening catalogue delineated that central principle:

> Since it is evident that the entrance requirements of the foremost colleges and universities represent the opinion of those best acquainted with such matters as to the subjects which should at least be included in school work, the prescribed course has been so arranged as to include the highest requirements for entrance made by any college.[41]

No school for girls had ever set such a stringent standard, and this policy immediately made Bryn Mawr a unique institution on the educational landscape. Although some existing girls' schools had begun offering college-preparatory courses to prepare students for the colleges and universities newly opening to women, no school required such a high level of preparation in *every* student it enrolled. Generally, college preparation for girls was tailored to the institutions they hoped to attend (some with less-demanding entrance requirements than others), and all schools open to girls offered "general" courses designed for students with no aspirations for higher education.

The Bryn Mawr School was the first school to demand that every student—

even girls of "average capacity," as early catalogues referred to them—master the most difficult subjects. The school's first catalogue announced that "the course of instruction is the same for all pupils." And as M. Carey Thomas explained at the Bryn Mawr School's first commencement, "the interest of girls going and the girls not going to college was the same," and hence "a complete preparatory course was advisable for both."[42]

The founders took exception to the fact that girls' schools—even those offering some college preparation—eschewed subjects required at the most serious boys' preparatory schools. Boys' preparatory schools required the study of both Latin and Greek (necessary for admission to the most competitive men's colleges and universities), while girls' schools typically made no such demands. But Thomas and her fellow founders believed that the study of Latin was "at the foundation of many of the most important studies" and that Latin "should be universally taught in schools, whether the children expected to go to college or not." And so all students at the Bryn Mawr School would be expected to study Latin; additionally, they would master either Greek or German—with no exceptions. In addition to languages, every Bryn Mawr student would be exposed to laboratory sciences, another area of study routinely neglected in many girls' schools.

Maintaining such requirements took determination and resolve in the face of a society that found too much study of such "male" subjects unnecessary, unreasonable, and sometimes even dangerous for girls and the roles for which they were being educated; it also required a willingness to lose students whose parents withdrew their daughters rather than subject them to such unprecedented intellectual demands. Millicent Carey McIntosh recalled overhearing a Bryn Mawr School Board of Managers meeting held in her mother's parlor in which her aunt, M. Carey Thomas, admonished the school's Headmistress Edith Hamilton, "Don't allow these soft Baltimore mothers to weaken their daughters by insisting that they drop Latin!"[43]

While instituting traditionally "male" standards of college preparation, the Bryn Mawr School founders simultaneously committed themselves to eradicating most vestiges of traditional girls' education. Their model school would contrast directly with "finishing courses" that had long typified much of girls' education. Activities with the slightest connotation of "female accomplishments" were anathema. Mamie Gwinn, for example, while noting that it would be nice for the Bryn Mawr School to have a piano for graduation ceremonies, jested that "we'll never consent to teaching music!" The founders appreciated

serious study in music or the arts. After all, they had personally devoted countless hours to the pursuit of "culture," and from its inception their school sought
to instill an appreciation of great art in its students. Garrett filled Bryn Mawr's
building with reproductions of great art and presented art lectures to students
using photographs from Thomas's, Gwinn's, and her own travels in Europe. But
the founders emphatically avoided what they saw as the insidious way that a
smattering of training for girls in the arts, a dilettantish "dabbling" in culture,
could take precedence over in-depth study in difficult academic subjects.[44]

Bryn Mawr School bulletins from the school's first decade announced that all
students would study Latin, French, English, history, science, and mathematics
throughout their course at the school. Greek or German was required of advanced students, and drawing and elocution were required of everyone. Requirements remained essentially the same during the 1890s, with a few
exceptions. Catalogues after the first no longer noted elocution as a requirement, although descriptions of English courses from later years suggest that it
may merely have been incorporated elsewhere rather than eliminated from the
curriculum. With the completion of Bryn Mawr's new building in the 1890s, all
students participated in gymnasium (which might include gymnastics, swimming, fencing, and archery). By the mid-1890s, the school had established a separate Primary Department for students six to ten years of age.[45]

To ensure the school's adherence to high intellectual standards—and to see
that each student truly mastered all subjects (rather than merely being exposed
to them)—the Bryn Mawr School would rely on outside examiners and examinations to measure students' achievements. According to the school's first catalogue, "the proficiency of the pupils will be tested not only by means of the
ordinary recitations and examinations, but also, from time to time, by means of
examination papers set by persons unconnected with the school."[46] Usually
these examiners were professors from Johns Hopkins University or Bryn Mawr
College. Such emphasis on outside evaluation by objective "experts"—which
Thomas saw as the mark of truly great educational institutions committed to
real rigor and which she also employed at Bryn Mawr College—would eradicate
any attempts to "soften" the school's curriculum to accommodate less talented
or motivated students.

Most stringent of all, not only would students be examined at the end of each
course they completed, they would each be required to pass Bryn Mawr College's entrance examination (modeled after Harvard's entrance examination) to
graduate officially from the Bryn Mawr School. Again, the founders enacted

such a policy as a means of maintaining the school's commitment to preparing every student for colleges of the highest level. Failure to pass the examination would render a student ineligible for graduation from the Bryn Mawr School— even if she had completed its entire course satisfactorily. According to the later reminiscences of one student at Bryn Mawr around 1900, messenger boys would deliver telegrams reporting examination results to each student's house imme-diately before the Bryn Mawr School graduation ceremony. "There has been more than one 'sob-story' in the annals of the Bryn Mawr School about a girl who would not go to commencement, even though her invitations to friends and relatives were out, because she did not pass her examinations."[47]

The Bryn Mawr School's emphasis on examinations had significant implica-tions for its faculty and the courses they taught. Bryn Mawr's examination poli-cies meant that the whole course of study at the school would be geared toward passing the Bryn Mawr College entrance examination and that a teacher's suc-cess or failure would be judged almost exclusively by the test scores of her stu-dents. In a series of letters during the summer of 1893, for example, the founders chastised a math teacher for her students' poor test results.[48]

While M. Carey Thomas argued that rigorous academic training was valu-able for all girls regardless of their intent to pursue higher education, the Bryn Mawr School's primary mission was the promotion of women's higher educa-tion. Although the school admitted students with no college aspirations (on the condition, of course, that they would meet the requirements for admission to Bryn Mawr College in order to graduate), the school favored students actively pursuing the goal of higher education. When they submitted the names of ap-plicants to the founders' Committee, who made all admissions decisions, the school's secretaries (as early headmistresses were called, perhaps to suggest their lack of independence from the founders in most school matters) routinely spec-ified which girls sought admission to the Bryn Mawr School for the purpose of preparing for college. Students with academic "deficiencies" who argued force-fully their commitment to overcoming their weaknesses and gaining admission to college were welcomed at the Bryn Mawr School. Thomas asserted that the school admitted "by favor" students who were seeking college admission, even if they were academically unprepared and would require special attention to help them succeed at the Bryn Mawr School.[49]

Not surprisingly, the founders were particularly interested in promoting at-tendance at Bryn Mawr College, which they believed to be the best college open to women. Upon the school's opening, newspapers across the Northeast described the Bryn Mawr School as specifically designed to prepare girls for Bryn Mawr College. In an effort to excite early Bryn Mawr School students about the possibility of attending Bryn Mawr College, the school sponsored student field trips to visit M. Carey Thomas and tour the college. In 1892, Bryn Mawr School Secretary Mary Colvin wrote to Thomas, expressing her students' excitement about their upcoming trip to the college. The Bryn Mawr School also made an exceptional offer to promote attendance at the college. Mary Garrett pledged the money to finance college scholarships for the best students graduating from the Bryn Mawr School every year: "The two pupils of each year who have completed the entire course most satisfactorily, will be entitled to four years' residence, free of expense, at any college at that time approved by the School," announced the Bryn Mawr School's first catalogue. No "scholarship girls," as they were called, attended any college other than Bryn Mawr, and, by 1896, the school catalogues specifically designated that the two scholarships would be for Bryn Mawr College. Undoubtedly, the school's scholarship program advanced the founders' goal of promoting higher education, served as a recruiting tool to attract Baltimore families desiring college attendance for their daughters, and provided Thomas's college with a flow of exceptionally well-prepared students.[50]

The founders realized from the outset that, if their school were to live up to its ideals, exceptional faculty would be essential. Throughout the nineteenth century, school reformers had complained that too many teachers in girls' schools were poorly trained and incompetent. From the perspective of the Bryn Mawr School founders in the 1880s, the situation had not improved much. They observed that many teachers of girls had received their training in state normal schools or lacked any form of higher education at all. The Bryn Mawr School, they insisted, would hire only high-achieving graduates of the best colleges open to women, women as devoted to the school's educational philosophy as they were. The school's secretary or, eventually, headmistress would be a scholarly figure, preferably with a doctoral degree, interested in pursuing independent research as well as in leading the model school.[51]

Vowing to avoid mediocrity, the founders, particularly Thomas, exerted enormous energy to recruit faculty members who would further their school's mission. This was no easy task in the 1880s. Marion Talbot responded to Thomas's inquiries about potential headmistresses for the new school that she knew of no one qualified for the position because "the number of college women who have had sufficient social experience is very small." But Thomas used her connections in the fledgling network of female college graduates, scholars, and educators to identify and attract high-quality teachers and leaders. To lure appropriately "scholarly" teachers, she even promised that the founders' family ties to Johns Hopkins trustees would ensure interested Bryn Mawr School teachers a close association with fellow scholars in their fields. And Thomas did recruit many exceptionally accomplished women. Early Bryn Mawr Secretary Mary Noyes Colvin had earned a Ph.D. in Zurich. Longtime Headmistress Edith Hamilton, who arrived at the school in 1896, had won Bryn Mawr College's highest honor upon her graduation—a European Fellowship for graduate study—and was working on her doctorate when she came to the Bryn Mawr School.[52]

Finally, the founders' commitment to forming an institution comprising scholarly women was significant in terms of its relationship to the level of instruction the students received and also for the teachers themselves, who could pursue socially acceptable careers as teachers in an age when the options for the earliest generation of female college graduates were limited. None of Bryn Mawr's teachers was married. The school would serve not only as a catalyst for girls to pursue higher education but also as an institution sustaining educated women who chose careers, self-support, and the daily companionship of other educated women rather than the traditional female option of marriage and domesticity. At a time when the lines between higher education for women (especially at women's colleges) and preparatory schools for girls were much more fluid than the clear distinctions between high schools and colleges today, many graduates of women's colleges (and sometimes their faculty) found employment at the Bryn Mawr School. Not surprisingly, given their clear connections, the Bryn Mawr School would increasingly come to rely on graduates of Bryn Mawr College to staff the school: by 1900, eight of the twelve teachers of academic subjects—including the school's headmistress—held degrees from Bryn Mawr College.[53]

Education, Health, and Reform

The Bryn Mawr School's primary mission was always to encourage the highest level of intellectual achievement among girls. From the founders' perspective, however, the achievement of that goal could only be possible if their model school devoted itself with equal intensity to improving the health and physical well-being of its students. Reformers had long observed the poor health that seemed to afflict women of the middle and well-to-do classes of nineteenth-century America. Catharine Beecher had blamed female ill health on factors ranging from women's poor diets and constricting corsets to inactivity and inadequate ventilation in homes and had proposed solutions including fresh air, better-balanced meals, dress reform, experimental water cures, and calisthenics (which she specifically recommended be incorporated into the curriculum of female academies).[54] Thanks to reformers such as Beecher, some schools for girls and women had adopted exercise programs by the mid- to late nineteenth century, but both the perceptions and the realities of fragile female health remained very real problems among educated women in the late Victorian world.

Many women associated with the Bryn Mawr School shared the health problems of the female population in general. Throughout their lives, founders M. Carey Thomas, Mary Garrett, Mamie Gwinn, and Bessie King all suffered from varying health problems. Moreover, the women with whom the founders corresponded (particularly in recruiting teachers for the school) filled their letters with references to poor health, from recurrent headaches to generally weak constitutions to past illnesses overcome. They also spoke of moving to different cities for health reasons and frequently referred to their responsibilities in caring for sickly mothers, sisters, and other female relatives. Worries about their daughters' health likewise consumed many mothers and fathers. Soon after the Bryn Mawr School's opening, the school's headmistress notified Thomas, "I am very much disturbed at the withdrawal of girls on account of ill-health," including reports of measles, headaches, and the need to travel to different climates to improve health.[55] Moreover, the all-too-real threat from deadly epidemics that frequently swept through cities such as Baltimore understandably fueled the anxieties of parents.

No doubt, concerns about the health of women and schoolgirls were legitimate, but some explanations for the phenomenon were dubious. Speculation about the links between the rigorous education of women and their health threatened institutions like the Bryn Mawr School, which were on the forefront of the movement to prove women's equal intellectual capacity. The popular superstition that too much mental exertion could be detrimental to women's physical well-being was nothing new. But the "scientific" arguments emerging by the 1870s—the very time when the doors of advanced education were beginning to open to women—and supporting such myths were new. Reflecting the recently circulating Darwinian theories of evolution, some proposals suggested that women were inferior to men both physically and mentally—lagging behind the opposite sex in the evolutionary process—and that women would only harm themselves trying to "catch up" with men.

Former Harvard Medical School professor Dr. Edward H. Clarke's *Sex in Education; or, a Fair Chance for the Girls* (1873) circulated widely among the educated classes. Based on a study of several Vassar College students, Clarke argued that, if women's "limited energy" were expended on too much study, their "female apparatus" would be at risk. Intellectual overwork would lead to a variety of serious ailments, including "neuralgia, uterine disease, hysteria, and other derangements of the nervous system." The message was clear: women's biology determined their mental capacities and ability to stand up under the rigors of serious education.[56]

Clarke's *Sex in Education* caused much debate and alarm, especially among women (and their families) undertaking or considering advanced education. As historian Rosalind Rosenberg has noted, "No one could easily dismiss arguments so deeply rooted in the principal intellectual assumptions of the day. And no woman in the 1870s or 1880s rejected the doctor's argument out of hand." Although many studies would later refute Clarke's findings, fear that he might be right plagued the earliest generations of college women. As M. Carey Thomas herself recalled, "We did not know when we began whether women's health could stand the strain of education. We were haunted in those days by the clanging chains of that gloomy specter, Dr. Edward H. Clarke's *Sex in Education.*" But Thomas's success in pursuing her intellectual dreams—and her commitment to providing similar opportunities for other women—convinced her of the error of Clarke's conclusions. While she and her fellow founders of the Bryn Mawr School did not deny that women of their day indeed suffered too many effects of ill health, they rejected the suggestion that women's problems were linked to too much education or that biology inevitably limited women's capacity for serious academic pursuits.[57]

Despite the founders' convictions, many parents of the middle classes still worried that certain kinds of education might indeed prove detrimental to their daughters' health—a worry that plagued the early Bryn Mawr School. Upon its opening, for example, one woman wrote to the founders, noting that, while she "heartily wish[ed their] enterprise success," she feared that "the excessive caution of physicians in dealing with the constitutions [of female children] that seem mysteriously and unaccountably frail" (combined with the "appalling indifference of the parents and the children") would prove a "most serious hindrance" to the school's goals. Her prediction of the reactions of parents to their daughters' experiences at the school proved accurate. Parents not infrequently cited health problems as their reason for withdrawing their daughters from Bryn Mawr. One mother specifically noted that she was enrolling her daughter in a different school because, despite her affection for Bryn Mawr and its exceptional teachers, she believed that the school's demanding courses and stringent marking, ranking, and examination systems had reduced her "sensitive" and "nervous" daughter to a "state of complete nervous exhaustion" when "such a strain" was simply "unnecessary." Even into the early decades of the twentieth century, the issue was still alive in the minds of some individuals: a leading Baltimore gynecologist, for instance, warned Bryn Mawr's headmistress that studying Latin was bad for her students' health.[58]

Realizing how such perceptions about the links between girls' education and their health could undermine their mission at the Bryn Mawr School, the founders determined that their model school would not only allay such superstitions but also prove that serious study and improvements in health could go hand in hand. Drawing on a genuine desire to combat girls' physical ailments, as well as a pragmatic understanding of the necessity to prove that the education they proposed to give girls would not be detrimental to their health, the founders designed an innovative "physical culture" program to complement the school's college-preparatory academic curriculum. If Dr. Clarke and his supporters had used "science" to rationalize retarding advances in women's education in the name of concern for their physical and emotional well-being, the founders would also rely on modern science—this time, science that the founders believed was sound and wisely applied—to disprove his theories and to enhance the goal of encouraging education of unprecedented rigor among schoolgirls.

M. Carey Thomas's interest in science in developing the Bryn Mawr School's physical culture program and curing female health problems was characteristic of her faith in science and the scientific method. Just as she wanted Bryn Mawr College to be an institution devoted to real scholarship and scientific research (as was the Johns Hopkins University, which she so admired), the Bryn Mawr School itself was to be rooted in the most scientific methods, whether in examination procedures or in physical exercise regimens. In Bryn Mawr's physical culture program, science, instead of curtailing women's intellectual pursuits, would be used to improve girls' health and open new educational opportunities to them.[59]

The Bryn Mawr School's commitment to physical culture was not unique in the most progressive female educational circles of the day, but its depth of commitment to the problem and its amazing allotment of physical resources to improving the health of girls from the youngest of ages were exceptional. "Physical culture is to receive as much attention as mental improvement," proclaimed a newspaper announcing the opening of the Bryn Mawr School's new building in 1889. The Bryn Mawr School became the first girls' school to employ its own physician, Dr. Kate Campbell Hurd, to direct its program. Dr. Hurd came to Baltimore from Boston's New England Hospital. When Thomas recruited her as the school's medical director, Hurd pledged that, if she accepted the position, it would be "with my whole soul and heart in the work, and with a determination to make the scheme of Preventive Hygiene a grand and telling success." Together she, Thomas, and Garrett would spend countless hours exploring emerging health and exercise programs across Europe and the United States in hope of combining the best developments into an innovative program at the Bryn Mawr School.

Mary Garrett financed Hurd's travels at home and abroad for over a year to gain firsthand knowledge of and training in the latest health trends. In the United States, Hurd took courses and daily private lessons from the famous Dr. Dudley Allen Sargent's School of Physical Culture in Cambridge, Massachusetts (the first school in the United States specializing in the training of gymnasium teachers) and visited Dr. Passe in Newport, Massachusetts, to explore the "Medical and Educational Swedish Movement." Her travels in Europe included visits to Paris and Baden to learn about baths and "especially the value of the spray and needle douches." In Stockholm, she reported herself impressed with Dr. Zander's Swedish system, convinced that his exercise machines not only helped the muscles but also cultivated "quick brain work and accuracy of attention and action." To Zander's system, Hurd credited the "strongly healthy generation of women" and "splendid looking children" she observed in Sweden.[60]

Bryn Mawr's efforts to improve the health of its students were manifested in its physical facilities. Relying on Hurd's reports, recommendations of Bryn Mawr College's gymnasium instructor Dr. Carrie Ladd, and personal consultations with Dr. Sargent, Thomas and Garrett spared no expense outfitting their model school with facilities and equipment, including Sargent's and Zander's machines, an indoor running track and swimming pool, dressing rooms and "needle baths" (showers), and an assortment of exercise ropes, rings, ladders, and dumbbells. Mary Garrett lavished attention on the smallest details—from the placement of windows for maximum sunlight to appropriate desk heights for different-aged schoolgirls—that might contribute to a healthy environment in the new building she financed for the school. As one announcement of the school's new building noted, even the "proportions of all the rooms are based on those adopted by French and other foreign Government Schools to secure the best ventilation, the height of ceilings vary according to size of rooms." The link between architecture and ideas—the connection between the school's commitment to new educational ideals and the physical environment in which they would be implemented—would be everywhere evident in the Bryn Mawr School's notable building.[61]

The Model School Building: Architecture as a Reflection of Ideals

The Bryn Mawr School opened its doors with Secretary Eleanor A. Andrews, a graduate of Newnham College of Cambridge University in England, and five teachers on 21 September 1884, in a three-story building at 715 North Eutaw Street, adjacent to the Johns Hopkins University. Almost immediately, however, Mary Garrett committed to financing a new structure to house the school. Using her vast financial resources, Garrett would spare no expense in erecting a model school building that would reflect—in fact, be an integral part of—the educational vision espoused by the founders. Thanks to her willingness to use her personal fortune to realize its goals, the Bryn Mawr School would have an exceptional building that physically manifested the founders' dreams and the school's ideals.

Ironically, the birth of Bryn Mawr's new building coincided with the unraveling of the close friendship and collaboration among the school's five founders. As dean of Bryn Mawr College, M. Carey Thomas lived in Pennsylvania and focused most of her attention on the college, although the Bryn Mawr School remained a significant, if less absorbing, interest. Mamie Gwinn, Thomas's special companion throughout her years of graduate training abroad, resided with Thomas at Bryn Mawr College. During the 1880s and 1890s, the relationship between Thomas and Garrett intensified, leading to jealous rifts between Mamie Gwinn and Mary Garrett as they vied for Thomas's attention. Likewise,

Julia Rogers, who had maintained a special relationship with Mary Garrett during the years of the Friday Evening meetings and the planning of the Bryn Mawr School, gradually grew estranged from Garrett as Garrett devoted more attention to Thomas. As a result of the deepening rift, Julia Rogers resigned from the Bryn Mawr School Committee around 1891. (Rogers would remain very active in Baltimore civic affairs, dedicating much of her interest and money to Goucher College.) In the 1880s, Elizabeth King was frequently in poor health and drifted away from active involvement in the school. Consequently, it was Garrett—both because she controlled the school's purse strings and because she would remain the one active founder residing in Baltimore—who would assume primary responsibility for both day-to-day decision making and oversight of the school's new building. Indeed, the school became her passion.[62]

Garrett hired New York architect Henry Rutgers Marshall (who had designed the building for the girls' school Brearley in New York and the library of Rutgers College, as well as many mansions for the rich) to design the new school building. Erected on Cathedral Street in a stylish residential section of Baltimore, where many of the city's private school patrons lived, the building housed the Bryn Mawr School from 1890 until the early 1930s (and was eventually torn down during modern urban renewal projects). Built of yellow brick imported from England, the imposing structure consisted of six stories, including a basement that housed a gymnasium and swimming pool, and a walled-in yard. An impressive entrance, stairway, and reception rooms, lighted by gas jets covered with Tiffany glass globes, dominated the first floor. The second floor, occupied by what Mary Garrett called the "silent study room" and an attached library, eventually housed 150 student desks as well as a headmistress's desk elevated on a platform. Classrooms—including a science laboratory and rooms specifically designed for reading and drawing—were on the upper floors. Bryn Mawr students (especially those in the lower grades housed in the topmost floors) climbed many stairs—a fact that would eventually not go unnoticed by concerned parents.[63]

The school was designed to contain all the necessities for undertaking serious study and for improving physical health. It had a swimming pool and gymnasium facilities and was also noted for being well ventilated and fireproof. The founders and the architect designed the school to promote very particular educational ideals. In her study of the architecture of the Seven Sister colleges, Helen Horowitz characterized M. Carey Thomas's building program at Bryn Mawr College as a rejection of the attempts of other female institutions, such as

Mount Holyoke, Vassar, Wellesley, and Smith, to adapt female domestic space to their educational facilities. At Bryn Mawr College, in contrast, Thomas "wanted to appropriate the library and the laboratory of men." Bryn Mawr College's physical campus reflected traditionally male educational architecture, reflecting Thomas's promotion of the identical intellectual abilities and available pursuits of male and female students. As Horowitz noted, "Bryn Mawr created special opportunities for women to enter the sacred groves of scholarship, but the groves had no gender." In many ways, the same could be said for the Bryn Mawr School.[64]

The Bryn Mawr School's building cultivated a particular atmosphere for the girls who would be educated there. Rather than creating a nurturing or domestic atmosphere, Bryn Mawr's building was designed to awe and inspire the youngest of girls, encouraging them to take themselves and their schoolwork seriously. Architecture emphasized the seriousness of a Bryn Mawr School education. Childish play or feminine softness would have no place at the school: "I don't think there was a carpet anywhere in the building and there were certainly no red-painted doors," recalled one Bryn Mawr graduate.[65]

To inspire Bryn Mawr students to the beauty of the world of learning and ideas, Garrett lavishly decorated the school building with replicas of great art brought back from her frequent trips to Europe. Marble statuary and plaster busts of Greek and Roman sculpture lined the hallways. A giant marble frieze of the Parthenon embellished the central study hall, a bust of Virgil and replicas of the Roman Colliseum and Forum adorned the Latin room. As one observer noted, "It is more than doubtful if any other preparatory school in the country has so generous a collection of Braun autotypes of the most famous paintings, to say nothing of many chromolithographs by the Arundel society of London." Additionally, "in every room are casts representing different periods of art; and care has been taken to make the pupils familiar, not only with Isis and Niobe and the nine Muses, or the works of Michael Angelo, but with sculptures in various parts of France and Germany—with the wonderful wood-carvings of the middle ages."[66] As an early graduate remembered, "The Winged Victory supervised our lunch-counter and the Elgin Marbles paraded around the study hall walls."[67]

One alumna recalled that, when she entered the Bryn Mawr School, she "stood in awe" in the face of its soaring ceiling, winding staircase, and innumerable statues peering down from their high niches in the walls; altogether, she felt like "a tiny atom in this great hall of learning."[68] Another graduate recalled how vividly her school's building impressed its educational expectations upon students:

> No child could walk through that heavy, iron-studded front door (which closed with a somber click-swuush!) without sensing that the building Stood For Something. Solid and spacious, it was furnished not for comfort or charm but for serious study—and it had Status. Among the city's private schools, we knew simply and without question that Bryn Mawr was the *best*. Others could be finishing schools ... or country-style boarding schools; they could teach manners, art, piano, horsemanship; *we* were all out for brains. Other schools might believe in being bright, colorful, attractive, warm; Bryn Mawr believed in being Important. Bryn Mawr School girls went to college, or if they didn't, no matter; they were educated as though they were going—and going straight through with flying banners to an A.B.[69]

A Vision for Some—Not All—Girls

The Bryn Mawr School founders saw themselves as enlightened women battling the prejudices, ignorance, and indifference of men and women who sought to limit the advance of education and opportunity for women. In many aspects, their self-image was correct: their exceptional vision for a new kind of education for girls and, indeed, a better kind of society for women remains impressive today. From the vantage point of the early twenty-first century, however, it is obvious that, while the model Bryn Mawr School was revolutionary in transcending many prevailing attitudes about gender, the school—like the individuals who created and maintained it—reflected the social and cultural norms of the well-to-do classes and perpetuated many of the prejudices of the day. In contrast to modern educational institutions that embrace diversity, Bryn Mawr actively sought to insulate its students from the "wrong" kinds of people.

Neither the school's founders nor its early administrators, faculty, or students transcended the common racial prejudices of the late nineteenth century. Although they had frequent contact with African Americans, the women of Bryn Mawr knew those individuals primarily as their subordinates: as the servants, nurses, chauffeurs, and janitors who staffed their homes and schools. While there were historic connections between the abolitionist and women's movements—and although an educational institution such as Oberlin College had opened its doors to African Americans and women simultaneously—the founders of the Bryn Mawr School never imagined that their school would advance the education of anyone other than white girls. Although M. Carey Thomas's own mother, drawing on her Quaker tradition, had supported the activities of some African American activists in Baltimore, her daughter evidenced a sometimes virulent racism, even against Bryn Mawr's own janitorial staff.[70]

The Bryn Mawr School Committee also scrutinized the religious affiliations of all applicants seeking admission. M. Carey Thomas reflected the rising anti-Semitism of the late nineteenth century among elite circles in the United States, which disconcerted both Mary Garrett and certain Bryn Mawr School administrators. When Jewish Sadie Szold—whom Secretary Eleanor Andrews described as "a quiet, ladylike girl, most interested about her work and promising to make a good student"—inquired at the school, Thomas and Mamie Gwinn (whom Garrett earlier described as the one "who has throughout been so emphatically against it") opposed her admission. In contrast, Mary Garrett (supported by Julia Rogers) wanted the school open to Jews. Szold did enter Bryn Mawr, but Thomas made it clear that she should be the last Jew admitted to the school: "I should on *no* account take them, and I register my *strongest* protest." In the margins of this letter to Garrett, she urged, "Cannot your action be withdrawn: we should not risk all that we care for in the success of the school for such a thing and I think at least I should have been allowed to give my reasons." The issue of a Jewish student's admission to the Bryn Mawr School caused significant strain in Thomas's and Garrett's relationship for months, a fact that, as Thomas biographer Helen Horowitz suggests, makes it difficult to excuse Thomas's anti-Semitism as mere conformity to the norms of her time and class.[71]

The Bryn Mawr School Committee admitted a few Jewish students, but Thomas wanted the numbers kept low. The school's policy became a matter of public controversy in 1890, when a reporter from the *Jewish Exponent* visited then Secretary Mary Noyes Colvin to inquire about the school's admissions policy for Jewish girls. According to Colvin, that reporter deliberately deceived her to undercover the school's alleged anti-Semitism, leading her to believe that he was a rabbi seeking admission for his daughter. In response to the reporter's queries, Colvin claimed to have followed the Bryn Mawr School Committee's instructions. She later explained, in a letter to M. Carey Thomas, that she had replied to the reporter's questions "*according* to your instructions that we took a certain number of Jewish girls, but that our number was filled." After the reporter's visit, an article criticizing the Bryn Mawr School for their exclusion of

Jews appeared. Public outcry followed (with reports of the controversy reprinted in other Baltimore papers)—so much that M. Carey Thomas was forced to address the *Jewish Exponent*'s accusations.

Publicly, Thomas denied any anti-Semitism (personally or on the part of the Bryn Mawr School), asserting that the school accepted all academically prepared students "without discrimination on grounds of race or religion." To prove her case, she pointed out that two of the school's best students were "Jewesses." If the reporter for the *Jewish Exponent* had been misled about Bryn Mawr's admissions policy, Thomas claimed, it was because the school's headmistress had a "misunderstanding of the regulations of the school."[72] Thomas and the Bryn Mawr School weathered this public crisis by using the school's headmistress as a scapegoat—much to Secretary Colvin's outrage, since she claimed to have been following Thomas's direct orders—and the school continued to admit a limited number of Jewish students. But the issue would reemerge later.[73]

The relationship between the Bryn Mawr School and the Jewish community provoked controversy; conversely, Bryn Mawr's status as a school for only the "better" classes seemed accepted as a norm of the day. When the school temporarily experimented with accepting boarding students (who would reside with Headmistress Colvin's sister), the Committee reserved the right to exclude any girls whose "character or manners made them undesirable associates for the other children."[74] A Bryn Mawr student essay discussing how "it is a marked feature of the common class of Americans that they have a very disagreeable way of speaking, which makes them unbearable," reveals the students' attitudes. Bryn Mawr's French teacher confided that she particularly desired a position at the Bryn Mawr School because she wished to be associated with the "ladies" of Baltimore rather than with her current students, who were of "a low class" and exhibited "the natural insolence with poorer people which is the fault of newly risen men and women without education trying to make up for it with show." And, when a newly hired teacher inquired about places to reside in Baltimore, she remarked that "if one lives in lodgings, while the people ought to be respectable, they need not be of one's own social station, as the average landlady claims to be. Social equality is often very uncomfortable, especially in business relations."[75]

The Bryn Mawr School founders, even though they espoused many revolutionary ideas about gender, did not tolerate women who broke certain social conventions. Thomas herself had sought advanced education at home and abroad at a time when to do so was certainly beyond the realm of acceptable pursuits for young women; she then rejected marriage in favor of following a public and demanding career. Likewise, Bryn Mawr encouraged what many considered an unacceptably "masculine" college-preparatory education for girls; moreover, the school employed college-educated single women in a society that still viewed marriage and motherhood as the "natural" paths for women. Yet, while they envisioned the school as helping women defy certain social convictions with which they disagreed, Thomas and her fellow founders condemned some women in similar situations whose behaviors or lifestyles seemed to flout other social mores. This high regard for many traditional women's morals and manners suggests that the school's founders—who themselves defied social convention by promoting higher education for women, pursuing careers, rejecting marriage and motherhood, living independently, and choosing other women as their primary companions—did not necessarily become more tolerant of other women whose behavior threatened reigning expectations for the behavior of middle-class women.

On the one hand, the Bryn Mawr School founders could—and did—make the argument that, because their undertaking in establishing a model preparatory school for girls was so unconventional and controversial, they could not afford to have their institution associated with smaller "scandals" that might turn public opinion even more decidedly against the school. Mary Garrett raised this issue in 1894, when two Bryn Mawr School teachers inquired whether it would be acceptable for them to ride bicycles in Baltimore. Garrett, who saw bicycling as a harmless activity with potentially good health benefits, thought the teachers' requests reasonable but still felt compelled to circulate a letter to her fellow Committee members to garner their response. Specifically, she inquired how they thought public opinion in Baltimore would respond to Bryn Mawr School teachers riding bicycles, noting that neither she nor the teachers in question wanted to involve themselves in anything which might "prejudice people against the School in any way."[76]

"Does Mrs. Irvine still wear her hair short and would she change?" Thomas inquired about a candidate for the school's headmistress, asserting that her question stemmed from the fact that the school Committee is "so revolutionary in all main points that I do not know whether our Head Mistress or Secretary could afford to differ from other people in non-essential trifles which arouse prejudice." And yet it is hard to attribute the Committee's concern with public opinion and reputation as only a pragmatic consideration aimed at avoiding ill will from the public. Repeatedly, the founders scrutinized the personal appearances, habits, and reputations of potential administrators, teachers, and students. "Background checks" were performed on every potential teacher and every potential student and her family. Thomas chastised one Bryn Mawr headmistress for not gathering enough background information on potential teachers, insisting that if she were proposing a candidate at Bryn Mawr College, she would present a complete history of that teacher's life since childhood and provide "unimpeachable personal references."[77]

Negative findings could and did lead to rejection: in a typical letter, Thomas concluded that it would "be unwise to admit" one little girl because her mother's "reputation leaves a great deal to be desired." Teachers with "questionable" habits—particularly those centering on their sexual behavior—likewise suffered from the founders' attitudes. A Miss O'Sullivan—although seen as an excellent candidate by Bryn Mawr's headmistress—was denied a teaching position because, according to Thomas, some evidence heard against her "was damaging in the extreme. It was probably a man's way of saying that she was fast." The Committee fired a French teacher likewise rumored to be "fast." Although the school's headmistress defended the teacher—"I know she has made an unfavorable impression in several instances, on account of her table manners, and her manners in general, but I have never heard any direct criticisms as to her being fast. Her life is a very quiet one"—the Committee claimed that the school could not risk negative public opinion. They denied dismissing the teacher because of her "personal character," writing to her that their actions stemmed only from "the difficulty you seem to have found outside of the school, in adjusting to American manners and ways of speech," which might arouse public "prejudices" that "would be of serious disadvantage to the school." The teacher emotionally defended her behavior, condemning the school's leaders for their intolerance, willingness to listen to "idle gossip," and indifference to her side of the story.[78]

The compilation of evidence inevitably raises questions as to whether the Bryn Mawr School was truly "revolutionary in all the main points," as M. Carey Thomas claimed it to be.[79] Certainly, the founders' conception of a new education for girls was revolutionary. The undeniably elitist variety of feminism the Bryn Mawr School and its founders sometimes epitomized, however, gives present-day observers pause. Like so many late-nineteenth- and early-twentieth-century reformers and the institutions they created, the Bryn Mawr

School perpetuated a host of prejudices at the same time it fought to overcome others. Sometimes, as with M. Carey Thomas's racism and anti-Semitism, the school reflected worse, rather than better, impulses of its day.

In the end, however, the Bryn Mawr School most significantly represents a major departure from traditional arguments for how and why girls should be educated. In rejecting prevailing conceptions of female difference in favor of an emphasis on women's essential likeness to men, the Bryn Mawr School established a new model for the education of girls that ultimately could have revolutionary implications not only for the education of certain kinds of privileged girls but for women and their place in society in general. One measure of exactly how exceptional that new vision was to be is the criticism it generated. The Bryn Mawr School would open to decidedly mixed reviews. Perhaps more telling than the inevitable scoffs from those who doubted the need for education for girls and women at all was the criticism from leading supporters of female education—just a very different conception of it. Many advocates of improved female education applauded efforts to take the education of girls seriously, but they differed from the Bryn Mawr School founders fundamentally in their conception of the intellectual nature of girls and the lives they should lead as adults.

A contemporary article in the *Kitchen Magazine* (a publication designed for women primarily filling roles in the traditional domestic sphere), discussing the opening of the school's new building, illustrates the issues that made Bryn Mawr exceptional and even controversial among both female and male supporters of serious and advanced female education. The article essentially agreed with the Bryn Mawr School founders that the existing state of girls' education was lamentable, that more money should be invested to improve schools for girls across the country, and that schools should pay more attention to improving the health of their female students. But the magazine's concurrence about the needs to advance girls' education stopped there: indeed, the article was damning with faint praise when it called Mary Garrett's work at the Bryn Mawr School "good as far as it goes."

Essentially, the *Kitchen Magazine*—while championing the expansion and improvement of education for girls—disagreed with Bryn Mawr's central assumption that girls should receive an education essentially identical to that of boys in the nation's best preparatory schools. Instead, they drew on older nineteenth-century separate spheres arguments premised on the ideals of female difference and even superiority—albeit an updated version of them—to justify their arguments. "Why does not Miss Garrett or some other philanthropist invest a quarter of a million in a model school of domestic economy, in which to prepare girls for housekeeping and home making?" they asked. In terms reminiscent of Catharine Beecher and a host of nineteenth-century reformers and those of the later Progressive Era, they argued that training in domestic economy should be a priority in the education of girls because "without pleasant, cosy, well-kept homes, the progress of the human race must be comparatively slow, and without thoroughly trained, competent housekeepers it is folly to hope for well-kept, pleasant homes." Drawing on arguments of social expediency, they claimed that society had a critical stake in improving the education of girls because their influence, as guardians of the domestic sphere, could ultimately redeem the public sectors of society.[80]

Older ways of thinking about women and their inherent differences from the opposite sex still held sway in late-nineteenth-century America. The Bryn Mawr School, however, represented an alternative way of conceptualizing the education of girls. The vision, the people, and the building were in place: the challenge would be to see the mission fulfilled.

CHAPTER TWO

Implementing the Vision
From Ideals to Institutional Realities

> During Miss Garrett's life time the school was practically in the position
> of an endowed school independent, essentially[,] of the public. It is no
> longer in that position: it is entirely dependent on the approval and sup-
> port of Baltimore people.
>
> —EDITH HAMILTON TO M. CAREY THOMAS,
>
> 10 NOVEMBER 1920

The founders of the Bryn Mawr School pioneered a new way of conceptualizing girls' education in the late nineteenth and early twentieth centuries. The
history of the school, however, is not only a story of ideals but equally a tale of
adapting the founders' dreams to the realities of a working school institution.
The complicated relationships between the vision and all the people who comprised the new school—the five young founders, with their lofty ideals; the administrators and teachers charged with operating the model school; the citizens
of Baltimore who could freely embrace what Bryn Mawr promised for their
daughters, or not; and the girls who would attend the school—reveal the enormous difficulty of implementing the Bryn Mawr vision. As the school's initial
decades illustrate, championing intellectual and educational equality for women
and transforming those ideals into a living school—populated with students,
teachers, parents, administrators, and donors, all with their unique personalities
and particular educational visions—are two very different things. The Bryn
Mawr School would be a complex compromise among those different people
and ideas.

From Vision to Reality: Difficult Transitions

Although the Friday Evening friendships of the five founders inspired the Bryn Mawr School, not all of the women would share equally in transforming the envisioned model school into a functioning institution. Just as plans for the new school were materializing, personal conflicts and loyalties were reconfiguring the women's relationships. Once their shared study and endeavors on behalf of women had provided mutual support and nurturing, but growing tensions now marred their earlier companionship. As a result, only Thomas, Garrett, and Gwinn remained during the actual implementation of the friends' plans for a new kind of school for girls. The growing intimacy between Thomas and Garrett eventually estranged Gwinn, and, in 1904, Mamie Gwinn left M. Carey Thomas, with whom she had lived for twenty-five years, and married Alfred Hodder. After Gwinn's marriage, Mary Garrett moved to reside with Thomas at the Bryn Mawr College deanery in Pennsylvania. From that time, Garrett, too, would be a fully absentee director of the school.[1]

The founders planned that the new Bryn Mawr School's every detail would enhance their vision for female education. Thomas devoted herself particularly to assembling an impressive faculty of female college graduates, while Garrett financed and directed the building of a magnificent new school structure. Because they believed in the uniqueness and superiority of their school, viewing their plans as so revolutionary that only they and a scant few other like-minded women could understand and appreciate them, they deliberately retained authority over every detail of the Bryn Mawr School's operation. Guarding their school against those who might alter, dilute, or destroy their plans was paramount, and their direct management, they believed, would be essential to the success of their mission.

But neither Thomas nor Garrett resided in Baltimore, and neither seems to have appreciated the amount of time and care the Bryn Mawr School would demand. During Bryn Mawr's earliest days, Mary Garrett had lavished attention on the school and its pupils—visiting regularly, planning and furnishing the new school building, even throwing sumptuous parties for students. But her recurrent bouts of illness and lengthy travels abroad (sometimes seeking cures and recuperation in Europe) interrupted her attention to the school, and she moved to Pennsylvania permanently in 1904. Thomas was first dean and then president of Bryn Mawr College, obviously an enormous responsibility, which kept her primary focus always the college, never the Bryn Mawr School. Despite their high hopes for the Bryn Mawr School and their reluctance to relinquish the implementation of those dreams to anyone else, Thomas and Garrett never consistently devoted their full energy to the school. Yet they continued to direct the school together from the Bryn Mawr College deanery until Garrett's death in 1915; Thomas would preside over the Bryn Mawr School's Board of Managers until her resignation in 1928.[2]

Thomas and Garrett did realize that the Bryn Mawr School would need an administrator to preside over the school and to facilitate communications between teachers, students, and families in Baltimore and the board headed at the deanery in Pennsylvania. For the position Thomas recruited highly educated women whom she considered representative of her ideals and capable of assuming day-to-day responsibility for running the school according to the founders' ideals.[3] From 1885 to 1895, four different secretaries would direct the Bryn Mawr School. But their authority over the business of the school was nominal. According to Thomas's niece, Millicent Carey McIntosh, the arrangement fit the situation:

> I can well understand why a school which insisted that girls should study Latin, which didn't allow them to drop subjects just because they didn't like them, preferred to have only a secretary who reported to Miss Thomas up in Bryn Mawr College. She, who was a hundred and twenty-five miles away, was safe from the rage of parents.[4]

But that situation often put the Bryn Mawr School secretaries in an untenable position. The correspondence between the succession of secretaries and Thomas and Garrett chronicles the frustration inherent in the secretaries' ambivalent position, as every teacher's schedule, every parent's query, every creditor's receipt had to be submitted to the board. Secretaries resented the Bryn Mawr founders' readiness to claim credit for the school's successes and to assign blame for its failures. The school's resulting administrative turmoil disturbed the school's teachers and supporters and did little to win the confidence of an already skeptical Baltimore public.[5]

Compounding its administrative problems, financial difficulties plagued the young Bryn Mawr School. While Mary Garrett's new building gave the impression of affluence, the Bryn Mawr School in reality did not generate enough revenue to support itself, even marginally. Early Bryn Mawr School records reveal constant financial worries. "There is not enough money in the bank to cash the teachers' cheques and they are now due," Thomas noted in 1895. "I must confess that I am rather in despair about the finances of the School," she confided elsewhere.[6] Bryn Mawr was fortunate to have a wealthy benefactor in Mary Garrett, who financed the school's building and continually paid its bills (a rarity for girls' schools, as noted by earlier educational reformers like Emma Willard and Catharine Beecher). But neither Garrett's substantial gifts nor her sometimes parsimonious management of the Bryn Mawr School's finances as treasurer of the board put the school in a secure financial position. Even Thomas's insistence that the Bryn Mawr School keep its teachers' salaries very low (ironically, given her championing of women's right to independence) by hiring primarily young graduates of women's colleges, who would work for less than more experienced teachers, did not save the Bryn Mawr School from debilitating debt that threatened the model school's long-term viability.[7]

The Bryn Mawr School's severe financial problems stemmed largely from its inability to attract an adequate number of students. Despite the founders' belief that Baltimore's girls needed a different kind of school, few Baltimoreans seem to have been interested in procuring a new kind of education for their daughters. Half-empty classrooms in the school's majestic building reflected the public's lackluster enthusiasm for the project. To combat public apathy and the shortage of students, the Bryn Mawr School board attempted to attract pupils with reduced or sometimes even free tuition. Although Mary Garrett—always a stickler for financial accountability—hoped the school could support itself through paying students, Mamie Gwinn reasoned that it might be better to accept a student for free or for half tuition when the school was not full.[8] At least Bryn Mawr could generate some revenue and, perhaps even more importantly, create the public illusion that the model school was succeeding. Likewise, Thomas decided against adopting a warning similar to Bryn Mawr College's admonition to families to pay their tuition fees in timely fashion—namely, a "Draconian clause about understanding and accepting terms and making oneself responsible" included in admissions information. That threat would be "much better omitted until the school is full," she concluded, clearly recognizing the imprudence of offending any parents (even those tardy to pay) who chose the Bryn Mawr School for their daughters.[9]

Despite its less-than-smooth transition from a vision to the realities of a functioning institution—despite administrative tangles, financial crises, and lukewarm public support—the Bryn Mawr School survived. Clearly, the school's progression from its shaky early beginnings to a thriving modern school signified an ability to overcome public skepticism and attract a core of support-ers. Even with Mary Garrett's money and willingness repeatedly to bolster the fledgling institution, the Bryn Mawr School simply had to have students to fill its classrooms and its coffers. Five women in Baltimore had decided to offer an extraordinary kind of education to girls. What kinds of families and girls would accept their offer?

Families and Students: A Portrait of the Bryn Mawr School's Constituency

No matter how lofty the founders' goals, how talented the school's teachers, or how impressive its building, the Bryn Mawr School could not succeed unless a critical mass of Baltimore parents enrolled their daughters in (and brought their money to) the model school. Reports of half-empty classrooms suggest that the early Bryn Mawr School was desperately short of students, but obvi-ously some families chose to support the school from its very beginnings. A dearth of documentation about students, parents, and their perspectives makes it difficult to uncover exactly who attended the early school and, most impor-tantly, their motives for embracing its goals for girls' education.

Given the school's primary mission of preparing girls for the most rigorous colleges open to women, the small but growing number of families seeking an elite college education for their daughters would have been the Bryn Mawr School's most obvious constituency. The Bryn Mawr School founders had deep personal ties to the Johns Hopkins University, and they cultivated connections between that respected institution and their own model school. The founders advertised that some of their own fathers served as trustees of the university to suggest the prestige of their school and enhance its (and their own) credibility. They eagerly recruited the daughters of Hopkins faculty members—even offer-ing them reduced tuition fees—because they were considered such desirable ad-ditions to the school. In the 1910s (by which time the Bryn Mawr School was well established and did not have to work as hard to recruit students), the school continued to grant substantial tuition reductions to all Hopkins professors (ex-cept "practicing physicians," who were considered able to pay the full cost of ed-ucating their daughters). Even as late as 1923, when Bryn Mawr was eliminating most scholarships and tuition reductions, the board voted to retain fee reduc-tions for Hopkins families.[10]

"Hopkins families" were among the Bryn Mawr School's core supporters from the beginning. As one alumna recalled, "Even in 1916, when I graduated from The Bryn Mawr School, the few Baltimore girls who even considered going to college were usually the daughters of men on the Hopkins faculty." A retrospective from the 1920s claimed that "for many years the school's academic standards have attracted the daughters of those who know how to value education ... [such as] professors at Johns Hopkins, people who are often not rich, but who have intellectual backgrounds and interests." According to another graduate, the Bryn Mawr School was even called "Little Miss Johns Hopkins."[11]

But Hopkins families alone could not sustain the Bryn Mawr School, particularly as they often paid reduced school fees. The school seems also to have drawn students from the broader middle classes who had college aspirations for their daughters. Historian Barbara Solomon noted that female collegians in the late nineteenth century were most likely to come from the growing middle classes rather than from the wealthiest sectors of society. Wealthy elites (from both established families and "new" money) tended to educate their daughters at home, in travels abroad, and in prestigious boarding schools, with the goal of preparing their daughters for good marriages and lives of leisure. In contrast, businessmen and professionals (including lawyers, doctors, professors, teachers, ministers, manufacturers, and tradesmen) "viewed college education for both sexes as the path to a fuller life, intellectually, socially, and economically."[12] And some families specifically hoped to provide their daughters with means of self-support. Many of the Bryn Mawr School's leaders fit this pattern. M. Carey Thomas came from a large middle-class family, respectable but not affluent. Headmistress Edith Hamilton, who would exert a strong influence over the school in the early twentieth century, came from a well-to-do family exceptional in its commitment to reform and to providing its four daughters with education that could make them self-supporting.[13]

The Bryn Mawr School attracted many families with similar goals. A 1916 graduate of the Bryn Mawr School (who later received a doctorate in experimental psychology from Bryn Mawr College) recalled that her mother opposed the idea of sending a girl to college—"taking a very dim view of what she called 'trying to ape men'"—but her father, a banker, viewed a college education as critical to his daughter's ability to support herself if she did not marry.[14] Furthermore, the founders generously supported many students they considered deserving, even when they could not afford private education. For instance, one Bryn Mawr headmistress requested and received a tuition reduction for Annie, the bright daughter of a widow who would probably need a college education to support herself. Another fatherless young girl whose mother was struggling to support their family specifically appealed to the school for reduced tuition so her daughter could become a teacher. Mamie Gwinn urged Mary Garrett that the Bryn Mawr School should educate for free the daughter of Bryn Mawr's French teacher, especially since there were not enough paying students to fill the school: "After all, what kind of girl is more in need of a college preparatory education than this small child of a self-supporting mother?"[15]

Bryn Mawr may have been the school of choice for some Baltimoreans who highly valued its rigorous college preparation, but such families did not provide enough full-tuition students to make the school a viable institution. In its earliest years, the Bryn Mawr School seems not to have attracted many wealthy supporters. According to one alumna, the early school drew students primarily from a segment of society that Baltimore's oldest, most prestigious families thought "did not 'matter at all.'"[16] But gradually, in the early decades of the twentieth century, the Bryn Mawr School began to attract more and more students from the "fashionable" part of Baltimore society. Eventually, the school would evolve into one of the largest, most popular, and most prestigious schools for girls in Baltimore.

Exactly why and how this happened is not clear. Perhaps some "fashionable" families were attracted by the Bryn Mawr School's connections to prominent Baltimoreans, particularly the families of the five founders. Bryn Mawr's reputation as the wealthy heiress Mary Garrett's school certainly added to its prestige. The school's connections to the Johns Hopkins University—both its trustees and its professors—may have appealed to others. Bryn Mawr's beautiful school building located in a fashionable residential section of town may have drawn other families. Too, the skill and charisma of Bryn Mawr Headmistress Edith Hamilton, who directed the school from 1896 to 1922, seem to have been key in winning the affection and loyalty of Baltimore's establishment.

But the Bryn Mawr School's increasing success in attracting students in the early twentieth century did not mean that all of those students would embrace their school's goals. Although all *Bryn Mawr School Bulletins* emphatically stated the school's intention to prepare all students for colleges of the highest standing, many students and their families had no such educational aspirations. School records and correspondence frequently lament the poor academic performance of Bryn Mawr students. Students failed required courses and examinations, left the school before completing its full academic course, and never sat for the Bryn Mawr College examination required for graduation. Not uncommon were the observations of a Johns Hopkins professor examining Bryn Mawr School students in 1889: the girls performed poorly, he claimed, showing a "lack of definiteness in answers" and demonstrating an only superficial understanding of the material. In 1895, Bryn Mawr School teachers sought to hold back many of their students for an extra year's work for fear that they would fail the required Bryn Mawr College entrance examination and hence damage the school's reputation.[17]

Scanty records make it difficult to document students' educational aspirations and college attendance, but it seems that the majority of girls who attended the early Bryn Mawr School were not interested in pursuing higher education. In 1887, the school's German teacher, who wanted her students to visit Bryn Mawr College to "be more able to sell the girls on what a lovely place it would be for them to go," worried to M. Carey Thomas that the school's pupils had very little knowledge of "the very great advantages of college life." A former student recalled that, while the Bryn Mawr School educated some "earnest, intelligent girls eager to prepare for college," it also enrolled "a number of daughters of Baltimore's fashionable families, intelligent, but some of them, alas, not really in earnest about education." A 1912 Bryn Mawr graduate reported that, although her class originally contained about forty girls, only twelve actually graduated.[18] Some students who passed the Bryn Mawr College examination and graduated from the Bryn Mawr School—and even won the school's highest honor, a scholarship to Bryn Mawr College—did not continue their education after leaving the school, preferring more traditional female paths in adulthood.

Many families who chose the Bryn Mawr School for their daughters obviously did so on their own terms. As one observer of Baltimore society noted decades later, Baltimore's elite had long preferred private education for its daughters, and attendance at the "right" schools cultivated lifelong connections in Baltimore's exclusive social circles. The Bryn Mawr School slowly—and, at this point, still tenuously—seemed to be gaining social prestige among some families.[19] While some families may have been attracted to the school because of its connections with prestigious social networks, they did not commit themselves to all of the school's goals. Many of Bryn Mawr's "fashionable" patrons used the school to educate their daughters for several years, never intending their daughters to pass the school's required examinations or to receive a graduation diploma. Some families preferred a European year abroad for their daughters rather than an academically rigorous final year of courses and exam preparation at the Bryn Mawr School.[20] Other families transferred their daughters to popular boarding schools for their final years of schooling. For these families, the Bryn Mawr School served purposes very different than college and career preparation; it provided one stage in preparing girls from elite families for more traditional female paths.

The patronage of these families was critical to the Bryn Mawr School's survival. Thomas's, Gwinn's, and Garrett's convictions led them to accept many worthy but not fully paying students, but the school desperately needed the steady source of revenue wealthy Baltimore families could provide. Ironically, while the growth of Bryn Mawr's socially prestigious constituency ensured the survival of the school, it also laid the ground for future conflict. After all, revolutionizing "fashionable" education for girls—not perpetuating it—was what the founders' Bryn Mawr School was all about. But the reality was that those Baltimore families most likely to embrace Bryn Mawr's goal of higher education were not among those most able to afford extended private education for their daughters.

Nurturing the School: Edith Hamilton's Story

After a decade of administrative troubles and financial difficulties, the arrival of Edith Hamilton as the Bryn Mawr School's new headmistress in 1896 greatly enhanced the school's ability to survive in Baltimore. A woman who shared the founders' love of learning and their belief in the power of education to transform women's lives, Edith Hamilton was committed to the founders' vision for their school. Just as important was that she proved adept at translating educational ideals into a thriving institution.[21]

Born in 1867 to a prominent Fort Wayne, Indiana, family (she and her relatives, including seventeen children, occupied three houses that encompassed three full city blocks), Edith Hamilton learned early the importance of education. Edith was the oldest of five children, and she and her three sisters studied literature, history, theology, and Greek, Latin, French, and German at home with their parents and tutors. Encouraged particularly by their mother to prepare for active lives, Hamilton and her sisters attended Miss Porter's School for Young Ladies in Farmington, Connecticut (as many relatives had before and would after them).[22]

Miss Porter's and the education imparted there contrasted with the education that would later be espoused by the Bryn Mawr School—indeed, Miss Porter's epitomized many of the "finishing school" characteristics that the Bryn Mawr School founders rejected. Sarah Porter (1813–1900) devoted her school to developing culture and character in its students. She rejected academic requirements, examinations, and grades; all classes and subjects were electives. Edith Hamilton later recalled that "we weren't taught anything." Similarly, her sister Alice expressed how "it is hard to make anyone who is not an old Farmington girl understand the love and loyalty we hold for Miss Porter's School, for some of the teaching we received was the world's worst." In contrast to the aims of education at the Bryn Mawr School, a Miss Porter's School education did not encourage students to wander from traditional paths. In fact, Edith Hamilton's ambition to go to college apparently disturbed Miss Porter, who opposed higher education for women.[23]

Despite the opposition of Miss Porter and that of some of her own family members, Edith Hamilton determined to go to Bryn Mawr College. Because her education was inadequate, she prepared for the college's entrance examination at home, studying especially the more advanced mathematics her formal schooling had neglected. Hamilton passed the Bryn Mawr examinations and excelled at the college. In 1895, she was awarded Bryn Mawr College's prestigious Mary E. Garrett European Fellowship, granted annually to the college's top graduate for advanced study abroad. Accompanied by her sister Alice (who herself received an M.D. from the University of Michigan and, in 1919, became the first woman ever appointed to the Harvard University faculty as a professor of industrial medicine), Hamilton proceeded first to the University of Leipzig and then to the University of Munich to study classics. As was the case when M. Carey Thomas and other women pioneered in higher education, Edith Hamilton found that her classmates reacted uncertainly, often with hostility, to her presence at the German universities. According to Alice Hamilton, her sister had to attend classes sitting in "a chair up on the lecturer's platform, where nobody could be contaminated by contact with her."[24]

While the sisters were studying in Germany during the 1895–96 school year, M. Carey Thomas offered Edith Hamilton the new position of headmistress (as opposed to the earlier "secretary") of the Bryn Mawr School. The school desperately needed a new administrator, and Thomas had confidence in Hamilton's abilities. Hamilton had planned to obtain a doctorate in Europe, but financial pressures in her family—and the fact that the Hamilton family had younger daughters to educate—helped persuade her to abandon her dreams of a Ph.D.

in exchange for an assured income. Hamilton accepted Thomas's offer, and she and Alice arrived in Baltimore in 1896. While Alice entered Johns Hopkins Medical School, where she studied briefly, Edith became the first individual outside the circle of founders to have a significant influence on the Bryn Mawr School. She would be its headmistress for twenty-six years, before she went on to achieve fame as a writer.[25]

A third Hamilton sister, Margaret, also graduated from Bryn Mawr College and studied biology and anatomy in Europe and at Johns Hopkins Medical School; she abandoned a science career (probably because of health reasons) and followed her sister Edith to the Bryn Mawr School. Margaret taught science at the school, headed its Primary School, and eventually acted as head of the school in the early 1930s. Margaret lived and worked closely with her sister at Bryn Mawr for two decades and remained at the school for nearly another two decades after Edith Hamilton departed, exerting considerable influence over the institution.[26]

As headmistress of the Bryn Mawr School, Edith Hamilton managed the daily details of school life, overseeing teachers and students, planning courses, shuffling schedules, organizing student activities, and seeing to the maintenance of school facilities. With its founders frequently absent, the school desperately needed a competent administrator. Hamilton tended to the details, but she sensed that her most important challenge would be to establish the fledgling institution by winning the trust and affection of critical segments of the Baltimore community.

Hamilton managed what she referred to as "the educational side of the work" but devoted herself equally to winning the support, affection, and loyalty of parents, students, alumnae, teachers, and the larger Baltimore public. As she wrote to Thomas in 1915, her early years at the school had been devoted to "the really big and important matters" that included "making teachers and pupils devoted to the school," "managing difficult parents," "building up a body of loyal alumnae," and "changing, really, the opinion of the public about the school." When Hamilton came to the Bryn Mawr School, the majority of Baltimoreans were skeptical about the new school, and one of her top priorities was to change their attitudes about rigorous college-preparatory education and expanded opportunities for women.[27]

Hamilton concurred with the founders that the Bryn Mawr School's central educational mission should be "to send as many Baltimore girls as possible to college." As she explained on the occasion of the school's seventy-fifth anniversary, she never questioned the rightness of maintaining Bryn Mawr's strict academic standards for all:

> The idea that we might be causing inferiority complexes never occurred to me.
> The notion had not yet invaded school precincts and my own experience, far
> from leading me to it, made me convinced that the Bryn Mawr College entrance
> examinations could be passed by every girl who was willing to work hard, very
> hard in some cases, I admit.[28]

Always Hamilton hoped to inspire her students to embrace learning and cherish the life of the mind.

During Hamilton's years at Bryn Mawr, the school maintained its rigorous central curriculum. In the first decade of the twentieth century, core course requirements were essentially the same as in the 1880s and 1890s. Because students were required to pass the Bryn Mawr College entrance examination to graduate from the Bryn Mawr School, coursework focused heavily on preparation in the subjects to be tested. All students studied English (with "great emphasis" on "voice production and enunciation"), Latin, French, and history (including ancient civilizations and European and American history) throughout their course of study. German or Greek was required of advanced students. Additionally, students studied geometry, algebra, and laboratory sciences. The school required everyone to take drawing and gymnasium; music was required of younger students but was elective for those in upper classes. By the 1910s, Bryn Mawr had expanded its offerings to include elective courses such as art, chorus, drama, home economics, and household chemistry.[29]

Like Thomas and Garrett, Hamilton understood how difficult it would be to maintain Bryn Mawr's standards in a community that did not agree on the best content for girls' education. "Utterly disregarding the popular demand," she wrote Thomas, the Bryn Mawr School was essentially "offering the people of Baltimore what they do not want: a first class college preparatory education for girls." Hamilton described herself and the founders as missionaries who would have to convert Baltimore to a new understanding of how and for what to educate their daughters. Together, Bryn Mawr's board, administrators, and teachers needed to coax and cajole Baltimore families into appreciating the value of a Bryn Mawr School education.[30]

As Hamilton repeatedly argued to the Bryn Mawr School board, winning over the support of Baltimore was not an option: it was a necessity, and it would not be easy. The Bryn Mawr School might have been able to impose its educational vision on Baltimore families in its earliest days, when Mary Garrett's money had put the school, in Hamilton's words, "practically in the position of an endowed school independent, essentially[,] of the public." But Garrett's money could not forever prop up the model school if a larger segment of Baltimore did not embrace and support the school on its own. While Garrett and Thomas argued that the Bryn Mawr School should simply require that students adhere to its high standards, Hamilton continually reminded them that financial realities made it difficult for the school to make demands. As Hamilton wrote Thomas in 1920, Bryn Mawr had run deficits continually from 1902 through World War I, with the exception of three years when the school's expenses were met only by deferring critical maintenance on the school building. Overwhelmed by debt and short of students, the Bryn Mawr School simply could not afford to act without regard to the wishes of the public. Ultimately, she argued, the institution would be "entirely dependent on the approval and support of the Baltimore people."[31] The challenge would be for Bryn Mawr to maintain popular support while remaining true to the founders' vision.

Families

Commitment to high academic standards for girls and dependence on the financial support of families did not coexist easily in Baltimore, a fact Hamilton feared that Thomas and Garrett did not appreciate. Hamilton urged them to consider the price of maintaining the Bryn Mawr School's standards. In a 1915 letter, Hamilton described the dilemma faced by the school when a prominent Baltimore family objected to mathematics requirements for its daughter:

> There is not another school in the country that would let Mary go[,] well connected as she is, rich, attractive, and an excellent language student besides; but, of course I must let her go if I cannot convince Mrs. Lee, and as Mary is thoroughly spoiled, an only child who will have a great deal of money some day, and as she detests her algebra … the odds are certainly against me.

Hamilton knew that the Lees would have no trouble finding a more accommodating school for their daughter. "Every other school I know would make the concession; would arrange a special course for Mary, would keep the good will of her family," but, of course, the Bryn Mawr School could not.[32]

Hamilton did not argue that Bryn Mawr should relax its mathematics requirements for Mary, but she did try to convince Thomas that the school could be more accommodating to families without abandoning its principles. Occasionally "bending" Bryn Mawr's standards and policies could garner the school much-needed loyalty and good will, ultimately helping the school achieve its goals. In another instance, Hamilton warned Thomas that the school risked losing more "well connected" students whose parents thought Bryn Mawr promoted its Primary School students to its Main School at too young an age: "For us to lose the children of such people ... educated people who care very much about their children's training would be a great misfortune to us."[33] Was Bryn Mawr's rule worth the loss of so many prominent families?

Hamilton particularly disagreed with Thomas on how to handle families who were late to pay their school fees. Thomas advocated strict policies as the best solution to a recurrent problem, and the Bryn Mawr School board periodically acted to improve the school's financial situation. Hamilton, while she obviously preferred families to pay their bills in full and on time, argued that sometimes rigid financial policies were short sighted and could easily backfire and harm, more than help, the school's long-term financial outlook. When Mary Garrett and the board proposed denying admission to the daughters of two popular Baltimore families because of their poor credit ratings, Hamilton objected. According to Hamilton, one of the little girls had a cousin enrolled at the Bryn Mawr School and was also a "friend of a number of the nicest children" at the school. Denying admission to the child in question would upset Bryn Mawr families, potentially losing their support. The other girl to whom the board proposed denying admission because of her family's credit rating hoped to transfer to Bryn Mawr from another Baltimore girls' school. Already at least one other child from that rival school had applied to Bryn Mawr in hope of remaining with her friend. If the Bryn Mawr School accepted the one girl in question, other students would follow. Hence, Hamilton reasoned to Garrett, she did "not believe that it would be wise policy to refuse either of those children."[34]

But the board rejected Hamilton's advice. Thomas believed that tolerating the financial delinquency of a few parents would encourage similar bad habits among the rest of the school's families. Arguing that her strict payment policy worked at Bryn Mawr College and could help secure a sounder financial basis for the Bryn Mawr School, Thomas ordered Hamilton to "enforce the rule in the catalogue that asked pupils to leave the school whose bills were not paid by the regular date." "Really troubled and anxious and unhappy" about the board's policy, Hamilton wrote to Thomas that "my own point of view" is "so different from yours in this matter" that "I feel that I must put it fully before you."[35]

"In my opinion the college and the school are in quite a different position," Hamilton argued. Trying to operate the Bryn Mawr School—a fundamentally local institution drawing students only from Baltimore families (even though Bryn Mawr's founders had hoped their model school would be of national interest and spark the formation of similar schools elsewhere)—like Bryn Mawr College was illogical. Hamilton offered the example of a Chicago judge whose daughter, Mary Brown, was stricken with typhoid fever and was unable to enter Bryn Mawr College. Despite the girl's illness, Bryn Mawr College—in strict accordance with Thomas's policy—demanded full payment of her college fees for the year.

> Of course I can perfectly understand the position of the college. The money was worth more to the college than Judge Brown's good will. What, after all, would it matter to Bryn Mawr [College] if she incurred a certain amount of ill will in the Chicago North Side? What would it really matter to her if North Side girls began going to Vassar instead? Bryn Mawr has all the rest of the United States to draw from; the ill will or good will of one set in one city is a negligible matter to her. The position of the school is altogether different; we are wholly dependent upon the good will of a quite limited number of people in Baltimore; every enemy we make is a serious danger to us. If Mary Brown's case had happened in the school instead of in the college it would have been better a hundred times over for us not to have exacted the payment of that bill.

Such harsh policy was doubly unwise at the local Bryn Mawr School because the school was still "offering the people of Baltimore what they do not want: a first class college preparatory education for girls." Because the Bryn Mawr School was "utterly disregarding the popular demand," it could not risk offending some of those few families who did embrace the school because they were late with their school fees.[36]

Hamilton pleaded with Thomas not to expel the daughters of prominent families for financial delinquency:

> To my mind such an action would be really terrible for the school[;] it would be hard for us to recover from it. These are people who have been connected for years with the school, who have always paid their bills, but who have often been late in paying them. They are on the friendliest terms with the school, they have many of them thanked me for the considerate behaviour of the school in regard

to late bills. To treat them as no drygoods shop or grocery shop would treat them, would be in my view an utterly wrong, a most mistaken, step to take.

Rather than alienating Baltimore families, Hamilton argued, the Bryn Mawr School needed to understand and accommodate them.[37]

Hamilton further argued that the Bryn Mawr School needed to be responsive to its environment, to react positively to changing conditions and times, rather than clinging to old rules. As she described it, Bryn Mawr should be "a living, growing school, able to meet new conditions" if it were to survive. As early as 1913, Edith and Margaret Hamilton noted two trends they believed demanded a response. First, Baltimoreans increasingly wanted schools to accept their preschool-aged children. In 1913, Edith and Margaret Hamilton informed Thomas of their desire to establish a "Baby Class" at the Bryn Mawr School. Numerous mothers who first tried to enroll their little girls at the Bryn Mawr School were going to other schools who accepted younger children—and inevitably those children remained at those rival schools rather than transferring to Bryn Mawr's Primary School when they were older. Parents who already had older daughters enrolled at Bryn Mawr and who wanted the school to take their younger daughters were particularly unhappy. "I hope very earnestly that you let us try this next year," Edith Hamilton implored Thomas. "Some plan seems to me absolutely essential to the success of the Primary department. The public demands a class for small children and they will go to other schools if we do nothing to satisfy this demand." Thomas, however, expressed "very grave objection" to the Hamilton sisters' plans, instructing them to concentrate on attracting students by making Bryn Mawr's Primary School the best school in town rather than by trying to capture a few "babies." While Hamilton pragmatically tried to position the Bryn Mawr School to accommodate families' demands, Thomas objected to any plans that might jeopardize the clarity of Bryn Mawr's mission. In the face of a public that she probably rightly sensed did not share all of her educational goals for their daughters, Thomas vetoed any plans for her model school to accept "babies" simply because their mothers wanted it.[38]

More significantly (even if they did not realize it at the time), the Hamilton sisters recognized the potential negative effects that changing residential patterns in Baltimore could have on the Bryn Mawr School. Seeing that more and more families were abandoning Baltimore's central city in favor of new suburbs, Edith and Margaret Hamilton proposed establishing a series of "feeder" primary schools in various suburban neighborhoods. Such schools could attract families of young girls, providing a steady flow of well-prepared students for the centrally located Bryn Mawr Main School. Lagging enrollments in the Bryn Mawr Primary School was a major concern for the school as a whole, since educating girls "from the cradle" assured full classes in the school's upper divisions, as well as cultivating long-term loyalty in families and students. Thomas and the Bryn Mawr School board were initially skeptical but, after much debate, consented to experiment. An outbreak of infantile paralysis (polio)—which made parents reluctant to send their little girls to any schools—ultimately defeated the plan. The Hamilton sisters' early analysis of trends in Baltimore, however, and their recognition of the need to respond to the shifting residences of prominent Baltimore families foreshadowed events that the Bryn Mawr School would have to face in the future.[39]

The most influential figures at the Bryn Mawr School in the early twentieth century—M. Carey Thomas, Mary Garrett, and Edith Hamilton—agreed that the school should maintain strict academic requirements and should encourage families to embrace new standards and aspirations for their daughters. But their attitudes and styles differed greatly. Edith Hamilton, perhaps because she was in daily contact with students and families or perhaps because of her personality, empathized with Baltimoreans. As her longtime companion and former Bryn Mawr School student Doris Fielding Reid described it, "Edith was able to see through the foolishness of some of the Baltimore attitudes to the real worth of a great many of its people." In turn, Baltimore families appreciated Hamilton: "Edith did not antagonize the Baltimore parents, as did many of the so-called 'advanced women' of that time." Hamilton remembered Bryn Mawr parents as "people who taught me so much" with "their wisdom and kindness."[40]

Removed from daily contact with individuals in the Bryn Mawr School community, Thomas and Garrett worried little about the negative sentiment their school's policies might create in Baltimore. Instead, they worried how easy it would be for Bryn Mawr to become "just another girls' school" if they relaxed the school's standards (if they excused a girl from gymnasium or math class, if they opened a "baby" class, if they let a bill go unpaid). The lackluster academic performance of many students, as well as the low rates of graduation and college attendance, during the school's earliest decades proved their suspicions justified. Their fears and mistrust of Baltimore families made them act defensively. Their tenacity in asserting their vision for the Bryn Mawr School kept the school from becoming a more conventional institution, a remarkable accomplishment in it-self. But their attitudes did little to win the loyalty of the Baltimore public that Hamilton believed critical to the school's success.

Women and Alumnae in the Progressive Era

Edith Hamilton understood the importance of cultivating families, and she also sensed the value of loyal alumnae. Hamilton, as a teacher personally de-voted to many of her students beyond their years of formal schooling, believed that a strong Bryn Mawr School alumnae association would benefit her former students. And, as a pragmatic administrator who perceived what it took to build a strong and lasting school institution, she knew that alumnae could greatly im-prove the school's chance of long-term success. By volunteering their time, sending their own daughters to the school, and raising and donating money, alumnae could enhance the school's public profile and make it strong. As Hamil-ton confided to Thomas when she proposed an annual "Alumnae Day" at the Bryn Mawr School in 1914, "I have realized in the last two years as never before, how very valuable to the school a strong Alumnae Association would be."[41]

M. Carey Thomas and Mary Garrett always expressed great pride in the Bryn Mawr School's "successes." Successes they defined as students who fulfilled the school's goals for its graduates: young women who went to Bryn Mawr College, who earned advanced degrees, who succeeded in their chosen professions. But Bryn Mawr School students who followed more traditional paths for women were a disappointment. As Thomas remarked of her Bryn Mawr College stu-dents, "Our failures only marry." Under such criteria, the majority of Bryn Mawr School students—most of whom never graduated from college and "only" married—deserved little note.[42]

Hamilton, however, had a different attitude. She was a teacher who saw her students in more personal terms—even the ones with lesser aptitudes or ambi-tions—and she hoped the Bryn Mawr School would inspire all of her students. She remembered her tenure at the school in such terms: "The atmosphere of the school was not dull or depressing. Again and again I saw that delightful thing, an awakening to the joys of knowledge. I became convinced that real education was a matter of individual conversion."[43] More pragmatically, Hamilton real-ized that often the school's more traditional graduates were the women most likely to remain in Baltimore, marrying, devoting themselves to volunteer work, and identifying strongly with the Bryn Mawr School rather than a college or career. Indeed, alumnae who remained close to home might well prove the most valuable in establishing the Bryn Mawr School in Baltimore.

Edith Hamilton's relationship to the Bryn Mawr School's alumnae is rooted in Progressive Era thinking about women and their relationship to society, particularly in the influence of the social settlement movement. Growing out of the desire of educated women simultaneously to help the less fortunate of society and to find useful, fulfilling employment for themselves, settlements offered a new model for the place of educated women in American society during the late nineteenth and early twentieth centuries. Following the example set by Jane Addams and her Hull House settlement (founded in Chicago during the same decade as the Bryn Mawr School), scores of educated women embraced, if not always the more radical elements of her platform of commitment to the poor, her general principle of educated women's service to society. After the establishment of Hull House as a place for women to live and serve the residents of surrounding poor neighborhoods, the number of settlements grew to more than a hundred in 1900 and more than four hundred by 1920.[44]

Although some men participated in settlements, women were the real force in the movement—and there they simultaneously developed and perpetuated particular notions about women's nature and place in society. The philosophy of Addams and her contemporaries combined both old and new notions about women. Essentially, these Progressive Era women accepted the notion of female difference, a legacy of separate spheres ideology. Notably, however, they did not view women's distinct natures as confining them to the private sphere. To the contrary, this group of highly educated and ambitious women embraced many of the ideas advocated by those like Thomas—believing in women's capacity for advanced education, in their ability and right to pursue careers, in their need for independence and self-support, in their right to an equal voice in the public world. But they rejected the notion that women and men were basically the same, instead arguing that women's nurturing, compassionate natures made them particularly suited for certain fields of study and work. Encouraging women to apply their skills to the betterment of modern society, they embraced "social housekeeping" as a means of extending women's distinct aptitudes, rooted in motherhood and the home, to the wider public sphere.

Edith Hamilton never lived in a settlement house or worked for the social reform that animated many settlement residents, but she did have close connections to the movement. Her sister Alice Hamilton was among the inner circle at Hull House, an intimate friend of Jane Addams, and a resident of the settlement part time even after she became a professor of industrial medicine at Harvard University Medical School. Younger Hamilton sister Norah illustrated Addams's *Twenty Years at Hull House*, and she and her mother Gertrude Hamilton, widowed in 1909, often resided there, as well. Using Hull House as a base, Alice Hamilton devoted herself to causes including female suffrage, workers' rights, socialism, and pacifism. From her perspective, her feminine nature suited her well both for reform and for her professional life as a doctor and scholar of industrial medicine. Edith and Alice Hamilton were close: Edith described her sister as "balm to my soul." Certainly, Alice's pursuits shaped Edith's thinking about society and the roles of women within it.[45]

Around 1910, Edith Hamilton launched the Bryn Mawr School Alumnae League: "an association of the Alumnae who had club work among the factory girls," as she described it to Mary Garrett in 1913. A 1910 Bryn Mawr School yearbook gave Hamilton complete credit both for conceiving of and organizing the league. The Alumnae League would undertake a myriad of activities, sometimes in coordination with the local YMCA or Red Cross: sponsoring a Girl Scout troop, directing Bible study groups for working girls, organizing charity rummage sales, and even "employ[ing] a trained, paid worker who lives in the neighborhood and directs the work." While obviously most of the alumnae in the Bryn Mawr School Alumnae League remained more traditional and conservative than Alice Hamilton and her peers at Hull House—returning to their comfortable homes and families each night—nonetheless they were exploring new models of womanhood. Particularly, the Bryn Mawr School gave students and alumnae who did not embrace the school's founding vision an alternative vision of how they might use their education. They were creating new roles, new avenues of useful female activity. And, as Hamilton realized, their activities were helpful not only to themselves and their community but also to their school.[46]

Throughout the 1910s, the school's alumnae grew more organized and conscious of their place in the Bryn Mawr School community. They viewed Bryn Mawr as "their" school and identified Edith Hamilton, rather than Bryn Mawr's founders and board, as its true leader. Their increasing identification with Hamilton, rather than with Thomas and Garrett, is probably not surprising. In the school's earliest days, Thomas and Garrett knew their students by name and followed their academic progress personally. The earliest Bryn Mawr School bulletins described the institution as "Mary Garrett's school," and, in the 1880s and 1890s, Garrett routinely visited the school and hosted lavish parties for her girls; likewise, M. Carey Thomas hosted Bryn Mawr School students during their visits to Bryn Mawr College. But the founders' personal contact with Bryn Mawr students had faded. Edith Hamilton invited Mary Garrett, for instance, to attend a 1913 meeting of alumnae, noting that "it would be felt as a very great honour and pleasure if you would and it is so long since you have been to any school function except Commencement." That same year, Thomas failed to attend even the Bryn Mawr School's graduation ceremony: "We were more disappointed than I can say not to have you at the commencement," Hamilton wrote Thomas. A combination of absorption in Bryn Mawr College and health problems—Mary Garrett suffered with leukemia from 1912 until her death in 1915, and Thomas underwent several operations on her leg, burned in a childhood accident, in 1913—only increased the founders' distance from the life of their school.[47]

Thomas's attitude toward Bryn Mawr School alumnae generated resentment. When the alumnae raised money for a scholarship fund in 1915, Thomas responded that surely a board member would have to be appointed to direct alumnae projects, since "the financial knowledge of the alumnae is very limited."[48] Hamilton frequently chided Thomas for her attitudes. In 1920, she admonished her that Bryn Mawr alumnae were perfectly capable of understanding their school's business—including its severe financial problems—and that they would respond generously if only the board would speak to them respectfully rather than condescendingly:

> The old days when Miss Garrett had to impose upon the people of Baltimore good education for girls and could not look for help in her great undertaking to any Baltimoreans have passed. The people now want good education for their daughters; they will support a college preparatory school for girls and they want a Board with larger representation from Baltimore.[49]

The issue of "larger representation from Baltimore" would escalate into the first round of a battle brewing between the Bryn Mawr School's local community of support in Baltimore and the president of the Board of Managers, M. Carey Thomas, in Pennsylvania.

As the Bryn Mawr School community solidified its identity, it demanded more power over its school. Specifically, Bryn Mawr School alumnae resented the fact that so few alumnae, and representatives from Baltimore in general, served on the school's managing board. By the 1910s, alumnae actively campaigned to garner some of the board's power. Edith Hamilton championed their cause. Letters between Edith Hamilton and Bryn Mawr School alumna Clara Murray Eager in June 1919 show that Hamilton was openly siding with the alumnae in their fight against the Bryn Mawr School board. Hamilton seems to have believed in the rightness of her cause, both for alumnae and for the school in general. Hamilton had had her own disagreements with Thomas and Garrett over management of the school, and many of her most loyal advocates were active Bryn Mawr School alumnae. Those alumnae would support her in future conflicts that might arise with the school board. In a real sense, increasing the power of Bryn Mawr School alumnae meant increasing the power of Edith Hamilton.[50]

At a 1919 board meeting, Hamilton argued "that the elevation to the Board of prominent Baltimore women would be a source of strength to the School and would greatly increase the local interest and support." In the fall of 1920, the Bryn Mawr School Alumnae Association wrote to their school's board, protesting that the board failed to appreciate the school's alumnae and their considerable efforts on behalf of the school. The board, in turn, was forced to discuss the "serious situation" stemming from alumnae discontent. In response to the brewing controversy, Hamilton admonished Thomas that the primary criticism of Bryn Mawr alumnae was that the school's board was "too small and too little representative of Baltimore, and in this, as you know, Margaret and I are entirely in agreement with them."[51]

Thomas, however, strongly and consistently opposed expanding the Bryn Mawr School's board. A very small group of individuals really committed to education could best govern the school, she argued in a 1919 board meeting. An enlarged board would not "be in sympathy with the maintenance of high college standards." And surely new board members elected from Baltimore would "be out of sympathy with the aims for which the school is founded and maintained." Thomas threatened those agitating for an expanded board that, while she and the current board were "willing to expend the time and effort required" to manage a school with Bryn Mawr's unique vision and standards, "we should feel no great interest in" the school "if its character were to be changed." But the pressure on Thomas to relent was great, particularly because the school's financial troubles were so acute that appealing to alumnae for aid seemed essential to

Bryn Mawr's survival. Fearing dire consequences for the Bryn Mawr School if they did not consent to alumnae demands, the board finally agreed that alumnae might have two seats on the Bryn Mawr School board.[52]

But Thomas's capitulation to alumnae demands was not complete, and she fought to control which alumnae might serve on the board. Thomas wrote to Hamilton that the board should take great care in electing new members, making certain that future alumnae members would be graduates of both the Bryn Mawr School and Bryn Mawr College and "investigating very carefully the character of such graduates" before their election. Particularly, Thomas had come to view Board Member Clara Eager, who was lobbying to open the board to alumnae, parents, and Baltimore citizens in general, as a troublemaker who should never have been elected to the board. With only Edith Hamilton and Clara Eager dissenting, the Bryn Mawr School board adopted a statement in 1920 reaffirming their commitment to keeping power on the board concentrated in the hands of a small number of women. Although they agreed to allow two alumnae representatives on the board, they included stipulations designed to preserve the Bryn Mawr School founders' original vision for the education of girls. For the present, one of the alumnae representatives to the board was required to be a graduate of a college in good standing; after 1925, both alumnae members were to be college graduates. In a letter to Thomas, Edith Hamilton objected to the provision because that stipulation (as Thomas well knew) meant that alumnae board members would not really be "representative," since "a very large majority" of Bryn Mawr School alumnae were not, in fact, college graduates.[53]

The immediate issue had been settled, but the antagonisms had not been mitigated. Alumnae wanted an even greater say in their school, and teachers and families, too, were beginning to register their protests. Edith Hamilton had made her resentments against Thomas public and was now speaking openly against the board's policies. And M. Carey Thomas worried, as she always had, that her model school's standards were being eroded, that the Bryn Mawr School was in danger of becoming "just another girls' school" rather than the model institution the founders had intended it to be.

Teachers

Both the Bryn Mawr School's founders and Headmistress Edith Hamilton understood the importance of high-quality teachers. In the school's earliest decades, Thomas went to great lengths to recruit talented teachers with impressive academic credentials who could uphold Bryn Mawr's academic standards. Many graduates of the Seven Sister colleges—with, not surprisingly, a good many from Bryn Mawr College—taught at the Bryn Mawr School and devoted substantial parts of their lives to the school, its students, and other teachers. And many of those teachers felt unappreciated for their abilities, loyalty, and hard work.[54]

While many teachers had expressed their enthusiasm for the founders' establishment of the Bryn Mawr School, unhappy teachers were prevalent at the early school. The turnover rate of Bryn Mawr School faculty (mirroring the school's rapid succession of secretaries before Hamilton's arrival) was very high. Many teachers—some who were dismissed and others who remained—shared a negative impression of their school's management. Even as they affirmed their respect for the founders' vision, they often characterized them as dictatorial and underhanded. Teachers lodged numerous complaints against the founders: that they reneged on employment agreements; that they interfered with teachers' judgments about curriculum, teaching methods, and grading; that they ignored teachers' suggestions; and that they arbitrarily dismissed teachers who had received no prior warning that their work was unsatisfactory.

Teachers expressed their discontent in letters to the Bryn Mawr School Committee in the 1880s and 1890s. Teacher Mary Augusta Scott warned that, if the Bryn Mawr School were to live up to its founders' vision—being "at once thorough in work, and liberal in spirit"—its managing Committee would have to learn to trust the skills and judgments of its teachers. Another teacher complained that, although the Bryn Mawr School founders had promised her a permanent teaching position, they later relegated her to "engagement by the week."[55] At least four other teachers expressed bewilderment and dismay at their dismissal.[56] Fired math instructor Charlotte Smith defended herself against accusations of poor teaching, asserting that, had the board "seen fit to indicate your disapproval of any of my methods[,] I would have willingly made any change you might have suggested." She concluded that she could not "but believe that the Committee have some reason for their action of which I know nothing."[57] Clearly upset by the Bryn Mawr School Committee's characterization of her as "a disgrace to the school which has been tolerated," Elizabeth Bickford (unlike Charlotte Smith) passively accepted the board's decision to fire her, leaving while still pronouncing her devotion to the Bryn Mawr School and her students.

But teachers' complaints had little effect on Bryn Mawr School policy. As Thomas instructed Edith Hamilton, the school's policy should be to hire bright, young graduates from the best women's colleges who, because they would be grateful for a position at a school like Bryn Mawr, would be willing to teach for very low pay. If those teachers—having gained some experience—chose to move on to schools offering more competitive pay, the Bryn Mawr School could easily replace them with other new college graduates.[58]

While Thomas saw many teachers as a dispensable commodity, Edith Hamilton rallied to their cause. From her perspective, Bryn Mawr's faculty was an invaluable asset to the school, and many of the teachers were her personal friends. Crushing teachers' enthusiasm and loyalty, she argued, stifled the school's ability to provide a good education to girls. Hamilton continually pleaded with the Bryn Mawr board to improve the working conditions of teachers. She repeatedly and unsuccessfully argued that the school should raise the low salaries it paid experienced teachers: "We cannot spend the money in any other way that will be so beneficial to the school as by keeping teachers who are in every way what we want, and making them loyal by paying them fairly." She later argued specifically that longtime English teacher Miss Hoyt—who "was perfectly aware that she could get more money elsewhere" but remained at Bryn Mawr out of a strong sense of loyalty to the school and its founders—deserved better pay.[59]

Hamilton's actions prove how deeply she believed in her own arguments to the board. On more than one occasion, she offered to sacrifice her own salary to increase that of Bryn Mawr's teachers. In a 1913 letter to Thomas, Edith Hamilton explained how her support for raising teachers' salaries would actually come at her own expense. Since Hamilton's contract guaranteed her a portion of any profits the school might make, increasing teacher salaries would certainly lessen the possibility that Bryn Mawr might make a profit and that she might receive a bonus. Hamilton particularly deplored the Bryn Mawr School board's practice of delaying salary payments to teachers whenever the school fell short of funds. Hamilton worried about the effect on teachers: "I do feel very strongly that we ought to pay the teachers if possible as they depend upon their monthly salaries for their living expenses," she wrote Thomas. In the face of a financial shortfall in 1915, Edith Hamilton proposed that, rather than delaying payments to teachers, she and her sister Margaret would forgo their salaries for the month and cover the school's expenses out of their personal funds.[60] Not surprisingly,

Hamilton's sympathy won her the support of Bryn Mawr's teachers, just as it had garnered the loyalty of its alumnae.

Administrative Conflict

Edith Hamilton supported teachers and alumnae because she believed their good will necessary to the Bryn Mawr School's success in Baltimore. Hamilton also had her own ongoing conflicts with M. Carey Thomas and Mary Garrett and would have welcomed a diminishment of their control over the school. From her earliest years at the school, Hamilton had also found herself in the difficult position that the school's prior secretaries had faced. While M. Carey Thomas respected Hamilton's intellect and ability when she asked her to head the school, she clearly intended to keep control of the institution in her own hands. The Bryn Mawr board, dominated by President Thomas and Secretary Garrett (until her death in 1915), required Hamilton to submit all matters concerning the school's operation—no matter how small—to the board for review. A voluminous correspondence between Hamilton in Baltimore and Thomas and Garrett in Pennsylvania comprises an extraordinary record of both everyday details of life at the Bryn Mawr School and more momentous issues and decisions shaping the school. The letters also illuminate the tensions—in style, personality, and philosophy—between the Bryn Mawr School's founders and its headmistress.

At the simplest level, the conflicts at the Bryn Mawr School stemmed from Thomas's and Garrett's insistence on retaining control over small details of school operation. Absorbed in their lives at Bryn Mawr College, they simply could not manage the school effectively, at least not in the detail they sought. Confident in their educational vision, as well as of their financial and administrative skills, they were reluctant to relinquish even the smallest control to Hamilton. Letters to Hamilton frequently expressed their distrust. Mary Garrett, for instance, "strongly disapprove[d]" of granting Hamilton freedom to purchase supplies for the school because she had "too little business knowledge." Thomas doubted Hamilton's ability to manage Bryn Mawr's staff. She wrote letter upon letter advising Hamilton on how to manage servants, repeatedly critiquing and reworking the Bryn Mawr School servants' schedules, despite Hamilton's insistence that Thomas's expectations were unreasonable. Thomas refused to accept Hamilton's cost estimate for refreshments to be served at the Bryn Mawr School's upcoming graduation: she declared Hamilton's enumeration of "100 sandwiches—4 kinds" too vague, demanding that Hamilton specify exactly what kinds of sandwiches and how many of each.[61]

Ironically, Thomas's and Garrett's letters often focused on petty details of administration and housekeeping rather than on issues of educational policy and philosophy. Following Thomas's instructions, Hamilton continually deferred to Thomas and Garrett in all manner of decisions, from purchasing necessary supplies or assembling a stage for a school play to admitting students or hiring teachers. But frequently answers to her questions were long in coming, leaving Hamilton and the school, at best, inconvenienced and, at worst, in dire straits. In response to Hamilton's repeated requests for the purchase of a filing cabinet, Garrett finally wrote, "We have been so overwhelmed with work connected with rebuilding the [Bryn Mawr College] Deanery and other college buildings, that we have been obliged to leave anything not absolutely necessary." "I found your letter of March 23rd ... had been filed unread, or rather had been laid aside by mistake with a pile of things," Garrett once acknowledged. In another instance, she confessed that "I must again plead guilty" to forgetting to mail critical reports on applicants seeking admission to the school. On another occasion, the Bryn Mawr School's phone was disconnected because Thomas and Garrett had neglected to pay the phone bill. Confusion often reigned: as Thomas explained in regard to decisions about the purchase of china for the school, "It was a misunderstanding between Miss Garrett and me. She thought I had sent it, and I thought she had."[62]

Sometimes they argued over the treatment of Bryn Mawr staff. In 1919, Thomas was angered when the school's longtime servant, Lee, requested time off to care for a sick daughter, and she wished to fire him. But Hamilton defended the elderly Lee as a "very old" and "valuable" servant and even volunteered to reimburse the school for the expense of hiring a substitute janitor during his absence. Thomas was unconvinced. She wrote Hamilton—in a letter labeled "STRICTLY CONFIDENTIAL"—that Lee had proved himself "exceedingly neglectful and careless" and "very sulky and insolent." Thomas argued that, based upon her experiences at Bryn Mawr College (and those of the college's repairman), "often a negro that has been satisfactory begins to go to pieces when he has been too long in one place ... When a negro began to go to pieces like Lee and become sulky defiant and idle," she asserted, it was not "safe to have him in a school where there were so many little girls." Hamilton's belief in the paternalistic responsibility of institutions to see to the welfare of their employees contrasted with Thomas's more callous and openly racist attitudes toward those she considered her inferiors.[63]

Day-to-day operation of the Bryn Mawr School proved difficult with no one with authority in residence in Baltimore, and Hamilton was frustrated, complaining that the Bryn Mawr School board prevented her from running the school effectively. Hamilton's correspondence with Thomas and Garrett also expressed her suspicion that the founders could be underhanded in their dealings with her and their school. At times, the tensions between Hamilton and Thomas and Garrett intensified to antagonism. Thomas and Garrett accused Hamilton of deliberately acting against their wishes for the Bryn Mawr School. Hamilton maintained that Thomas and Garrett broke their promises, lied, and blamed her for their mistakes.

In a typical dispute, Hamilton, Garrett, and Thomas argued over who was to secure estimates for school expenses. Angered at Thomas's and Garrett's criticisms of her, Hamilton poured out her frustrations in a 1912 letter to Mary Garrett and all but accused her and Thomas of lying:

> At times such as these, when my own recollection of what took place in a Board Meeting is so entirely at variance with yours, I do deplore the fact that I never have minutes of the Board Meetings. I must always depend upon my memory, and as you see, it is occasionally quite different from what you and Miss Thomas remember.

In 1913, the three women argued over whether Hamilton had been authorized to offer employment to a new teacher. Hamilton maintained that she had been given explicit permission to hire the teacher at a board meeting and demanded a copy of the meeting's minutes to prove it. Hamilton again expressed her belief that she needed written records of decisions so that she could protect herself: as she wrote Garrett, "If you are not willing to trust my memory ... I must be guarded."[64]

Evidence suggests that at least sometimes Thomas did knowingly lie to protect herself, blaming Hamilton for unpopular decisions in order to deflect criticism. When the father of a Bryn Mawr School student disputed the school's fee payment policy, Hamilton referred him to Thomas—informing him rightly that the Bryn Mawr School board oversaw all financial matters. Instead of taking responsibility for Bryn Mawr's policy and the displeasure it caused, however, Thomas wrote to that father, "I think that you must have misunderstood Miss Edith Hamilton because although I am President of the Board of Managers of the Bryn Mawr school all financial matters are decided by Miss Hamilton the Head Mistress except such as are referred to the board for its decision." Correspondence reveals that Hamilton was rarely granted such control.[65]

Thomas's and Hamilton's correspondence expressed their alternating respect and antagonism for one another. From the early 1910s, Hamilton had periodically expressed her desire to leave the Bryn Mawr School. Thomas always dissuaded her. "You know how I feel about you leaving the School into which you have put your life," Thomas wrote Hamilton in 1914. "Now when fruition is at hand it would be a shame to give it up." But their relationship was never easy. This may have been at least partially because of their personalities. Helen Horowitz's biography of Thomas documents Thomas's history of contentious behavior, and Alice Hamilton's biographer suggested that Edith Hamilton was of a "moody" nature. Margaret Hamilton, who lived with her sister throughout their years of work together at the Bryn Mawr School, worried that Edith seemed to have "so many bitternesses and upset, even morbid feelings inside of her." And when Edith Hamilton eventually did leave the school in 1922, Alice Hamilton wrote to their sister Margaret that "I do wish Edith's temperament were a little stiller, a little less tempestuous and extreme. My heart sinks when I look ahead for her."[66]

In a 1915 letter concerning when Edith and Margaret Hamilton (who was by then heading Bryn Mawr's Primary Department) should return from their summer vacation to prepare for the school's fall term, Edith Hamilton typically assumed that Thomas and Garrett were deliberately slighting her. Hamilton and Thomas disagreed on how early the Hamilton sisters needed to return to Baltimore, but the incident provoked feelings in Edith Hamilton that seem far out of proportion with the question of whether her vacation would be cut a few days short. In a particularly emotional letter, Hamilton catalogued her resentments, berating Thomas for her lack of trust:

> It is perfectly impossible for you to see that we do our duty to the school. You cannot check up the time we give or the effort. I might come to the school late every day in the week and I doubt if you would ever know. You must, perforce, trust us, but this letter means that you do not, really, or that you do so only when you must.

Edith Hamilton had long made clear her resentment of Thomas's and Garrett's lack of faith in her (and, by extension, her sister's) judgments and abilities, but this letter was notable in the depth of frustration it revealed. Hamilton's tirade against Thomas continued:

> Your letter has taken me back to my first unhappy years at the school when of course I was on trial but when I should have done better work for you if you had made me feel that you had confidence in me instead of precisely the reverse. I have often wondered why you treated me like that. It seems to me certain that I should not get the best work from a young teacher if I made her feel that I was watching her in an attitude of hostile criticism, and that my first assumption always was that she was wrong. Again and again during those first years I wanted to say to you that you were in the illogical position of trusting me—of necessity—in all the really big and important matters of meeting criticisms against the school, of managing difficult parents, of making teachers and pupils devoted to the school, of building up a body of loyal alumnae, of changing, really, the opinion of the public about the school, as well as of planning the courses and doing all the educational side of the work, while at the same time you always made me feel exactly as you have now done that you did not trust me and that you had to watch me to see that I did my duty.

Hamilton emotionally characterized her work of almost two decades at the Bryn Mawr School as taking place in the shadow of Thomas's mistrust and hostility.[67]

Beyond its revelation of ongoing conflict and emotion, Edith Hamilton's dramatic letter offers perceptive insight on a central irony at the early Bryn Mawr School. Although Thomas and Garrett wanted to control the implementation of their vision at the school, ultimately their physical distance from the school forced them to entrust many of "the really big and important matters" to a headmistress. And that headmistress had gradually won the affection of many individuals in the school community. Just how loyal that community was to Edith Hamilton and how distrustful they were of the Bryn Mawr School board generally and of M. Carey Thomas particularly would become starkly apparent at the time of Hamilton's departure in the early 1920s.

The Widening Rift: Edith Hamilton's Departure

In the early decades of the twentieth century, the Bryn Mawr School went through a period of turmoil. On 3 April 1915, after years of illness, Mary

Garrett died. The ramifications for the Bryn Mawr School were significant. With her death, the school lost its most significant benefactor. Garrett gave roughly $300,000 to the Bryn Mawr School during her lifetime. Although she made provisions for the school upon her death, no longer could Bryn Mawr turn to her as it had so often in the past to cover its debts and provide additional income in times of need. In her will, Garrett gave Bryn Mawr its building outright, clear of debt. Apart from a few specific provisions, she left the bulk of her estate to M. Carey Thomas, who she was confident would make "an appropriate and wise use" of the gift. As Helen Horowitz suggests in her biography of Thomas, Garrett intended Thomas to use the wealth—estimated at more than one million dollars—to support the institutions and causes to which they had devoted their lives. Tellingly, if Thomas had predeceased her, the Garrett fortune would have gone to the Bryn Mawr School, Bryn Mawr College, the Johns Hopkins University School of Medicine, and the National American Woman Suffrage Association. The Garrett family contested the will, but the courts eventually ruled in Thomas's favor, and once Garrett's fortune was in her hands, Thomas controlled the money to use as she chose. That financial power affirmed Thomas's control over the Bryn Mawr School at an important juncture in its history.[68]

Mary Garrett's death devastated Thomas. At the height of her grief, she faced a professional crisis—an open and hostile challenge to her power at Bryn Mawr College. While Edith Hamilton and Bryn Mawr School teachers had long chafed under Thomas's managing hand, the Bryn Mawr College faculty in 1915 made public their own complaints. They accused Thomas of, in the words of a newspaper editor, having the "habit of dealing arbitrarily with the careers of members of her faculty" and having "produced a state of intimidation in the college in which no one ventures to speak in protest." Thomas's foes were vocal, and their accusations garnered the serious attention of the public and the college's own board. Reports of Thomas's imperious behavior appeared in the headlines of the *Philadelphia Public Ledger*, and the Bryn Mawr College directors launched an investigation. Thomas was fighting for her career. Ultimately, Thomas weathered the storm and emerged still head of the college, although the board made changes that limited the power of its president in favor of its faculty. But the fight had tarnished her reputation publicly and put a tremendous strain on her personally. Revelations of Thomas's behavior and her struggles at Bryn Mawr College probably confirmed the resentments of many members of the Bryn Mawr School community and may well have emboldened them in their own battles to limit Thomas's power in Baltimore.[69]

Then, after years of being at odds with the Bryn Mawr School board, Edith Hamilton announced her intention to resign as headmistress of the Bryn Mawr School. Although Hamilton had discussed the possibility with Thomas in the past, she now seemed more determined to follow through with her plans. Whether because of her conflicts with Thomas, feelings of overwork at the school, ill health, or a combination of all, Hamilton apparently informed the board of her intentions as early as 1919, and the board discussed her resignation at their meetings in both October 1919 and October 1920, though apparently without any clear understanding of exactly when Hamilton planned to depart. In the spring of 1922, Hamilton announced that poor health made it impossible for her to continue her full duties as headmistress of the Bryn Mawr School during the upcoming school year. She offered the board a choice: she could take a vacation and then continue working part-time during the following year, or she could depart permanently at the end of the school year. The board quickly replied that Hamilton should leave immediately rather than prolong her exit. Apparently without controversy, at their regular meeting in February 1922, the board passed a resolution praising Edith Hamilton's years of service to the Bryn Mawr School and proceeded to discuss potential candidates to replace her as Bryn Mawr's headmistress.[70]

The matter of Edith Hamilton's departure, however, did not end quietly there. News of Hamilton's resignation sparked heated controversy and public scandal that shook the Bryn Mawr School community in the months to come. As the Bryn Mawr community had matured in the early twentieth century, its devotion to Edith Hamilton had grown. During the spring of 1922, old resentments against the Bryn Mawr School board erupted as parents, alumnae, and teachers protested Hamilton's departure. The facade of civility between the Bryn Mawr School board—particularly M. Carey Thomas—and the school community shattered.

Throughout the controversy, the Bryn Mawr School community—alumnae, teachers, families, and Hamilton herself—portrayed Edith Hamilton as the victim of M. Carey Thomas's malice. But the reality was more complex. There is no evidence that the Bryn Mawr School board (or Thomas personally) pressured Hamilton to resign, although once she had stated her intention to leave, they preferred her immediate departure. Edith Hamilton had spoken of departing for years, and Thomas had urged her to stay. But from the moment the Bryn Mawr School board accepted her resignation, Edith Hamilton was displeased: displeased with their preference for her early resignation, displeased with Thomas's behavior, displeased with the search for Bryn Mawr's next headmistress. Her experiences of twenty-six years gave her reason to be suspicious of Thomas, but Hamilton did seem exceptionally sensitive—interpreting the board's every move as a personal affront, as a slight and a sign of their ingratitude. Whether because of troubling events of which we have no record or because she harbored mixed feelings about leaving the school she had headed for so many years, Hamilton engaged in battle, calling on the Bryn Mawr School community to vindicate her. Because of their loyalty to Hamilton and their already deep distrust of Thomas, parents, alumnae, and teachers championed her cause.

In March 1922, several Baltimore men with daughters at the Bryn Mawr School organized a meeting of families and friends of the school. Those in attendance passed resolutions praising Edith Hamilton's personal qualities and professional abilities and planned a farewell gift for their headmistress. In a more unusual move, the fathers passed a resolution demanding that Edith Hamilton be allowed to select her successor. Soon both Bryn Mawr School alumnae and teachers joined Bryn Mawr fathers in endorsing the resolution. That measure, submitted to the Bryn Mawr School board in March 1922, clearly signaled the Bryn Mawr School community's distrust to the board. Not surprisingly, the Board of Managers denied the request. Instead of appeasing the school community, M. Carey Thomas took personal affront and engaged in a public battle against Hamilton and her supporters. Newspapers in Baltimore and Philadelphia followed the controversy for weeks. Popular opinion clearly supported Hamilton.[71]

"Says Dr. Thomas Wants to Be Boss: Seeks to Control Bryn Mawr School, Miss Hamilton Asserts," read one newspaper headline. "Dr. Thomas Threatened to Close School, Charge Fathers of Students in Baltimore Institution," reported a Philadelphia newspaper. Hamilton was reported as saying that Thomas had declared "she would close the doors of the school" before accepting Hamilton's choice for Bryn Mawr's next headmistress or yielding her authority to the demands of parents and alumnae. The *Baltimore American* outlined Thomas's angry confrontation with Edith Hamilton at the home of a prominent Bryn Mawr School family, the Reids, where Hamilton was residing during the conflict: "During the interview, it is said, Miss Thomas became exceedingly angry and, according to Dr. Reid, shouted so that she could be heard all over the house. She charged that Miss Hamilton had violated the ideals of Miss Garrett and herself and declared that she had completely mismanaged the school." The Reids had close personal ties to Hamilton and were hardly objective observers, but their portrayal of Thomas mirrored the reports of Thomas's behavior in other newspapers and by various Bryn Mawr School groups who came to Hamilton's defense.[72]

Soon the Bryn Mawr School fathers, who had initially organized to honor Hamilton and exert influence over the future of the school, were launching a concerted campaign against Thomas reminiscent of the one at Bryn Mawr College only a few years earlier. One socially prominent father charged that the Bryn Mawr Board of Managers was "an organization dominated by a single mind"—M. Carey Thomas. Another father, who chaired the protest committee, was quoted as demanding Thomas's total withdrawal from the Bryn Mawr School. Surely her work as president of Bryn Mawr College, he sarcastically quipped, was enough to satisfy her.[73] The message of Bryn Mawr fathers was clear: while they had entrusted their daughters to the Bryn Mawr School under the guidance of Edith Hamilton, they did not want their daughters educated in a school dominated by M. Carey Thomas.

Not easily intimidated, Thomas denied all charges leveled against her and counterattacked, claiming that she and Hamilton had "worked together on the Bryn Mawr School Board for 26 years in harmony and friendship." Edith Hamilton, she claimed, would never have made such accusations against her "if she had not been nervously broken-down and ill."[74] Almost a decade later, Thomas described the events, from her perspective, to the Bryn Mawr School board:

> The statements by the fathers of former and present pupils at a meeting called apparently for the purpose of general abuse showed on the part of most of the fathers present (I was told by a personal friend who was there) bitter antagonism to, and shocking misunderstanding and flagrant misrepresentation of, the educational ideals of the Bryn Mawr School which had been operating in their midst for the past 38 years and had made their daughters into Baltimore women of whom they and the School are so justly proud.[75]

Bryn Mawr School teachers, who had a history of conflict with the school board and of devotion to Edith Hamilton, joined the fray. After their own meeting, most teachers declared themselves willing to resign from the Bryn Mawr

School in protest of the board's refusal to consider their wishes for Hamilton's successor.[76] When the teachers' pleas went unheeded, most did refuse to sign their employment contracts for the following school year.

By April, Hamilton and Thomas were refusing to be in the same room together: Thomas would not attend Bryn Mawr School board meetings with Hamilton present, so Hamilton resigned her seat as headmistress on the board before the end of the school year.[77] Soon after, the board appointed a new headmistress, publicly rejecting Edith Hamilton's candidate despite the protests of the Bryn Mawr community. The public outcry diminished, however, and, by the start of the following school year, the community seemed willing to put the controversy behind them. Notably, however, both alumnae and parent groups had organized and asserted themselves as never before in the school's history, and they would continue to exert their influence in the decades to come.

Bryn Mawr School teachers probably emerged the weakest from the battle. In May 1922, Thomas urged Bryn Mawr "Teachers and Staff" that board members "hope very much that all the teachers and staff will be willing to sign their agreements as soon as possible now that this important question [of hiring a new headmistress] is settled." Although Thomas apologized that "due to misunderstanding" the board had neglected to inform teachers of their offer to a new headmistress, that apology was hollow. Indeed, her letter proceeded to warn protesting teachers that Bryn Mawr would replace any teacher who refused to sign her contract within five days. The Bryn Mawr School's new headmistress, she added, had already compiled a list of replacements for any recalcitrant teachers.[78] The teachers, their jobs at stake, capitulated.

That the Bryn Mawr School community overwhelmingly supported Hamilton in the battle between her and Thomas is clear. But the exact nature of Hamilton's behavior is less so. Edith Hamilton seems to have resigned from the school during a time of personal crisis and illness. According to her sister Alice, who was in consultation with Edith's doctor, Edith was suffering from not only hardening of the arteries but also "occupational fatigue," and she needed rest.[79] Moreover, Edith Hamilton's resignation coincided with the intensification of her relationship with Doris Reid.

Doris Reid, a 1912 graduate of the Bryn Mawr School, was the daughter of Edith Gittings Reid (a writer and close friend of Edith Hamilton's) and Harry Reid (a geology professor at Johns Hopkins University). Edith spent the summer before the controversy traveling with Doris in Europe. Upon their return to Baltimore, Edith, in poor health, left the home she shared with her sister Margaret and moved in with the Reid family. The confrontation between Hamilton and Thomas reported in the newspapers took place in the Reid home. As Edith and Doris began a lifelong relationship, the other Hamilton sisters were not happy with Edith's choice, viewing Doris as a bad influence on their sister. Indeed, Alice blamed Doris—whom she characterized as "young and her judgment poor"—for pushing Edith into impetuous actions at the Bryn Mawr School. Alice wrote to Margaret: "I of course will never say such a thing to anybody but you but I can't help seeing that because of this affair with Doris Edith first destroyed your home and now may destroy your work. It all comes back to the Doris affair in the end."[80]

Edith Hamilton's actions caused tension between her and the sisters to whom she had always been so close. Specifically, Margaret Hamilton had lived and worked with Edith as a teacher and as head of the Bryn Mawr School Primary School for more than twenty years, and Edith's fight with Thomas threatened Margaret Hamilton's own position at the school. As Alice wrote to Margaret, "Sorry as I am for [Edith], I am much sorrier for you." Alice's sympathies in the matter clearly lay with Margaret, for, as she saw it, "Edith wants another year's salary, you want your work ... I cannot help feeling that part of [Edith's] worry is a realization that she went too far, presumed on the hold that she had over the [Bryn Mawr School] Board and sees now that she gave herself up into their hands."[81]

Alice never denied the validity of Edith's complaints against Thomas. As she interpreted the situation, "Baltimore got very much excited over it, for the impression got about that Edith's hand had been forced and they all do dislike Miss Thomas so much." Furthermore, she advised Margaret to distance herself from Edith's actions because she feared Thomas would unfairly dismiss Margaret because of her sister's actions. In the end, despite Alice's advice, Margaret did offer her resignation to the Bryn Mawr School out of loyalty to Edith. In the wake of the controversy, however, Margaret returned to the school at the request of parents, alumnae, and the board. The Bryn Mawr School board appointed Margaret Hamilton to a group of five faculty members created to oversee the transition to a new headmistress, and, in the 1930s, she would for several years serve as the acting head of the school.[82]

In the end, despite all the drama, Edith Hamilton left the Bryn Mawr School and soon after moved to New York City, where she lived the rest of her life with

Doris Reid. Alice wrote to Margaret in 1923 that she was not corresponding with Edith: "When I think of writing to Edith I seem paralyzed, there does not seem anything to say. I cannot keep pretending that all is right between us, when so plainly it is not." Alice noted her intention to visit Edith during trips to New York, however, "in case there should be a softening." Although her relationship with her sisters remained strained for several years, and they believed that Reid exerted too much influence on her, Edith's life stabilized, and the sisters seem to have mended their friendship by the mid-1920s. Alice wrote sister Norah in 1925, after a visit, that Edith "was so like her old, old self."[83]

In the 1930s and 1940s, Edith Hamilton skyrocketed to fame in her second career as a scholar and writer about classical mythology. *The Greek Way, The Roman Way,* and *Mythology* earned critical and popular praise. In 1950, Hamilton won the National Achievement Award, and she was elected to the American Academy of Arts and Letters. She received honorary Doctor of Letters degrees from Yale University, the University of Rochester, and the University of Pennsylvania. She enjoyed television interviews and invitations from the White House and, in 1957, at the age of ninety, was made an honorary citizen of Athens. She died in 1963. At age ninety, Alice Hamilton reminisced about her sister: "She was, of course, far more gifted than I and I always knew it and admired her and we were deeply intimate as sisters so near of age usually are."[84]

Surely Hamilton's subsequent fame made her even more hallowed in halls of the Bryn Mawr School, where she was revered above the school's founders during most of the twentieth century. Tributes from former students signify the place she occupied in the school's collective memory:

Miss Hamilton—even to the younger children, before we entered the lighted circle of her classes—was a figure of high, mystical power. When she slipped into the study hall, and took up her place at the desk, to read or mark papers, her mind remote from us and our infinitesimal concerns, the buzz and rattle of the ordinary regime sank to perfect stillness; and a hush ever followed her swift passage as she swept by us on the stairs.

I think I do not exaggerate, or speak only for myself, when I say that she brought in with her the air of having come from some high centre of civilization, where the skies were loftier, the views more spacious, the atmosphere more free and open than with us.

And to many of us she was the means of a higher gift than culture. Even a heedless school girl is aware, if dimly, of a noble and religious nature.[85]

Neither Mary Garrett nor M. Carey Thomas received such admiration or praise from the school they created.

Foreshadowing a New Bryn Mawr School

The war over Edith Hamilton's departure marked an important reconfiguration of the Bryn Mawr School community. Bryn Mawr teachers, parents, and alumnae did not garner the kind of control over the future of the school that they sought. Although they generated public acrimony against M. Carey Thomas—simultaneously almost deifying Edith Hamilton in the school's memory—they were not granted a voice in selecting Bryn Mawr's next headmistress. The Bryn Mawr board did make attempts to appease the school community— agreeing to investigate "the whole subject of cooperation between members of the school corporation, teachers, alumnae and parents." They justified maintaining the status quo at the Bryn Mawr School, however, because of supposed lack of "sufficient information to act at the present time."[86]

In the long run, however, parents and alumnae gained important new footholds at Bryn Mawr. Their protest groups—if initially unsuccessful—would eventually evolve into parent and alumnae organizations that would gain more and more influence at the school in decades to come. Although they might have lost the "first round" with Thomas, they ultimately would comprise a power base that the Bryn Mawr board could not ignore. Significantly, prominent Bryn Mawr School fathers took on increasingly important roles in shaping what the founders had intended to be a school run exclusively by females—indeed, often leaving mothers and alumnae to follow. The role of fathers (particularly successful businessmen) in organizing protests surrounding the transfer of power from Hamilton to a new headmistress foreshadowed a subsequent increase in male influence at the Bryn Mawr School, especially in financial affairs. Teachers, in contrast, gained no new influence at Bryn Mawr. Always they feared losing their jobs—for many, critical sources of self-support that, without positive recommendations from Bryn Mawr, would be virtually impossible to replace. With little leverage against Bryn Mawr's board—and with parents and alumnae consumed with issues other than teacher status—teachers would remain the least organized and least influential element in the Bryn Mawr School community.

The Bryn Mawr School founders had dreamed big, envisioning how a model school could transform the education, expectations, and experiences of girls and women. To them, credit for the Bryn Mawr School vision is owed. But Edith Hamilton's skill was invaluable in translating the founders' vision into a working institution. From one perspective, Hamilton's diplomacy may have weakened the Bryn Mawr School's most revolutionary aspects. That was what M. Carey Thomas justifiably feared. And sometimes Hamilton's drive to make Bryn Mawr a thriving Baltimore school—as well as her affection for Baltimoreans and their daughters—did lead her to soften the model school standards, making the school reflect the wishes of the community rather than leading that community to a new understanding of how and why girls should be educated. Yet, without Hamilton's flexibility—and the loyalty she inspired in so many Baltimoreans—the Bryn Mawr School might not have survived beyond its earliest years.

In the decades after Hamilton's departure from Bryn Mawr, that delicate balance between the founders' ideals and popular demands would become more difficult to maintain. With the growing voice and influence of Bryn Mawr School families and alumnae, M. Carey Thomas and the Bryn Mawr board—faced particularly with the school's ever-more-debilitating debts and increased competition from rival girls' schools in Baltimore—would face tough choices.

CHAPTER THREE

Transforming the Vision

The Bryn Mawr School Community and New Educational Ideals

> When circumstances over which we have no control seem to the Board to make it impossible to conduct a self supporting School with these high standards we have an absolute right to close the School. No one can question this right. It is the only self respecting action to take ... It would be better to close it and let the experiment stand for what it had accomplished. — M. CAREY THOMAS, 2 JANUARY 1928

In the late nineteenth century and especially in the early decades of the twentieth century, women's visibility in American public life, their access to advanced education, and their employment outside of the home rose dramatically. In 1920, the seventy-year struggle for women's suffrage culminated in the ratification of the Nineteenth Amendment. But as significant as that victory were the broader social trends reshaping the place of women in society. By the 1920s, young women flocked in record numbers to institutions of higher learning—both to the flourishing women's colleges and to the increasing number of co-educational state universities and normal schools. Female employment and participation in the professions simultaneously rose. "Modern" women enjoyed unprecedented social freedoms. Cultural images that would have shocked the late Victorian world of the Bryn Mawr School's founding—such as the "flappers" who cut their hair, shortened their skirts, fraternized with men, and openly smoked and drank—suggest how dramatically society's conception of women and women's conceptions of themselves had shifted in but a few short decades.[1]

The original Bryn Mawr School was the product of a different generation. As American culture changed, so would educational expectations and ideals for the middle-class and well-to-do girls that the school served. The challenges of adapting to the ideals of the twentieth century would be numerous and significant. Paradoxically, new attitudes toward the education of girls would simultaneously support Bryn Mawr's once unique commitment to preparing all girls for college and challenge its determination to maintain a rigorous program that emphasized the intellectual identity of the sexes and encouraged girls to challenge traditional female roles in society. With the Bryn Mawr community exercising its new-found strength, the school would evolve into a well-established institution that suited the new lifestyles and landscapes of the nation in general and the city in particular. Just as twentieth-century America was different from the society of Bryn Mawr's founding, so would be the new Bryn Mawr School's understanding of the role it should play in interpreting the nature of girls, their relationship to society, and the education they deserved.

A New Headmistress

When Amy Kelly was appointed as the new headmistress of the Bryn Mawr School in April 1922, she stepped into an unenviable position. Following in the footsteps of a revered longtime headmistress would have been difficult for anyone. But given the circumstances of Edith Hamilton's departure, Kelly's position was particularly tenuous. Edith Hamilton had supported a former Bryn Mawr School teacher to head the school, and the Bryn Mawr School community viewed Kelly as M. Carey Thomas's choice. The acrimonious battles surrounding Hamilton's departure had left the school community divided and vulnerable, and how it would survive a change in leadership was uncertain.

No one questioned Amy Kelly's credentials as the new scholar and teacher to head the Bryn Mawr School. After receiving an undergraduate degree from Oberlin College and a master's degree from Wellesley College, Kelly taught at Wellesley as an associate professor of English literature. At the time of her appointment as the Bryn Mawr School's new headmistress, she was writing a biography of Eleanor of Aquitaine, a book she published to high acclaim after her years at the Bryn Mawr School.[2]

Despite the controversy that preceded her appointment, Amy Kelly proved herself a capable and effective leader for the Bryn Mawr School community. Although Kelly never won the hearts of the school quite as had Edith Hamilton—and she subsequently never achieved the stature of Hamilton in the school's collective memory—she quickly earned the respect and trust of the diverse and recently warring factions at Bryn Mawr. The sympathy she showed families, alumnae, and teachers assured the community that, contrary to their fears, she sought to make the school responsive to its concerns. Simultaneously (and in contrast to Edith Hamilton), Kelly maintained an amicable relationship with the Bryn Mawr School board. When, for example, Kelly wanted Thomas to meet with the Bryn Mawr School faculty to discuss their concerns (this time about inadequate sports facilities and the need for more music in the school), she cajoled, rather than scolded, the cantankerous Thomas: "Don't you think it would be pleasant and profitable to have the school invite the Board of Managers to tea?"[3] Kelly helped heal old rifts.

To move beyond past conflicts and hurts—and understanding as keenly as had Edith Hamilton that the Bryn Mawr School had to attract more students if it were to thrive—Amy Kelly continued Hamilton's mission to win the devotion of families and the support of the local community. Kelly would lead the school in adapting to new educational values and urban patterns that were transforming Baltimore and many cities across the nation. Ironically, although the departure of Hamilton and appointment of Kelly had seemed a victory for M. Carey Thomas and her vision for the Bryn Mawr School, Amy Kelly would in reality preside over a period during which Bryn Mawr—its philosophy, its physical configuration, and its relationship to the larger society and women's places within it—would be transformed by forces unimagined by Thomas or anyone else within the school community just a few decades earlier.

Changing Trends in Women's Education and Place in Society

Changes in the educational landscape were apparent at all levels and in all sectors of society in the early decades of the twentieth century—and had distinct implications for girls and women. The nation's public school system underwent major renovations during the Progressive Era. New reverence for "science" applied to the social order dictated that schools that had evolved unsystematically, often from nineteenth-century common schools, be consolidated into centralized school systems directed by bureaucracies of trained "experts." "Social efficiency," a much-lauded Progressive ideal, mandated that students be differentiated and classified—according to age and grade, aptitude and intelligence, future life roles, and gender. The nineteenth-century ideal in public schools had seated all students (male and female, from a range of backgrounds) together to receive a "common" education, but this approach seemed too unscientific and inefficient for the modern world. Students, it was now believed, needed educations tailored specifically to their future roles in society. These attitudes were particularly prevalent in increasingly popular secondary schools.

The growth in secondary education in the United States in the early twentieth century was steep. The U.S. Federal Census of 1870 counted 129,404 students attending both public and private secondary schools; in 1920, the U.S. Commissioner of Education reported 650,000 students enrolled in secondary education—a fivefold increase. In the earlier nineteenth century most secondary education had been private, but the vast majority of the new growth came in public high schools.[4] High schools enrolled a relatively small percentage of American youth in the early twentieth century: in 1920, less than one in five American youths graduated from high school. By 1930, however, the numbers had risen to almost one in three, and by 1940, approximately half of young Americans were graduating from high schools.[5]

Girls had long been welcome in public schools, and by the late nineteenth century they were a majority of high school students. In the early twentieth century, their presence and place in high schools received new scrutiny, particularly because educators worried that boys' achievement rates lagged behind girls'. Whereas nineteenth-century educators had feared that education beyond rudimentary levels might damage female health and well-being, now the concern was that girls had been too successful. Educators worried that too many female students and teachers had "feminized" high schools.[6]

In addition to measures like introducing competitive athletics as a way of "masculinizing" the institution, high schools began new programs of differentiating students by gender. Many women joined school reformers in calling for courses that would prepare girls for their largely domestic lives. These reforms were based not on a presumption of different intellectual abilities of the sexes—a belief that had been prevalent in the nineteenth century but that had been dispelled by girls' and women's success in all kinds of schools—but on the notion that every student's education should be suited to his or her future roles in life. Since, despite the increasing prominence of women in American schools and the public sector, the vast majority of educators and parents still understood marriage and motherhood to be the primary focus of women's lives, female-specific subjects, such as the new study of home economics, populated the academic landscape for girls and women as they had not since the old days of female academies.

The "feminization" of education that so concerned educators in the late nineteenth and early twentieth centuries was associated more closely with public than private secondary education. While public high schools attracted more girls than boys, private secondary schools enrolled about even numbers of boys and girls in the early twentieth century. Educators worried that girls were dominating public coeducational high schools, but leading private school educators and patrons remained largely in single-sex environments. In 1910, 49 percent of all students in private schools were in single-sex institutions—a percentage that rose to 56 percent by 1929. Ironically, women enrolled in private secondary schools (which were overwhelmingly single sex) often experienced less sex-differentiated education than did their peers in public high schools. Perhaps because the more affluent classes that supported private schools were less interested in vocational education than were public school administrators, girls in private schools were more likely to be enrolled in the same courses as boys than were girls in public schools. In 1929, for instance, less than 2 percent of all girls in private high schools enrolled in home economics courses, in contrast to 30 percent of girls in public high schools in the 1920s.[7]

The new study of home economics, which grew in popularity in the first half of the twentieth century, symbolizes the continuing debates about the places of girls and women in educational institutions and in society. Based on a new incarnation of the notion of female difference so opposed by M. Carey Thomas, the new "female" field—intended to combine the study of science and the study of economics and to apply the combination to the social and domestic worlds—was seen as an innovative place of research and real-world application for women. Hull House veteran and later director of the Federal Children's Bureau Julia Lathrop viewed the 1924 establishment of Vassar College's Euthenics program devoted to the study of the home as a progressive step for women and their influence in society. A smaller group of skeptics feared the implications of reasserting female difference after years of fighting to prove women's intellectual abilities. Vassar psychologist Margaret Washburn warned that "you are driving women back into the home, from the slavery of which education has helped us to escape."[8] In spite of the worries of a few, this renewed differentiation of the curricula—based on perceptions of the different places women and men would occupy in society—remained the vogue among both female and male reformers.

The redefinition of women's proper places in colleges and universities

coincided with the tremendous growth in women's participation in higher education. In 1870, approximately 11,000 women were enrolled in institutions of
higher learning; by 1920, that number had soared to 283,000. Indeed, women
comprised around 47 percent of American undergraduates by 1920. More than
90 percent of those women attended coeducational colleges and universities. As
historian Barbara Solomon notes, "The denigration of college as an option for
women evaporated, and its desirability became established." But historian Lynn
Gordon warns that the presence of women in large numbers did not mean that
women enjoyed equality on college campuses: particularly at coeducational
schools, women's access to academic classes and extracurricular activities was
often limited.[9]

Going to college in the 1880s did not necessarily mean the same thing as
going to college in the 1920s. The pioneering generation of female college
graduates in the 1870s and 1880s had defied traditional expectations about
women's nature and place in society by their "masculine" pursuit of higher education and, in doing so, had raised questions about their femininity and what
roles they could assume in the family and in society. As going to college became
more commonplace, however, college women were no longer perceived as pos-
ing such great challenges to traditional female roles and expectations. Indeed,
by the 1920s, proponents of college for women often specifically rejected many
of the characteristics of the early college graduates (which M. Carey Thomas
epitomized). A 1929 collection of essays on *The Education of the Modern Girl* by
educators from women's colleges and college-preparatory girls' schools suggests
how the social and cultural connotations and implications of college attendance
for women had evolved in the decades between the Bryn Mawr School's founding and the 1920s:

> Fifty years ago the strong-minded woman who dared to stride out in the waters
> of higher education was eyed a little askance by those who were not certain that
> she was quite womanly. Even twenty years ago the college woman was consid-
> ered distinctly advanced, and one expected her to stride along in her stitched golf
> skirt at the head of the suffragette parades. To-day, the American girl goes to col-
> lege as a matter of course, her right to higher education unquestioned, her social
> position unaffected.

While confirming the growing desirability of college for many girls, Dorothy
Waldo (headmistress of a girls' school herself) emphasized what she considered
the positive differences between the new generation of "American girls" flock-

ing to college campuses by the 1920s and their earlier counterparts. The prior generations of "strong-minded women" who "strided," donned unfeminine "stitched golf skirt[s]," and marched in "suffragette parades" contrasted unfavorably to modern college girls who proved "that one need not be unwomanly and unfeminine in order to be educated." To the contrary, she argued, modern college women felt no need to reject their womanliness and "proved to be excellent home-makers"—with lower rates of divorce than their less-educated counterparts—as well as valuable volunteers in community women's clubs and schools.[10]

Given the real gains in women's education of the past decades and yet the simultaneous reassertion of difference and traditional femininity, it is not surprising that women's roles in society were full of contradictions, too. Growth in women's education had coincided with growth in their participation in the paid workforce and the professions. By 1920—when women comprised about half of the college population and received about one-third of all graduate degrees— they made up about 20 percent of the labor market. (Notably, however, the vast majority of women employed outside the home were working-class women. Only about 12 percent of all employed women were professionals, and by far the greatest increases in female employment in the early 1900s were among immigrants and African Americans.) From 1890 to 1920, women's participation in the professions increased by an impressive 226 percent, at a time when men's increased by only 78 percent. And yet women's employment and particularly their access to the professions did not keep pace with their gains in education.[11]

Women found it particularly difficult to gain access to the traditionally male professions. In 1920, women comprised less than 2 percent of lawyers in the United States. And, although women had made substantial inroads into the medical profession in the nineteenth century, they faced continuing obstacles and even setbacks. By 1910, 6 percent of the nation's physicians were female but, in the face of quotas on the number of female students admitted to medical schools (formalized at 5 percent across the nation in 1925), women's participation in the medical professions—except as nurses—steadily declined. Female physicians dropped to about 4 percent of all doctors by 1930.

Some educated women continued to find employment as professors in colleges and universities. Although women earned approximately 33 percent of all graduate degrees in the 1920s, women comprised just under 8 percent of the professors in the United States. Moreover, female academics were clustered primarily in women's colleges or in departments deemed suitably "feminine" at coeducational institutions. Women scientists almost never found employment in the science departments of coeducational colleges and universities or in industry and were instead channeled into female colleges, home economics departments, or nursing schools.[12]

Despite the dreams of educators like M. Carey Thomas, despite the rigorous curriculum offered at institutions like Bryn Mawr College, and despite the real successes of some professional women, the vast majority of even educated women still tended to cluster in female fields. In 1920, 75 percent of female professionals were teachers or nurses. These fields—established as suitably feminine in the nineteenth century—were joined by social work and librarianship as the primary professions for women. Such employment trends mirrored the education women received at the nation's colleges and universities: while women received over two-thirds of all degrees in education, nursing, home economics, and librarianship, men received over 90 percent of degrees in engineering, business, agriculture, law, medicine, pharmacy, and the physical sciences.[13]

Teaching continued to dominate women's employment choices, as it had in the nineteenth century. A 1912 study found that 54 percent of the graduates of five women's colleges entered the teaching profession.[14] The 1918 census of nearly twelve thousand women graduates of nine eastern colleges who had ever been employed found that an overwhelming 83 percent had worked as teachers. As noted educator Willistine Goodsell observed, "Teaching is, of course, the path of least resistance for those women who desire to utilize as promptly as possible the information that they have acquired in college as a means of gaining a livelihood."[15]

Nursing quickly became the second largest female profession behind teaching: in 1900, about 94 percent of nurses were female. Associated with the settlement work and social housekeeping philosophy of the Progressive Era, the new field of social work—which college women and settlement residents were instrumental in developing—appealed to many twentieth-century young women. As early as 1900, 75 percent of social workers in the United States were female. While the growing social service bureaucracies of the early twentieth century created a host of new jobs for female social workers—again, seen to be the "natural" choices for such work because of their feminine nature—women dominated the lower rungs of the bureaucracies, which tended to be run by men. Alice Parsons described the promise clerical work held for many educated women in the 1920s:

Those of us who were in college in those days heard prodigious rumors about this great new possibility opened up to women. Girls who didn't want to teach were no longer faced with the alternative of going home and twiddling our thumbs. They might, if they studied typing and stenography and were very clever and efficient, become the Confidential Secretaries of men who were doing frightfully interesting things.

Even as the numbers of women pursuing advanced education and professional pursuits grew, an air of antagonism to the old feminism and career women of earlier generations prevailed. Women's magazines like *Ladies' Home Journal* and *McCall's* (although ironically run by career women themselves) tended to denigrate careers in praise of traditional domestic skills and paths that they claimed would lead to the greatest satisfaction for women.[16]

These cultural shifts, though obviously taking place far beyond the confines of the Bryn Mawr School's classrooms, would have significant implications for the institution. As the educational landscape (both in Baltimore and in the larger nation) expanded at all levels, private schools for girls would have to assess their place within it. As, gradually, families' expectations and aspirations for their daughters changed and as girls themselves came of age in new times with different possibilities for education and work open to them, schools like Bryn Mawr would have to redefine what they were all about.

Changing Urban Landscapes and New School Models

As women's opportunities for education and employment grew, the interconnected forces of industrialization, urbanization, and immigration transformed the landscape of the late-nineteenth- and early-twentieth-century United States. For some Americans, the ongoing changes promised a better future. Others remained skeptical, even frightened, of their impact. Although the privileged world of the Bryn Mawr School was isolated from some of the harshest realities of society, urban trends would affect the institution significantly. Indeed, alterations in the Baltimore landscape, particularly, would force Bryn Mawr to create a new place for itself in the education of the city's daughters.

Baltimore reflected many of the challenges facing cities across America. Between 1870 and 1900, Baltimore's population doubled, from a quarter to half a million inhabitants. The large immigration of Germans, first, and then "new immigrants" from southern and eastern Europe—combined with an even larger migration of African Americans lured to Baltimore by the promise of jobs and better futures—fundamentally altered the composition of the population.[17] Like other cities, Baltimore found itself unprepared to cope with its surging population. A dearth of city services and public health measures led to alarming urban blight. Prejudice discouraged many Baltimoreans from addressing the plight of the city's new and more ethnically and racially diverse residents. Problems of inadequate housing and transportation, hopeless overcrowding, poor or nonexistent sanitation systems, and substandard public schools escalated alarmingly in poor city districts.[18]

In response, some middle-class and well-to-do citizens began seeking remedies for the host of problems surrounding them. Responding to the increasingly apparent necessity of reconfiguring modern urban life, a diverse group of Baltimore reformers—with a variety of motivations—addressed a host of political and social concerns. Some prominent Baltimore men led "good government" campaigns, opposing rule of their city by corrupt political machines and promoting fair elections and efficient municipal administration. Social reformers embraced causes ranging from improved housing to disease prevention, from building playgrounds to regulating child labor. Johns Hopkins University President Daniel Coit Gilman headed Baltimore's primary social reform organization, the Charity Organization Society, founded in 1881. Various churches and volunteers from Johns Hopkins University, the Woman's College (later Goucher College), and the Bryn Mawr School Alumnae League established about a half-dozen settlement houses offering services to residents in Baltimore's poorest neighborhoods. Still other individuals focused their efforts on city planning and public improvements. They built roads and developed transportation systems and improved Baltimore's notorious sewage system, with miles of open sewers that threatened public health. Others established parks and promoted "city beautification." Whether motivated by genuine concern for the poor, by religious convictions, or by pragmatic assessments of the relationship between urban problems and their own quality of life, a key constituency of Baltimoreans—including many with connections to Baltimore educational institutions such as Johns Hopkins University, Goucher College, and the Bryn Mawr School—committed themselves to improving the landscape of their city during the Progressive Era.[19]

Public education drew the attention of another coalition of reformers. Overall, Maryland schools in the early twentieth century were noted as substandard.

As a port city flooded with immigrants, Baltimore's schools particularly felt the pressure of overcrowding and poor conditions. A 1913 study of American school systems ranked Maryland as having one of the worst educational systems of the forty-eight states (ranking it 36th in "general efficiency," 46th in "average school attendance," and 47th in tax dollars spent per pupil). The 1910 Federal Census gave the state poor markings for its high illiteracy rate, low school attendance, and mixing of different aged children in the same grades. As a result of publicity and subsequent public outcry, legislation, with reform focused on removing school control from local political boards and placing it in the hands of educational "experts," ameliorated conditions in following decades.[20]

Some reformers and entrepreneurs dreamed of creating new environments that would provide escape from the problems of modern urban life. In Baltimore, ambitious beautification schemes took shape. Pledging to avoid the crowded and unhealthy conditions that had come to characterize the old city center, Baltimore annexed large tracts of undeveloped land on its outskirts and began planning new living spaces. Baltimoreans were developing new suburban models of residential spaces and lifestyles, made possible, of course, by new transportation systems and the family automobile.

In 1891, a group of Baltimoreans incorporated the private Roland Park Company for the purpose of creating a new "country" residential development. They hired as a consultant Frederick Law Olmsted Jr., whose famous father had designed New York's Central Park, Stanford University's campus, and George Vanderbilt's Biltmore Estate. Olmsted, a major innovator in the design of twentieth-century suburbs, planned the new Roland Park suburb on the model of an extensive park, seeking harmonious blending of man-made elements with nature. Ideally, Roland Park residents would enjoy the benefits of both country living and close proximity to city amenities. The company built business blocks set back from streets to provide convenient access to grocers, drugstores, post offices, and the like but banned other, undesirable businesses from their neighborhoods. The developers established institutions such as country clubs, women's and garden clubs, and even schools that fostered the new lifestyle. With its winding streets, spacious parks, meticulous landscaping, and house facades complementing the natural landscape, Roland Park provided an increasingly attractive new living option for Baltimore families.[21]

The population shift in Baltimore was clear and dramatic. Before World War I, only 8 percent of Baltimore's Social Register families lived in the outer suburbs, but almost half of such families resided in Roland Park Company suburbs by 1932. As one observer noted, "It is no idle jest that Baltimore society is moving further and further out; from all signs soon there will be no Baltimore society, literally speaking, as everyone will live in the country."[22] Increasingly, the old city center—in Baltimore as well as other urban areas—was left to business establishments and the poor and less well-to-do. The suburbs' quiet streets, clean air, and open spaces proved alluring to Baltimore families fleeing what they viewed as the invasion of their city neighborhoods by "undesirable" populations of poor whites, recent immigrants, and African Americans. The minimum costs for suburban houses of two to five thousand dollars ensured that virtually none of Baltimore's African Americans moved to the area, and the company used covenants and deed restrictions to keep from selling properties to Jews and Catholics. Even as late as the 1930s, some local merchants reportedly refused to do business with the only Jewish family living in the Roland Park Company suburb of Guilford.[23]

The development of suburbs as alternatives to urban living had dramatic ramifications for schools in American urban centers. The growing flight of families left urban public schools primarily to the poor. In Baltimore particularly, where many of the more affluent families had always preferred private education for their children, the growth of the suburbs spurred a movement and redevelopment of educational institutions as they followed the residential patterns and preferences of their constituents. By the early 1900s, for example, the Johns Hopkins University was already planning a move from its original city location.[24]

The growing popularity of suburbs influenced not just the location of schools but also new philosophies about the best ways to educate and nurture children. From suburban perspectives, city private schools were not only inconvenient but also beginning to seem antithetical to the raising of happy, healthy children. Echoing the fears of many observers of modern city life, both educators and families were coming to see the urban environment as detrimental to children's physical health (due to poor sanitation, stagnant air, and disease), psychological health (because noise and overcrowding encouraged mental agitation and nervousness), and moral health (through association with encroaching businesses and "undesirable" populations). Integrating education with country or suburban living promised both to protect children from the ill effects of modern urban blight and to nurture them into healthier persons.

Such educational trends were evident in large cities across America, but Baltimore would lead in developing a new suburban educational model that would increasingly dominate private, nonreligious education for both girls and boys in the early and mid-twentieth century. If the Bryn Mawr School had pioneered in developing a new model of education for girls, the Country School for Boys of Baltimore City (renamed, in 1910, the Gilman Country School for Boys in honor of supporter and Johns Hopkins University President Daniel Coit Gilman) represented the first U.S. experiment with a new kind of suburban "country" education. Established in 1897 (coinciding, not coincidentally, with the development of both Progressive reform and suburban Roland Park in Baltimore), the school promised to educate boys in a homelike, country atmosphere unavailable in either city day schools or boarding schools. Mrs. Francis King Carey is credited with initiating the school so her son could both remain at home and be educated in the country. Although the school would prepare students who aspired to higher education, the Gilman Country School primarily emphasized how its unique environment would protect the health and character of its students. Indeed, it proposed, country surroundings—conducive to afternoons engaged in sports rather than wandering dangerous city streets—could improve both the mental and physical well-being of children.[25]

According to a 1911 *New York Evening Post*, Gilman School was the "oldest and most successful" of a new breed of country schools springing up in cities and suburbs across the nation, replacing older city day schools, as well as both city and country boarding schools. Although Baltimore's Country School was for boys only, it clearly established the "country-day" model of education for children of both sexes. New country-day schools for girls quickly followed. In Baltimore, the Roland Park Company established the Roland Park Country School to provide new suburban families with a girls' school close to their homes and suited to their lifestyles. By 1937, more than one hundred schools in the United States explicitly embraced the country-day philosophy (which would come to designate emphasis on a combination of academics, extracurricular activities, and close parental involvement as much as location), and they even united in a special Country Day Headmasters' Association.[26]

The country-day ideal developed when private schooling as a whole was becoming less prominent in the broad educational landscape. In 1900, almost 18 percent of secondary school students attended private schools, but only about 7 percent did so by the end of the 1920s. One survey in 1920 concluded that perhaps two-thirds of private schools with enrollments over one hundred were Catholic.[27] If public high schools dominated the education of American adolescents and parochial schools comprised the majority of private schools, a very small but influential group of Americans continued to support secular private schools. In contrast to public education, which was overwhelmingly coeducational, private schools were by far the most likely to be single-sex institutions.

As the country living movement flourished—manifested in burgeoning suburbs and the country-day educational ideal so well suited to them—older private city schools would be forced to take note. Private day schools, which relied on local neighborhood clientele, would have to adapt to changing city landscapes, and they would be pressured to modify their philosophies in accordance with new theories of schooling. The ramifications for the Bryn Mawr School—a city school founded on a philosophy in many respects at odds with the popular country-day model—were great. Interpreting and adapting to them would not be easy.

Change at the Bryn Mawr School: Adapting to New Times and Trends

On the surface, the fulfillment of the Bryn Mawr School's founding vision seemed closer than ever by the 1920s. Evidence suggests that more and more families once skeptical of Bryn Mawr's pledge to promote rigorous academics were coming to view the school's college-preparatory course as essential. Bryn Mawr records from the late 1920s referred to "the increasing number of graduates going on to college" rather than pursuing mere "'finishing' courses." Similarly, a 1929 notice of a meeting on "Choosing the College" noted that "in the past few years that number of girls who have gone from the Bryn Mawr School to various colleges has shown a marked increase."[28]

Paradoxically, by the 1920s families' motives in sending their daughters to college did not necessarily coincide with the Bryn Mawr School founders' vision of what higher education might do for women and their place in society. When the Bryn Mawr School opened its doors in 1885, its requirement that every graduate prepare for and pass the Bryn Mawr College entrance examination had been exceptional. As Edith Hamilton had sensed, the Bryn Mawr School was "offering the people of Baltimore what they do not want: a first class college preparatory education for girls," even as late as 1915. But by the 1920s, as Hamilton also noted, the Bryn Mawr School no longer had to convince Baltimore families of the value of advanced education for their daughters: "The old days when Miss Garrett had to impose upon the people of Baltimore good education for girls and could not look for help in her great undertaking to any Baltimoreans have passed. The people now want good education for their daughters; they will support a college preparatory school for girls." Bryn Mawr's once radical educational proposals were becoming mainstream, even fashionable.[29]

Although women in M. Carey Thomas's and even Edith Hamilton's generations who obtained college and graduate degrees were pioneers, by 1920 women were commonplace on many college campuses.[30] In Baltimore, a city the Bryn Mawr School founders had decried for lacking quality female education, the success of Goucher College had contributed to changing attitudes. As Dr. Lilian Welsh, professor of physiology and hygiene, remarked at a Goucher fundraiser in the 1910s, Goucher graduates were playing prominent roles in social, educational, and charitable work in the city and, as homemakers, were helping solve the problems of the modern home and family. Welsh, in contrast to Thomas, celebrated the training of women for the specifically female realms they would occupy in life.[31] Clearly, Baltimore's embrace of higher education for women did not necessarily mean its acceptance of the more radical elements of the vision of Bryn Mawr's founder.

As the popularity of college education for women grew, so did the number of schools offering college preparation. Once the Bryn Mawr School's rigorous academic curriculum had made it exceptional, but increasing numbers of girls' schools were integrating college-preparatory courses into their programs. Once many Baltimore families who hoped to send their daughters to college had looked to the Bryn Mawr School, but now they had many options. And that meant serious competition for the Bryn Mawr School.

Unfortunately for the Bryn Mawr School, at the very time it needed to prove that it remained the best (if not the only) place to prepare Baltimore girls for college, its curriculum and examination policies were increasingly out of step with modern college and university admission processes. In the late nineteenth and even the early twentieth century, many colleges and universities accepted graduates of select schools judged to be of good quality "by certificate," meaning that graduation from particular schools guaranteed admission to particular colleges. Bryn Mawr College had broken with the norm among the Seven Sister colleges in rejecting admission "by certificate" and requiring that all of its applicants pass its own admission test. With the growth in higher education, however, and with increasing pools of applicants not just from established private schools but from public high schools (which were enrolling greater percentages of Americans), colleges and universities grew to rely more heavily on standardized admission testing.

Because a Bryn Mawr School diploma required passing the Bryn Mawr College entrance examination, Bryn Mawr School graduates enjoyed automatic acceptance by Bryn Mawr College and also other popular women's colleges that recognized the school and the Bryn Mawr College examination. Ironically, by the second and third decades of the twentieth century, the Bryn Mawr School's stringent academic requirements were actually making admission to many colleges more difficult. As early as 1916, for example, Smith, Vassar, Wellesley, and Mount Holyoke together agreed to use College Board examinations as a key admission factor, and they (along with other colleges and universities) were increasingly reluctant to accept the Bryn Mawr College entrance examination in their place. In 1925, both Smith and Vassar began refusing to substitute Bryn Mawr College examinations for College Board tests.[32]

Consequently, Bryn Mawr School students who wished to attend colleges other than Bryn Mawr College faced multiple examinations. From the perspective of the school's founders, preparing for two sets of examinations—both the standardized College Boards and the Bryn Mawr College entrance examination—should have presented no dilemma, as examinations were essential instruments in learning and in preserving high academic standards. As M. Carey Thomas once confided to Margaret Hamilton, "The more the merrier in the case of examinations." Indeed, Thomas reasoned that taking Bryn Mawr College examinations could actually benefit students sitting for College Board tests: "They can regard the Bryn Mawr examinations as trial examinations if they like." But students, parents, and Headmistress Amy Kelly were distressed. Families viewed the Bryn Mawr School's testing policies as extreme and unwarranted. As Kelly reported to the Bryn Mawr School board, studying for multiple examinations meant that "family plans for the summer are completely disarranged," and "doctors disapprove of the strain of three sets [of examinations] within four months."[33]

Other girls' schools could actually offer easier admission to many colleges and universities. In 1924, Kelly explained the situation to the Bryn Mawr School board:

> Last year the parents of the Vassar candidates strenuously objected to having
> their daughters meet the strain not merely of taking two sets of examinations in

their junior and senior years but of making the quite different preparation in the ground covered in Physics and Mathematics and the adjusting to the difference in emphasis in French and Latin ... Girls preparing for Vassar will certainly go to another school rather than face the almost impossible difficulty of meeting both requirements. This would seem to me to suggest to the public, which does not understand the technicalities involved, that we cannot prepare girls for Vassar in the Bryn Mawr School.

Kelly particularly feared rumors circulating in Baltimore that parents who hoped for their daughters to attend Vassar should not enroll them in the Bryn Mawr School.[34]

Most ironically, Kelly reported that Baltimore families no longer assumed that the Bryn Mawr School was the best place to prepare for Bryn Mawr College—despite the historic connections between the two institutions. "Why is the Bryn Mawr School distinguished as offering a special preparation for Bryn Mawr College, when pupils can go to the Roland Park School [the newer Baltimore girls' school offering college preparation] and gain admission to the college on College Board examinations?" she queried Thomas in 1926, saying it would be absurd if the Roland Park School offered easier entry than the Bryn Mawr School to Bryn Mawr College. Kelly perceived the seriousness of the matter: "It may be the counsel of timidity, but I do seriously fear the competition of the Roland Park School, if we make another [examination] requirement which offers no guarantee of admission to college but seems merely another handicap in a race already beset with difficulties."[35]

The Bryn Mawr School's examination dilemma evaporated when Bryn Mawr College abandoned its own entrance examination in favor of College Board tests in 1927. The Bryn Mawr School's historic requirement that each of its graduates pass that examination would be no more. As a result, the Bryn Mawr School could adjust and update its own curriculum to prepare students for the single standardized test of the College Board.[36] But new flexibility in testing policies would not position the Bryn Mawr School to compete with other educational trends—namely, the demand for "country" atmosphere that was growing so popular. In Baltimore, girls' schools like the Roland Park Country School, which, as Kelly noted, was "near the fashionable residence districts and in the country making it very attractive to people with a considerable social following," presented a new and previously unknown threat to the Bryn Mawr School.[37]

In its earliest decades, the founders and administrators of the Bryn Mawr School had fought the perception that the school's academic demands might endanger girls' health, nerves, and marriage prospects; now the school's city location, rather than the content of its curriculum, seemed potentially harmful to students. As early as 1911, Edith Hamilton noted the "serious problem for our girls in the city" as Baltimore's "streets become less desirable as places for our girls to spend their leisure time." Hamilton specifically cited the vice of newly established movie theaters. Other school reports discussed the menace of businesses, auto showrooms, cars, and trolleys—with their accompanying noise, dirt, and danger—for Bryn Mawr's youngest students. Laments about the deterioration of the school's once serene neighborhood were widespread among school officials, alumnae, and parents. The Bryn Mawr School's constituency objected particularly to "the Negro invasion" at the school's "very doors."[38] With its neighborhood changing, with its constituency fleeing to the suburbs, and with new country-day philosophies rising in popularity, the Bryn Mawr School faced growing pressure to reconfigure itself.

Fresh air, green playgrounds, and expansive athletic fields were in short supply at the city campus of the Bryn Mawr School. Of course, the Bryn Mawr School—committed from its earliest days to improving female health—had required physical culture classes for all students when many parents saw too much exercise as detrimental to their daughters' well-being. But the emphasis on exercise in new country-day models of education differed significantly from the old Bryn Mawr desire to combat female ill health. Modern educators and families promoted physical recreation not just for its health benefits but also for its development of strong character and balanced personality in children of both sexes. While the old Bryn Mawr School had relied on methodical exercise regimes, undertaken with a sense of seriousness and purpose, newer theories stressed the importance of fresh air and "play." From the perspective of the 1920s, Bryn Mawr's once so innovative exercise methods and facilities seemed dreary and outdated to both students and educators, satisfying none of the new demands for outdoor activity. The pool and elaborate exercise equipment of which Bryn Mawr's founders and early physical education directors had been so proud fell into disuse as competitive outdoor sports such as field hockey, lacrosse, and tennis, unknown at the early Bryn Mawr School, surged in popularity.[39]

Given such trends, both Edith Hamilton—who concurred that "fresh air and exercise are absolutely essential to health"—and Amy Kelly experimented with solutions to the problems presented by the school's city location. When the Gilman Country School established its "open air school"—designed, on the advice of doctors, to provide students with fresh air, even on the coldest of days, as they studied—Bryn Mawr opened its own out-of-doors classrooms, ingeniously situating its youngest pupils on the roof. (The sight of shivering, blanket-wrapped students attending classes outside on cold winter days rendered this particular innovation a short-lived fad in the second decade of the twentieth century.)[40] The Bryn Mawr School also tried developing a "country annex" at Montebello, the estate that Mary Garrett had left to M. Carey Thomas. The 1917–18 catalogue advertised the advantages of the school's "Week End Country Place," describing how Bryn Mawr students enjoyed nature, tennis and hockey courts, picnics, and "weekend parties" at the Garrett estate. In an effort to attract more students and compete with the fashionable boarding schools many prominent families still preferred for their daughters, Bryn Mawr School leaders even contemplated opening a country boarding division for students at Montebello.[41]

School officials also struggled to incorporate athletics into school life, and, indeed, organized sports such as hockey, basketball, and lacrosse proliferated at Bryn Mawr from 1910 to 1930. According to Bryn Mawr seniors in their 1929 yearbook, "We are especially proud of our athletic achievements … Our athletics have been the best part of school."[42] But securing athletic fields adequate for those activities was difficult for the city school. As early as 1910, the Bryn Mawr School had advertised its country athletic fields for "out-of-door sports" played every afternoon and on Saturday mornings.[43] At M. Carey Thomas's insistence, the school attempted to practice and play at Montebello, but that solution proved unacceptable. Montebello was an hour away from the school's city location, and it was too time consuming and expensive to transport students between the school and the country estate frequently. Furthermore, some members of the Bryn Mawr community feared relying on the use of Montebello too heavily because M. Carey Thomas—not the Bryn Mawr School—controlled the estate, and Thomas could choose to sell the property at any time. Bryn Mawr periodically rented athletic fields around Baltimore and played its hockey games at the borrowed country estate of a Bryn Mawr School family.[44] But parents continually pressured the school to improve its sports program and facilities, and competing with suburban schools that had their own playing fields proved increasingly difficult.[45]

Outdoor activities and athletics comprised a major cornerstone of the

country-day philosophy, and emphasis on general "aesthetic" education constituted another essential element of the new educational model—at least for girls.
Certainly, the Bryn Mawr School's founders had themselves appreciated the arts
and sought to instill a similar appreciation of culture in their students, but they
had been concerned that training in female "accomplishments" could erode
concentration on strict academics. Families in the twentieth century, however,
wanted a broader range of extracurricular offerings for their daughters, and
Bryn Mawr teachers and administrators generally concurred on the desirability
of expanding school activities to include dramatics clubs, art studies, and, eventually, music instruction.[46]

As a result, the Bryn Mawr School expanded its mission to students. While
adhering to its original goal of preparing girls for college, the school now
trained and entertained girls with a wide variety of activities. Indeed, the contrasting emphases in Bryn Mawr School catalogues from the 1880s to the second decade of the twentieth century is striking. Catalogues from Bryn Mawr's
first decade exclusively enumerated academic requirements, whereas catalogues
from the 1910s described a variety of student activities and "Afternoon Study
and Play." The optional "afternoon school," which met from 3:15 to 5:45 p.m.,
consisted of study halls, outdoor games and exercises, and art and music lessons.
It even offered the Bryn Mawr School's first female-specific courses in "Household Chemistry" and "Home Economics." Such extracurricular subjects and activities proved immediately popular and, while initially kept strictly separate
from the standard academic day, quickly evolved into an integral part of the
school. Even M. Carey Thomas—usually resistant to any plans she deemed
threatening to Bryn Mawr's academic standards—wrote Edith Hamilton that
her niece, Millicent Carey (later McIntosh), was "delighted with the afternoon
plan" and its provisions for both study and recreation.[47]

The Bryn Mawr School developed a full-fledged music program in the
1920s. In the 1880s, Mamie Gwinn had pledged that the Bryn Mawr School
would never consent to teaching music, and, even as late as the 1910s, the school
argued that music took too much time away from college preparation in its
upper grades. A 1917–18 Bryn Mawr School catalogue noted that music was
"required in the primary school and the first intermediate class" but was optional for older students, but the Bryn Mawr School board agreed to require
some musical instruction for all of its students by the early 1920s.[48] Indeed, by
1922, Bryn Mawr's leadership had perceived the lack of music at the school as a
deficit:

The School needs more appreciation of music as a part of the school life. The pupils sing very badly and their repertoire is limited to about fifteen of the most familiar hymns. The cultural value of carefully selected and carefully prepared music in morning exercises we are at present almost completely missing.[49]

The school leaders proposed to integrate music into the regular curriculum, establish a school choir, and offer voluntary choral work on Wednesday afternoons. Bryn Mawr engaged a new director of music (Mr. Surette, head of Concord School of Music and "musical adviser in a number of the women's colleges"), who periodically visited the school and offered voice lessons to students. Soon music became a routine part of daily morning exercises—new hymnals were even ordered for opening exercises—and a choir and glee club were popular by the mid-1920s. In 1927, the Bryn Mawr School agreed to rent pianos so its students could take private lessons from the prestigious Peabody Institute's music teachers.[50]

With its competitive athletics, music program, afternoon school, and ever-expanding extracurricular offerings, the Bryn Mawr School was becoming a very different kind of place. The once strictly academic Bryn Mawr, according to a 1922 account, faced the problem of "competition of academic and non-academic interests in a day with too few periods to accommodate both interests." So plentiful were student activities—"captain-ball, basket-ball and hockey, choral work, dramatics and teachers' appointments"—that the school entertained the idea of shortening the length of its classes to accommodate them all. It was probably Headmistress Amy Kelly who expressed frustration that the competition between academic and extracurricular activities "produces most undesirable friction and puts any person with executive duties in an impossible situation as umpire." (Scheduling problems also arose because so many students commuted a considerable distance from their suburban homes to Bryn Mawr's city location.)[51] Although Bryn Mawr still asserted its old priorities—claiming that extracurricular activities would not come at the expense of sound college preparation—the school consciously refashioned its public image. As one publicity piece argued, "Although the Bryn Mawr School offers no general course, but only a program of studies preparing for college examinations, it has from the beginning provided for the development of aesthetic skills and appreciations in art, in dramatics, and in music."[52] The old Bryn Mawr School would not sell well in the new Baltimore, and Bryn Mawr leaders tried to update their school's image.

Redefinition: Competition, Crisis, and a Country Campus

The early Bryn Mawr School had been a "missionary" institution convincing Baltimoreans to embrace an education for girls that they essentially did not want. The modern Bryn Mawr found itself in the reverse position, trying to become exactly what its community *did* want in a school. Necessity was transforming the once pioneering Bryn Mawr School from a leader to a follower in the realm of girls' education.

Fearing the exodus of families to the suburbs and their schools, Edith Hamilton had long urged the school's board to respond. As early as 1913, she had specifically relayed her concerns about "the school that is beginning to be our rival, the girls country school Roland Park." More and more parents, she knew, were reluctant to send their daughters to a school located in the very city neighborhoods they were abandoning. Edith Hamilton and her sister Margaret argued that the Bryn Mawr School had to maintain the loyalty of families in the county. Establishing primary schools in suburban neighborhoods to "feed" into Bryn Mawr's Main School in the city might provide a novel solution. Bryn Mawr, Margaret Hamilton suggested, "should be willing to spend money here for the sake of making its way into a most desirable neighborhood"—particularly Roland Park.[53]

But plans for Bryn Mawr's country primary schools never materialized, and competition from rival girls' schools intensified. Margaret Hamilton lamented to Thomas that she wished "the finances of the school had permitted me to start my country primary schools this year. It would have made such a scenic advertisement for the school."

New country-day schools offering convenient suburban locations, lush bucolic settings, impressive athletic fields and facilities, and wide–ranging cultural and extracurricular activities continued to draw more students away from the Bryn Mawr School. The establishment of one "non-college preparatory school," with a proprietor (Mr. Hillyer of the Calvert School, a popular local primary school) who "knows how to make his school very fashionable, and to sacrifice good education to give the parents what they wish for their children," presented "the worst blow the Bryn Mawr School has ever had." According to Margaret Hamilton, Bryn Mawr would be "face to face with a fight for the next few years." And when Bryn Mawr's director of physical training, Miss Elock, resigned to open a new boarding school offering a "general" (rather than college preparatory) course, Headmistress Kelly worried. She realized that the new school's very different philosophy should not place it in direct competition with Bryn Mawr, but already about half a dozen students had left Bryn Mawr. While the students Bryn Mawr had lost to the new school were not academically bright students, she feared that "there may be some exodus later, of course, especially if one or two popular girls decide to make a change." Kelly also noted rumors that Edith Hamilton was encouraging support for the new school but that she was "convinced from statements by both Miss Elock and Miss Margaret Hamilton that this is positively not the case."[54]

New country schools that did offer college preparation—optional, flexible, and with fewer rigid requirements than those of the Bryn Mawr School—presented an even greater threat. While once the Bryn Mawr School had stood alone as the school preparing Baltimore girls for college, now other schools promised to train girls for higher education—and in a popular country atmosphere. "After noting the rapid growth of the Roland Park Country School and noting the loss this year of two excellent pupils to this school because it offers much better facilities, I feel sure that we are going to fall behind in numbers if we do not extend facilities," Headmistress Kelly warned the Bryn Mawr board soon after her arrival at the school. In 1924, Kelly visited the Roland Park School, surveying particularly its gymnasium, and reported her findings to the Bryn Mawr board. Bryn Mawr took note when a local newspaper reported that "three classrooms, a gymnasium, and a studio will be constructed during the summer at the Roland Park Country School to take care of increase in enrollment." Kelly maintained in 1926 that Roland Park Country School did not lure away Bryn Mawr's best students—it "at present merely rids us of some material poor from the academic point of view"—but she warned that Bryn Mawr had to take steps to ensure that the loss of its students did "not become a landslide as it might if the social pull became stronger than the demand for good work."[55]

Competition from country-day schools was hastening a crisis at the Bryn Mawr School. Declining enrollments—which exacerbated the school's long-standing financial problems and deepened dissatisfaction among families—forced decisive action if the once model Bryn Mawr School was to survive in the changing landscape of the twentieth century. Together the school's once fractured community of support would unite behind a new plan to save the Bryn Mawr School by transforming it into a bona fide country-day academy for girls.

By the mid-1920s, the Bryn Mawr School was making efforts to establish a new campus in Baltimore's burgeoning suburbs. By 1927, a potential property for a new campus had been located, and by the following year the Bryn Mawr School was seriously evaluating its finances in preparation for a move. Bryn Mawr's Parents' Association (a direct outgrowth of protest meetings at the time of Edith Hamilton's resignation) discussed and debated "plans for the future of the school." Bryn Mawr School alumnae orchestrated fund-raising and moving campaigns, often independently of the school's official efforts. After one controversy, Bryn Mawr's board specifically agreed in 1928 not to interfere with its alumnae's fund-raising activities. Voicing their long-standing frustration with the school's management—and what they perceived as its reluctance to move forward with plans—families and alumnae particularly pressured the Bryn Mawr School to act decisively.[56]

Aware of its precarious standing and of the suspicions of parents and alumnae, Bryn Mawr's board acknowledged that it had to be perceived as responsive and quick-acting to maintain the loyalty of its constituency. The board repeatedly assured the Bryn Mawr community of its commitment to their plans for transforming the school. By 1928, the Bryn Mawr School owned a new country campus and operated its Primary School in a renovated house on the country property. But funds for erecting new school buildings to house the majority of Bryn Mawr's students remained woefully short. In the spring of 1928, the Bryn Mawr School held its commencement exercises in the county to symbolize the imminence of its move. Even so, unhappy families threatened that fall to abandon Bryn Mawr unless construction of its new Main School building began within two years. In an effort to appease parents, the school borrowed money to ready athletic fields at the county property for the school's sports programs, even though classes continued to be held in the city building.[57]

Money, however, remained the critical issue. Pamphlets—such as "The Bryn Mawr School: Its New Country Site and Its Financial Needs" and "The Bryn Mawr School: A Frank, Business-like Statement of Its Financial Need for $300,000"—outlined the problem.[58] As a female institution—historically run both by and for women—the Bryn Mawr School faced particular difficulties. With Mary Garrett's backing, the original Bryn Mawr School had been an exception to the rule in female education—for, in controlling her own fortune, Mary Garrett had been free to establish her school as she saw fit. Certainly, women's colleges and girls' schools had grown more prosperous by the early twentieth century. And yet the Bryn Mawr School struggled financially.

Fund-raising proved extremely difficult. Bryn Mawr alumnae enthusiastically launched a myriad of fund-raising schemes. They hosted a treasure hunt, a lawn dance, and a card party; they sponsored a horse show, and they organized Christmas and rummage sales. But they netted only small proceeds from their parties and sales, profits more suitable for small projects than for erecting new school buildings. In retrospect, their hopes to finance a new country campus by such measures seem naive.

Men within the Bryn Mawr School community proved more adept at raising large sums of money than did alumnae. The fathers who had originally organized in protest at the time of Edith Hamilton's resignation took the initiative in overseeing the school's fund-raising and financial planning, somewhat ironically, given the school's historic commitment to keeping power exclusively in the hands of women. M. Carey Thomas had always preferred female leadership, as she reminded the Bryn Mawr School board in 1928: "I feel very strongly that the Board of Managers should be women and whenever possible former pupils of the Bryn Mawr School. Women really care for and follow the education of their girls. Men do not." But, in the absence of a benefactor like Mary Garrett and keenly sensing its need, the Bryn Mawr School turned with increasing frequency to fathers and husbands, who had more extensive business experience and contacts. Even M. Carey Thomas conceded the wisdom of seeking the advice of men, proposing the formation of some kind of male "business association" to advise the school on financial matters. Concurring on the need for male expertise in "all questions involving capital expenditures or investments or liens on the school property," Bryn Mawr's board formed an official "Men's Advisory Committee." Financial necessity and shifting attitudes gave men new status within the country-day Bryn Mawr School.[59]

Landscape and Architecture: A Reflection of Educational Models

The Bryn Mawr School's country campus contrasted sharply with its old city building. For decades, Mary Garrett's model school building had stood as a monument to the Bryn Mawr School founders' educational ideals. A virtual fortress of learning, the Bryn Mawr School building had been designed to promote serious study and produce strong, healthy women—never to nurture or coddle childish, feminine sensibilities. Grandeur and austerity—more than "homeyness" or warmth—characterized the building. By the 1920s, however, that intentional design and atmosphere of the old school represented a past that the modern Bryn Mawr hoped to overcome. To families attracted to the country-day ideal of incorporating fresh air, open spaces, recreation, and nurture into the learning process, Bryn Mawr's old building seemed out of date. They deemed a new kind of school campus essential to implementing the country-day philosophy they now embraced.[60] The Bryn Mawr School's two physical settings symbolized the shifting educational ideals influencing the school and serves as a metaphor for distinctly different models for the education of girls.

In direct contrast to Mary Garrett's Bryn Mawr School building, the new Bryn Mawr campus was specifically designed to be as unimposing and "un-institutional" as possible. "We have kept in mind the desire of your committee that the building should have as little of an institutional quality as is possible," the new campus's architect assured Headmistress Kelly. The suburban Bryn Mawr would be housed not in a single building but in numerous small-scale structures, as the desired atmosphere could "be obtained more readily if the general scheme is broken up into smaller units," reasoned the architect. The Bryn Mawr School embraced his recommendations. As one report explained, the "essential idea" of the new country Bryn Mawr was "to provide for the child's whole day with a regime of recitation, lesson preparation and play in an atmosphere as little as possible institutional." Those goals could best be achieved in "small buildings low and home-like in appearance"—"small and domestic" in type—with "easy access to the out-of-doors." An alumnae magazine described the new campus: "All the school houses are small, sunny, quiet and informal with only two floors and easy access to out-of-doors." All the "houses" are "delightfully planned to make the most of the setting and the climatic condition that permit outdoor life through most of the year."[61]

As in the residential neighborhoods of suburban Roland Park, all of the school buildings—constructed of native Maryland stone rather than the brick and marble statuary of the city Bryn Mawr School—were to blend as unobtrusively as possible into the natural landscape. Green athletic fields, tennis courts, nature trails, gardens—perhaps even an ice-skating pond—would complement the natural environment. In addition to new accommodations for outdoor recreation, Bryn Mawr planned for a new music unit with rooms for the chorus and orchestra, as well as individual practice, and for an art studio and exhibition area for student art.[62]

A 1933 Bryn Mawr School bulletin compared the school's original building unfavorably with the new country campus:

> The graying statuary will be lonely in its halls but the kindly eyes of Miss Mary

Garrett will turn from the cold stairwell to gaze on an orchard hedged in with lilacs. Miss Edith Hamilton will come out from her dark niche and smile when she thinks of the contrast between the concreted yard and grimy shrubbery she honored by the name of "The garden" and this one when the sun slants in from dogwoods and roses.[63]

The modern Bryn Mawr School generally spared little sentiment for its old model school building and all it had symbolized.

Indeed, the Bryn Mawr School made few attempts to link the new school with its past. Perhaps more than anything else, Mary Garrett's classical statuary represented the original Bryn Mawr School, epitomizing all of the founders' lofty views for their model school. But Bryn Mawr made no attempt to incorporate those symbols of the past into its new campus. "What are we going to do with our reproductions of classical sculpture?" school officials wondered in 1929.[64] Rather than cherished reminders of Bryn Mawr's founders and their vision, Garrett's treasures proved burdensome, relics deemed unsuitable for the new country campus. During the next three decades, the Bryn Mawr School's large collection of classical reproductions were stored, loaned, and eventually sold or given away. Some "bas-reliefs" went to another local girls' school, Garrison Forest, and the once prized reproductions of the Parthenon friezes that had graced the old school's central study hall were loaned to the rival Roland Park Country School and eventually sold to the Roland Park alumnae in 1947, for what Bryn Mawr considered a ridiculously low price of three hundred dollars. In 1954, the Bryn Mawr School board reported that it had finally "been successful in giving away all the articles that have been in storage."[65]

A Lingering Voice from the Past

M. Carey Thomas's reactions to the plans at her school are suggestive of the significance of the changes under way. For more than four decades, Thomas had exerted a definitive influence over the school she considered her own. Although usually absorbed in her responsibilities at Bryn Mawr College, she had always asserted her model for the education of girls at the Bryn Mawr School. She had offered a personal model of intelligent and independent womanhood, and always she had demanded that the Bryn Mawr School fulfill its founding vision of offering a truly exceptional education for girls. When Baltimore's reception had been lukewarm at best, when applicants were few and seats were empty, when school fees went unpaid and deficits mounted, when students failed examinations and trickled away to more traditional girls' schools and womanly pursuits, Thomas had persisted.

But by the 1920s, Thomas's influence was waning. Although ostensibly she had reinforced her control over the school during the battles surrounding Edith Hamilton's resignation, the controversy had actually strengthened the parent and alumnae groups who were leading Bryn Mawr's campaign to become a country-day academy. Characteristically, Thomas would not give up her power—and her vision—without a fight.

Thomas witnessed the Bryn Mawr School's plans to move to the county suburbs with skepticism. She saw Bryn Mawr's city school building, the one her dear Mary Garrett had erected as an embodiment of and monument to the founders' educational vision, as the heart of the Bryn Mawr School. To abandon the model school building would be to abandon the school's very essence. Unmoved by arguments about the necessity of following Baltimore's well-to-do population to the suburbs and accommodating their demand for country-day education, Thomas accused Bryn Mawr parents and alumnae of trying to destroy her school. She charged Bryn Mawr's administration with cowardly catering to the demands of the less-enlightened members of the school community. Thomas issued a final, desperate threat that she considered her only chance to save her Bryn Mawr School from the community that wanted to remake it: she declared that she would close the school rather than allow it to change.

As the executor of Mary Garrett's will and thus holder of the Bryn Mawr School's outstanding mortgage on its city property, Thomas had real financial power over the institution. She could foreclose on the school's city building, refuse to release the property for sale, and leave the school without funds to establish its new campus. To exert her control she also could promise to set up or withhold an eventual endowment for the Bryn Mawr School from the Garrett fortune she managed. Thomas mustered all her resources for the confrontation.

In December 1927, Thomas wrote to Amy Kelly and the other members of the board that she would rather close the Bryn Mawr School than see it "become less good little by little" until "it had become a ghost of itself."[66] In early January of 1928, she reiterated her threats: "When circumstances over which we have no control seem to the Board to make it impossible to conduct a self supporting School with these high standards we have an absolute right to close the School. No one can question this right. It is the only self respecting action to take." The original Bryn Mawr School, Thomas proclaimed, had been founded as a grand experiment in the education of girls with the hope of proving that a girls' schools of the highest academic order could survive and become self-supporting. But, from Thomas's perspective, Baltimore had shown its true colors, disdaining the exceptional education and opportunities Bryn Mawr sought to offer its daughters. Thus, the founders' and their Bryn Mawr School's mission had failed. Although it would be "a deep grief to me to see the School close," Thomas concluded, "it would be better to close it and let the experiment stand for what it had accomplished." Indeed, "it would be unbearable to have it continue with a different policy and lower standards."[67]

Appalled by her threats, the school's administrators and board members rallied to dissuade Thomas from drastic action. Eight days after Thomas's pronouncements, the Bryn Mawr School sent a delegation to visit her in an attempt to change her mind. They argued that the Bryn Mawr School could raise money and move to the country and still uphold its high academic standards. The Bryn Mawr School, they tried to convince her, could remain true to its founding principles, even as a country-day school. While still vocally skeptical, Thomas—apparently out of lingering affection for the school, its headmistress, and some board members—agreed to give the school an opportunity to prove her fears groundless: "Still if there is any possibility ... of securing help to continue the School on its present lines by appealing to the Baltimore public," she wrote, "I do not wish to stand in the way."[68]

Although Thomas agreed not to close the Bryn Mawr School, she insisted that measures be taken to protect the school's high academic standards, which, she argued, "must be safeguarded under any reconstruction scheme." Such safeguards including reaffirming Bryn Mawr's longtime policy of concentrating power in a small managing board comprising women chosen for their educational accomplishments and their commitment to high standards in girls' education. As she had in the past, Thomas tried to ensure that the influence of less-well-trusted parents and alumnae would be confined to advisory committees. Specifically, Thomas asked that her niece Millicent Carey McIntosh be appointed to the Bryn Mawr School board. McIntosh was a graduate of both the Bryn Mawr School and Bryn Mawr College, and she eventually served as dean of Bryn Mawr College, headmistress of the Brearley School for girls, and president of Barnard College. McIntosh had Thomas's affection and trust. Thomas believed that her niece, if anyone, would hold the Bryn Mawr School true to its founding ideals. In accordance with Thomas's demands, the Bryn Mawr School pledged to "always maintain and operate its School in faithful conformity" with it founding ideals or, in keeping with the provisions of Mary Garrett's will, forfeit its property to Bryn Mawr College or Johns Hopkins University. In return, Thomas agreed not to stop the sale of the school's city property. As an additional incentive for maintenance of academic priorities, which Thomas feared were threatened by moving schemes, Thomas pledged $100,000 to the Bryn Mawr School on the condition that the school match her gift and use the funds to establish an endowment. The gesture, according to Thomas, was "a spur" that "seemed necessary to rescue the academic side of the school."[69]

Ultimately, Thomas did not stand in the way of the Bryn Mawr School's transformation schemes. Surely, the attention and patience of Headmistress Kelly soothed Thomas's fears. When Thomas, for instance, declared herself very disappointed with the buildings rising on the school's new grounds in 1932, Kelly assured her that her displeasure stemmed from a "wrong impression." Kelly addressed each of Thomas's concerns about all manner of building details—the elevation of structures, the chimneys, the windows and shutters—and offered to give her a personal tour of the country campus to prove her fears ungrounded.[70] Millicent McIntosh, too, always allayed her aunt's worries about the future of the school.

In the end, relatively little came of Thomas's attempts to "rescue" the Bryn Mawr School from itself. The Bryn Mawr School board gradually yielded more power to various members of its community, permitting their perspectives to guide the school and the education it offered to Baltimore girls. Despite Thomas's efforts to spark the growth of an endowment to protect the school's "academic side," Bryn Mawr used the first fifty thousand dollars it raised (in repudiation of Thomas's conditions) toward the purchase of its new county property. Although the Bryn Mawr board reassured Thomas that, after purchasing the new property, establishing an endowment would be its first priority, that promise came to naught. Expenses incurred by continuous improvements to the new campus, combined with the onset of the Great Depression of the 1930s, destroyed all realistic plans for an academic endowment in the near future.[71]

M. Carey Thomas resigned from the Bryn Mawr School board in 1928, after her final battle with the school over its country-day transformation. Although she remained interested in the school, her influence waned thereafter. On 2 December 1935, Martha Carey Thomas died at the age of seventy-eight, and an era at the Bryn Mawr School came to an end. The Bryn Mawr School had harbored hopes of a substantial endowment, specifically the $100,000 Thomas had promised to leave the school in 1928. Because of financial reverses and Thomas's own profligate spending, however, little remained of the fortune Mary Garrett had left Thomas, and the intended bequest to the Bryn Mawr School never materialized. Thomas's legacy to the Bryn Mawr School would be in the vision and high standards for girls' education that she had established and insisted the school maintain throughout her life.

Continuing Crises: The Depression Years

Just as the Bryn Mawr School's moving campaign was gaining momentum, the Great Depression strangled the school's efforts to remake itself. Debt and declining enrollment had placed the school in a tenuous position in the 1920s and had made building the new country campus difficult. The Bryn Mawr Men's Advisory Committee had urged caution, warning against spending money to improve the school's new campus before selling the old city building. But the school had moved ahead, in an effort to hold the loyalty of its wavering constituency. Already overextended, Bryn Mawr found itself in even more dire straits in the wake of the 1929 stock market crash. Suddenly the value of Bryn Mawr's city property was seriously eroded, with no potential buyers in sight. In September 1931, the Baltimore Trust Company, which held significant Bryn Mawr School funds, closed its doors. Given the scale of the financial crisis, many Bryn Mawr School families found themselves unable to pay their daughters' school fees on time, if at all.[72]

Statistics paint a grim portrait of the Depression's effects on Baltimore. By Christmas 1931, eight thousand Baltimore families were on public relief; the following year, the number had risen to eighteen thousand families; and by Christmas 1933, twenty-three thousand—or one in six Baltimore families—were on relief. On 25 February 1933—in the wake of more bank failures—the governor of Maryland closed all banks in his state to halt runs on deposits.[73] Financial turmoil abruptly thwarted many of the Bryn Mawr School's ambitious plans, and, in the midst of the crisis, a core component of Bryn Mawr supporters struggled to hold the school together.

The clearest portrait of the Bryn Mawr School and its hardships during the Depression emerges from the early 1930s correspondence among Headmistress Amy Kelly, Margaret Hamilton (then head of Bryn Mawr's Primary School), and Elizabeth Thomas (head of Bryn Mawr's Main School). During the critical

1932–33 school year, the Bryn Mawr School granted Amy Kelly a sabbatical. Kelly spent the year traveling in Europe, and she corresponded frequently with Margaret Hamilton and Elizabeth Thomas about the school's situation.

Shortly after her return in 1934, Kelly resigned as Bryn Mawr's headmistress and returned to teaching at Wellesley College.[74] Although it is not clear whether financial disagreements contributed to Kelly's departure, Bryn Mawr's handling of its financial troubles in the early years of the Depression had clearly led to conflict with its headmistress. During Kelly's sabbatical year in 1933, Kelly and Elizabeth Thomas had corresponded about the difficulty Kelly experienced receiving her salary. While in Europe, Kelly cashed her salary check in April 1933, not realizing that the Baltimore bank on which the check had been drawn had failed. The American Express office that cashed Kelly's check tried to force Bryn Mawr to cover the amount out of another account. Elizabeth Thomas, describing the school's dire financial situation, wrote to Kelly that Bryn Mawr would pay its teachers only half of their salaries in the upcoming months. "To have to pay again your cheque made a deep hole in our balance," she noted, and argued that the school could not pay Kelly. Kelly sympathized with the school: she assured Elizabeth Thomas that "I do appreciate the situation of the school and I realize fully how hard the problems are and how much you are doing to care for the whole situation." She hoped "you will not find all this peevish and fussy," but Kelly expressed her frustration at being expected to refund the money from the salary check she had cashed. By the spring of 1933, the Bryn Mawr School had reduced Kelly's salary, but the school did not fully pay her even that salary.[75]

As late as 1938, Kelly (then at Wellesley College) was corresponding with the Bryn Mawr School's accountants about the money she believed was owed her. In a series of letters in 1937 and 1938, Kelly outlined how she believed the school had reduced her salary more than she had agreed to and "without my knowledge of the circumstances in which I was making those concessions." The Bryn Mawr School (which acknowledged that it still owed Kelly money) hoped to cancel its indebtedness to Kelly for a sum of $153.64. But Kelly objected: "I am not prepared to make any further sacrifices, and I shall hold the school responsible. I should deplore taking issue with the school in the matter, but I feel that sufficient time has elapsed for a final settlement." Not until October 1938 did the school finally settle with Kelly for $383.37.[76]

Janet Howell Clark was chosen as Kelly's successor in 1935. Clark had deep ties with the Bryn Mawr School community: she was a graduate of both the Bryn

Mawr School (1906) and Bryn Mawr College (1910), as well as a Bryn Mawr School parent and board member. She also had impressive academic credentials: she had earned a doctorate in physics from Johns Hopkins University and taught at both Bryn Mawr College and Smith College before returning to teach at John Hopkins School of Hygiene. Clark taught at Hopkins for over a decade, establishing herself as an authority on the biological effects of radiation, before becoming Bryn Mawr's third headmistress. But only three years after her appointment at Bryn Mawr, she left to accept a position as dean of the College of Women and professor of biological science at the University of Rochester, where she remained until her retirement in 1952.[77]

In the absence of a continuous leader during the 1930s, Margaret Hamilton and Elizabeth Thomas managed the school's daily activities. Margaret Hamilton ran the school's country campus, where the Bryn Mawr Primary School operated. Elizabeth Thomas, a distant relative of M. Carey Thomas's family, a graduate of Goucher College, and longtime Bryn Mawr School mathematics teacher, secretary, and business manager, oversaw the school's city property, where Bryn Mawr's older students still attended classes.[78] Together Hamilton and Thomas undertook all kinds of economies—cutting teacher and staff salaries, dismissing servants, closing music rooms to save fuel and cleaning expenses, and discontinuing all tuition reductions—to keep the Bryn Mawr School open. Margaret Hamilton, who had been at the Bryn Mawr School for almost forty years, served for four years without pay before retiring in 1935.[79]

When the Depression hit, the Bryn Mawr School owned two campuses: the county property that housed the youngest students and the city building that served the older ones. Financial realities prevented a swift and complete move to the country campus, but many Bryn Mawr families were impatient. One influential alumna, it was reported in 1932, was rallying "prominent parents" to agitate for the school to keep additional grades in the county. Because of "pressure brought to bear by the parents and the board," administrators agreed—despite scheduling difficulties—to keep one more grade in the county in an effort to "try to stall this exodus" of parents threatening to enroll their daughters in other suburban schools.[80]

Parents, it seemed, were "more emphatic than ever" that their daughters be educated near their suburban homes. Some parents liked their daughters near their brothers (often enrolled at the Gilman Country School) and viewed transporting their daughters to Bryn Mawr's city campus as too difficult, particularly because the Depression was forcing them to make do with fewer household servants. The decision to house additional grades in the county proved "a very pop-ular move" and "forestalled some of the withdrawals that were inevitable other-wise," but families were only temporarily appeased. Just a few months later, one father—warning that families were "very much upset by a somewhat indefinite announcement" at Bryn Mawr's commencement of the school's plans to move the entire Main School to the county—threatened to send his daughters to an-other school unless Bryn Mawr acted immediately. He was "confident that many other parents feel the same way" and threatened that "the reported indefinite-ness of the announcement yesterday will cause a falling off in the number of children to be entered for next fall."[81]

The Bryn Mawr School had real reason to fear an "exodus" of students be-cause it was happening. During the 1930s, Bryn Mawr (like other private insti-tutions) inevitably lost some students whose families could no longer afford the luxury of private education for their daughters. But more students left the Bryn Mawr School to enroll in different kinds of private schools for girls—schools of-fering what families perceived as advantages that Bryn Mawr did not. In 1932, Bryn Mawr lost twelve students to other Baltimore schools, as well as additional students departing for boarding schools. While some of those leaving Bryn Mawr for other Baltimore schools may have entered free public schools, at least half enrolled at rival girls' schools—especially Roland Park Country School and Garrison Forest School, both of which were country-day academies.[82] During the following school year, Bryn Mawr lost a devastating thirty-eight students: eight girls transferred to public schools, at least three went to boarding schools, three to finishing schools, one on a European year abroad, and six to rival Bal-timore private schools.[83] Clearly, the Bryn Mawr School's greatest loss of stu-dents during the Depression came not from the economic hardships of families but from the preference of more and more Bryn Mawr families for a different kind of education for their daughters.

And so—despite inadequate funds, mounting debt, and no relief in sight—the Bryn Mawr School went forward with its moving plans in order to stem the dramatic loss of students that would surely lead to its closing. In 1933, in re-sponse to "almost a united approval from parents," moving the Main School im-mediately seemed "the best and really only thing under all the circumstances." The Bryn Mawr School would thus direct all of its limited resources to that overriding goal. Inevitably, the grand architectural schemes for the new campus developed with such enthusiasm in the 1920s were put aside in favor of building less expensive, temporary (or so it was planned) structures.[84]

Moving plans superseded everything. Money M. Carey Thomas had designated "to rescue the academic side of the school" by establishing an endowment were instead used to cover moving expenses.[85] Funds that alumnae had, since Edith Hamilton's era, raised for scholarships for Bryn Mawr School students were also diverted for improvements to the country campus. In October 1932, the Bryn Mawr School alumnae authorized the board to seek permission from all donors to various scholarship funds to release their donations to be used to cover moving expenses and debt. In December 1932, the four thousand dollar principle of the Edith Hamilton Scholarship Fund was released for general use.[86]

As Bryn Mawr's board, administrators, alumnae, and families united behind the goal of building a new campus, Bryn Mawr School faculty saw their salaries cut again and again. According to Elizabeth Thomas in 1933, Bryn Mawr teachers had been "most courageous and splendid" in the face of the school's financial crisis, evidencing a most "earnest desire to serve the school of which they are most fond." Simultaneously, she noted, they questioned their deep salary reductions when they did not see similar economies elsewhere.[87]

Elizabeth Thomas and Margaret Hamilton had always worried about the plight of Bryn Mawr School faculty members—almost all of them single and self-supporting. Realizing that "if we cannot do something drastic we shall have to close," a distressed administrator (probably Thomas) wrote Amy Kelly in 1932 that Bryn Mawr would have to dismiss some teachers and cut the salaries of those remaining. Despite her personal reservations, Thomas saw no alternative but to follow the advice of the Men's Advisory Committee in late 1932 by cutting teachers' salaries more drastically than previously. As Bryn Mawr's enrollment fell the following year, the school dismissed more teachers in 1933. Thomas worried about teachers for whom she felt real personal affection. Because of her expensive illnesses, longtime teacher Miss Parker would have little on which to live after being dismissed, and she had no family to whom she could turn for support. Other Bryn Mawr teachers had lost all of their savings in bank failures, and by 1933 their salaries had been cut by 50 percent.[88]

While teachers accepted as necessary the draconian reductions to their salaries in the early 1930s, they would come to resent the Bryn Mawr School's readiness to spend money on its physical plant rather than on its faculty. After meeting routine operating expenses, they argued, teachers' salaries—not physical improvements to the school campus—should be the school's priority. In a letter to the Bryn Mawr School Board of Managers in April 1933, teachers emphasized their repeated willingness to sacrifice and accept significant salary cuts in an effort to do their part to save the school. But they resented Bryn Mawr's decision to cut their salaries by 50 percent in the middle of the 1932–33 school year when the school was spending so much money erecting new buildings.[89] Ironically, at the very time when teachers' salaries were plummeting, they were being expected to work longer hours supervising afternoon programs. When Bryn Mawr moved to the country campus, it extended the ending of its school day from 1:30 to 4:45 p.m. to offer many electives, extracurricular activities, and study halls, and teachers were expected to supervise those afternoon activities with no additional compensation.[90]

While administrators like Margaret Hamilton (who did not take her salary for several years) worried that teachers' salaries had been reduced below a "living wage" and that their morale was very low, building the new country campus remained the Bryn Mawr School's priority.[91] In comparison to families and alumnae who had successfully pressured the Bryn Mawr School to adopt the educational model they preferred, teachers remained relatively powerless members of the Bryn Mawr School community, with little leverage within the institution that employed them. Teachers (despite the sympathy of some administrators and occasional conciliatory statements made by the Bryn Mawr School board) had little choice but to accept the school's policies or quit (not a very realistic option for most self-supporting teachers, given the scarcity of jobs during the 1930s). As late as 1938, the Bryn Mawr School board was still discussing—but not acting upon—teachers' requests to return their salaries to pre-Depression levels and to be granted representation on the Bryn Mawr board, along with alumnae and parents.[92]

The Country-Day Bryn Mawr

Despite tensions and hardships, the day-to-day work of teachers, administrators, and students continued throughout the 1930s as it had for decades. In reality, what students did in their classrooms in the country had not changed very significantly. Course requirements for students at the end of the 1930s were very similar to those for students in the early 1920s. (It is difficult, however, to assess the exact nature of what was taught in courses and to judge teachers' expectations for their students' performance.) Bryn Mawr College's discontinuation of its own entrance examination in the 1920s, during Amy Kelly's tenure as Bryn Mawr School headmistress, had already given the school more freedom in tai-

loring the curriculum of students to their interests and the colleges they hoped
to attend, and that trend continued. Bryn Mawr School catalogues from the late
1930s and early 1940s noted the flexibility: "In the Upper School the work con-
sists of strictly college preparatory courses but the increasing flexibility of the
college entrance requirements makes it possible to adjust the work in the upper
classes to suit the special interests and abilities of the individual pupils."[93]

In the late 1930s and early 1940s, all Bryn Mawr students took English,
French, and Latin throughout their years at the school. Greek, required of all
Bryn Mawr students at the original school, was offered as an alternative to Latin
or as an elective; German could be substituted for certain science or history
courses (though it was noted that students preparing for Bryn Mawr College
should take German). Students studied history (the history of ancient Greek and
Roman civilizations, European civilizations throughout the centuries, and
American history), mathematics, and laboratory science (with, again, special
note that students preparing for Bryn Mawr College needed physics). Music and
art were required for students in lower grades but were elective for advanced
students. Physical education was mandatory for everyone.[94]

Mirroring the trend evident during Edith Hamilton's years at Bryn Mawr,
the school continued to expand its athletics and arts programs, and student organizations multiplied. Perhaps most in contrast to the founders' Bryn Mawr
School was that the country-day educational model addressed the needs and interests of students far beyond the traditional classroom. The country-day Bryn
Mawr granted students somewhat more flexibility in planning their academic
curricula; even more, it greatly expanded the extracurricular opportunities available to them. Students and parents alike seemed pleased.

By the end of the 1930s, the Bryn Mawr School had successfully transformed
itself in the Baltimore suburbs. Responding to shifting educational theories and
residential patterns, Bryn Mawr had conceded to the demands of its community
and adopted the country-day model of educating girls. As the decade drew to a
close, the entire Bryn Mawr School resided at its country campus, although not
in the buildings the community hoped one day to erect. Bryn Mawr continued
to prepare girls for college, but students now also enjoyed a wide range of activities at their school. None of the changes had come easily.

CHAPTER FOUR

An Establishment Vision
The Bryn Mawr School in the Mid-Twentieth Century

> We wonder if you realize how many of the women in our community
> have gone to Bryn Mawr School and how many are civic leaders as well as
> home-makers. They are our best example in talking about the advantages
> of private school education.
> — SUGGESTED LETTER TO FRIENDS
> OF THE SCHOOL, 1953

The cultural expectations of girls and their families and the range of opportunities—both educational and professional—open to them shifted considerably during the first half of the twentieth century. During this period, the Bryn Mawr School came to reflect U.S. society in ways its founders would never have imagined. The educational landscape in the mid-twentieth century was paradoxical for women. On the one hand, it was dynamic, marked by unprecedented growth and prosperity; on the other hand, it could be conventional and restrictive. At the Bryn Mawr School, the spark of the founders' dreams for rigorous academic training and college preparation remained alive, but the context had changed. The country-day educational model had allowed the school to tailor its offerings to its constituency and to individual students and to broaden its extracurricular offerings significantly. Those trends would accelerate to suit the times. Once the founders' educational goals had stood in contrast to society's expectations; now the Bryn Mawr School more often epitomized, rather than defined itself against, the times and trends shaping the education and lives of girls and women.

Education and Opportunities in the Mid-Twentieth Century

More Americans than ever were being educated by the mid-twentieth century. Both the postwar baby boom and cold war concerns about national security fueled the growth of the educational system at all levels. Thanks in part to the G.I. Bill, the greatest expansion in higher education the nation had ever seen occurred after World War II.[1]

Girls and women participated in the educational expansion. In 1930, about 55,000 women received Bachelor of Art degrees; by 1960, 139,000 B.A.s were earned by women.[2] Women sometimes, however, occupied a smaller percentage of the spaces in educational institutions than men. Girls and boys graduated from high schools in roughly the same numbers (in contrast to earlier years, when girls had been the majority), but they did not pursue higher education at the same rates. In 1950, women were only 31 percent of all college students, a low not seen since 1880. Still, more women had access to higher education in the United States than in any other modern country in the mid-twentieth century. But society's expectations and public obstacles limited women's choices as to how they could apply their education in the workplace and in public life.[3]

At the graduate level, the numbers of women receiving advanced degrees grew steadily: M.A. degrees granted to women quadrupled, and the number of Ph.D. degrees earned by women tripled. In 1930, fewer than 6,000 women earned master's degrees; in 1960, 24,000 master's degrees were obtained by women. Likewise, 350 women earned doctorates in 1930; 1,030 received doctorates in 1960. As at the undergraduate level, despite increases in real numbers, the percentages of women graduate degree holders declined, in part because of the number of World War II veterans returning to college campuses. In 1930, women received 16–18 percent of graduate degrees; in 1950 and 1960, however, they were granted only 10–12 percent of advanced degrees. In 1920, women received one of seven doctorates granted; by 1956, they obtained only one of ten doctorates.[4] Although women temporarily gained access to science and professional programs because of a shortage of male students during World War II, the gains were quickly reversed in the post–World War II period. In 1949, 12 percent of medical school graduates were women; by the mid-1950s, only 5 percent were female. Likewise, women comprised 27.7 percent of academic personnel in 1940 but only 22 percent by 1960.[5]

Statistics reveal clear patterns in female education, but the social and cultural

expectations shaping women's opportunities and choices are complex. Both contemporary observers and historians have explored the rise of domesticity, albeit
an updated one, in the 1950s. The new "feminine mystique," as Betty Friedan
described it in her 1963 best-selling book, defined women—despite decades of
their expanding participation in education, the workforce, the professions, and
public life—solely in terms of their roles as wives and mothers.[6] Associated with
post–World War II affluence, rising marriage rates and falling marriage ages,
and the soaring birth rates of the baby boom, the new culture of domesticity
centered women's lives in their homes and in the burgeoning suburban landscape (accessible to a much broader range of Americans than were earlier exclusive enclaves like Baltimore's Roland Park). As wives and mothers, women
participated in a range of community activities—volunteering in schools,
churches, libraries, and women's clubs—but their activities tended to be apolit-
ical, in contrast to the embrace of social causes that had animated many female
reformers of M. Carey Thomas's, Mary Garrett's, and Edith Hamilton's generations. More than two decades after the victory of woman's suffrage—seen as
critical to female equality by generations of reformers in the nineteenth and
early twentieth centuries—women's political participation was very low: women
held less than 5 percent of public offices.[7]

Despite the cultural emphasis on domesticity, women's employment outside
the home was rising after World War II, with middle-class, married women entering the labor force faster than any other group. In 1950, 27.9 percent of the
labor force was female; by 1960, 37.1 percent was female.[8] Although college
women of the post–World War II generation were likely to be married by age
twenty-two, they were also likely to work outside the home. In contrast to the
employment trends of earlier decades, education actually made women more
likely to be employed. By the early 1960s, two-fifths of female high school graduates worked outside the home—but almost three-fifths of college-educated
women were employed. While women as a group continued to have limited
access to graduate training and traditionally male professions, more and more
women pursued careers: from 1940 to 1960, the number of professional women
increased by 41 percent.[9] Most women (both professional and otherwise), however, continued to work primarily in female-dominated—and hence lower-
paying and less prestigious—fields. And they tended to justify their employment
not in terms of their right to independence, self-support, and personal fulfillment, as women like M. Carey Thomas had hoped, but within frameworks more

acceptable in the reigning culture, like the advantages brought to their families by mothers' incomes.[10]

American culture—promulgated by women's magazines, the new medium of television, and the advertising industry—celebrated the new domesticity. In a 1956 *Look* magazine celebrating women, the editors waxed poetic about the modern American woman who "marries younger than ever, bears more babies and looks and acts far more feminine than the emancipated girl of the 1920s or even '30s. Steelworker's wife and Junior Leaguer alike do their own housework." These women of the 1950s were compared favorably to earlier generations of "feminists"—a word of opprobrium—who were alleged to have been discontented with their femininity. The celebration of housework and domesticity coexisted, somewhat paradoxically, alongside the social desirability of higher education for women, as well as the growth in female employment, in the culture of the midcentury.[11]

Obviously, the context, the connotations, and the implications of education for women had changed. In 1956, Emeritus Professor of Economics Mabel Newcomber (Vassar College) explored the contradictions in women's places in colleges and universities and in the larger society in *A Century of Higher Education for American Women*. Her study catalogued the demographic trends influencing women's place in higher education. "Today half of the young women of this country are married by the age of 20, that is, before they can graduate from college," a reality that "affects the daughters of the well-to-do and the well-educated as much as the others." If college women married before their senior year, they were not likely to graduate unless they attended the same school as their husbands, and even then they proved less interested than their male counterparts in either intellectual pursuits or career preparation. "For the majority of women students who graduate, and many who do not," Newcomber argued, "the important factors are academic interest and the conviction that the college training will make them better wives and mothers and widen their job opportunities." "Job opportunities" were usually perceived in terms of suitably "feminine" employment fields: in 1956, more than three-fifths of female college graduates chose studies in education, nursing, home economics, or secretarial training.[12]

While women had proved they could achieve academically at the same levels as men, Newcomber observed, the attitudes of both students and educators were markedly different than those of their predecessors: for modern women, after all, "the challenge of pioneering is gone." Young women and their families in the mid-twentieth century valued higher education for women. Newcomber observed that "more and more college men regard a college-educated wife as an asset, socially and economically" and that all concurred that an educated wife helped her husband in business, cultivating the right contacts and potentially increasing his income. Higher education could enhance social pedigree: engagement and marriage announcements routinely listed a woman's college as part of her social background. And yet, Newcomber pondered, "the immediate value of higher education for homemaking is not altogether clear." Newcomber argued that educators needed more clarity in the purposes of the education they offered their female students. Whether women should be educated like men—given the very different attitudes, goals, and future roles of male and female students in the 1950s—was still debatable.[13]

After decades of women's increasing participation in high schools, higher education, professions, and public life, society in general and many educators in particular reopened old questions about the purposes of female education and the merits of liberal education for women. The questions were the same ones that the Bryn Mawr School's founders had contemplated, though in a very different social and cultural context. Based on studies suggesting that college women often felt discontented and unprepared for the lives of domesticity that usually followed their formal education, some educators tried to resolve the contradictions by calling for a new "feminine" education in colleges and universities in the 1940s and 1950s. They argued that women needed—in fact, deserved—a curriculum more closely connected to their future roles in life. To support their position, they pointed to surveys suggesting that, although more women were attending college—and many of them assumed that they would hold some kind of job after their graduation—most, too, intended to end their employment upon marriage. The educators noted that most families and their daughters valued marriage and motherhood as the ultimate goals for women.[14]

Lynn White, president of Mills College for women, became a national proponent of the new feminine education. White criticized what he described as "our present peculiar habit" of educating our daughters "as if they were men." While he acknowledged that women needed preparation for employment before marriage, he opposed women seeking advanced degrees, and he promoted an education designed primarily to prepare women to enrich their homes and communities. "Feminine" studies he advocated included training in "the theory and preparation of a Basque paella, or a well-marinated shish kabob." Although few educators went as far as White, the move for "feminine" education spread to most educational institutions in the 1950s. Advocates of curricula identical to that taught to men and professional career preparation for women—the educational model championed by the Bryn Mawr School founders—found themselves on the defensive.[15]

Although some educators resisted the trend to sex-differentiated education and defended women's rights to the same liberal education that men enjoyed, their objections were often subdued and qualified, leaving their students with an ambiguous message about the kinds of education and social roles they should pursue. Historian Barbara Solomon used Barnard College President Millicent Carey McIntosh—a Bryn Mawr School "success story" and a very influential member of the school's board from the time of her appointment in 1928 through the 1960s—as an example of an educator who advocated equal education and career preparation for women yet simultaneously accommodated the renewed emphasis on domesticity. "A girl does not need courses in baby tending to prepare her for motherhood," McIntosh argued, "but she does need a philosophy which does not belittle the home as a place unworthy of her best, and does not glorify the job as important beyond everything else."[16]

McIntosh's commitment to furthering serious educational and professional opportunities for women—just as her aunt had hoped—was clear. As her aunt M. Carey Thomas had intended, McIntosh upheld the Bryn Mawr School's high academic standards, but she did so with attitudes different from those of the schools' founders. Indeed, her relationship to her society and the expectations for women within it contrasts notably with that of M. Carey Thomas. Thomas—who had worried that marriage and motherhood would hinder her niece's professional work—seemed driven to challenge the prevailing culture and its attitudes toward women. Perhaps because of the opportunities made possible by her aunt's generation, McIntosh—who successfully combined a distinguished career with a marriage—was more comfortable with her culture's often contradictory expectations for women and their place in the educational and social landscape.[17] Thomas's and McIntosh's perspectives are suggestive of the changing attitudes of the Bryn Mawr School about its relationship to the girls it was charged with educating.

The Bryn Mawr School continued to see itself as an institution shaped by a special history and guided by a special mission. The school's commitment to

preparing its students for college continued, and the school proudly acknowledged the educational and professional accomplishments of many of its graduates. At the same time, however, the country-day model, the renewed emphasis
on femininity in the larger culture, and the social expectations of the school's
elite suburban clientele all shaped the character of a Bryn Mawr School education. By the mid-twentieth century, the Bryn Mawr School was beginning to
epitomize exclusive private girls' education.

Leadership and Institution Building at the Bryn Mawr School

The 1930s had been a tumultuous decade at the Bryn Mawr School, and the
institution needed leadership to help secure its financial position, improve its
suburban campus, and plan for the future. As the board searched for a new headmistress in 1938, Millicent McIntosh proclaimed that the Bryn Mawr School's
new leader would have to be a woman of "distinction" to help the school fulfill
its "peculiar destiny."[18] McIntosh, who would exert great influence on the
school during the 1940s and 1950s, sought a headmistress who would be, in the
tradition of prior school leaders, a scholar as well as a teacher, a leader who appreciated Bryn Mawr's heritage.

When the Bryn Mawr School board appointed Katharine Van Bibber as the
school's new headmistress, it indeed chose a woman whose educational background mirrored that of the school's prior and current leadership. Van Bibber,
like McIntosh, was a graduate of Edith Hamilton's Bryn Mawr School, the
school's top graduate in 1920 and winner of its college scholarship. Like Hamilton and McIntosh, Van Bibber graduated from Bryn Mawr College, where she
won the college's prestigious European Fellowship. After receiving a master of
arts degree from Columbia University, Van Bibber had served as assistant head
of the Brearley School under Millicent McIntosh. Van Bibber became headmistress of the Bryn Mawr School in 1939, and she would lead it for more than
two decades, until her retirement in 1963.[19]

Both Van Bibber and McIntosh believed in the continuity between the Bryn
Mawr School's past and present, but they sought to incorporate new educational
theories and practices into the essence of the old school. From their perspective,
the founders' model school and the mid-twentieth century country-day academy were not so very different. The country-day Bryn Mawr, they believed,

could and should maintain high academic standards. It also needed to update its attitudes and continue to build its support within the community.[20]

When approached about her interest in becoming Bryn Mawr's new headmistress, Van Bibber agreed to consider the position only on the condition that the board address the long-standing grievances of the school's faculty. Van Bibber worried, as had M. Carey Thomas, that too much absorption in physical improvements to the school's country campus threatened the academic quality of the school. She tried to reassert academic priorities by focusing on the need for retention of excellent teachers—which would only be possible if the school treated its faculty better. Teachers deserved representation in the school's management, she argued, and their salaries should be raised before any new building projects were undertaken. Van Bibber was not completely successful in this quest: as she wrote years later, the Bryn Mawr School's refusal to pay its teachers a living wage inhibited her ability to attract good teachers, forcing her to rely only on older women with independent means or young alumnae still living at home to staff the school. As late as the 1960s, Bryn Mawr relied on many mothers of students as part-time teachers, rather than on well-paid, full-time faculty members.[21]

Van Bibber also understood that, despite Bryn Mawr's successful creation of a suburban campus, the school's position in Baltimore was still precarious. Upon her appointment as headmistress, Van Bibber requested that the school board contemplate a complete reorganization of the Bryn Mawr Primary School. Bryn Mawr had long relied on its Primary School to feed students into the Main School. The Primary School had suffered lagging enrollments during Edith and Margaret Hamilton's years, but hopes had been high that the move to the country would reverse the trend. At the end of the 1930s, however, the Primary School's declining enrollment posed a threat to the entire school.[22]

Van Bibber encouraged loyalty and unity within the school's community. By the time she became headmistress, Bryn Mawr families and alumnae were well organized and practiced at participating in the life of their school, but Van Bibber encouraged closer association between Bryn Mawr's parents' association and alumnae and its teachers and administrators.[23] She understood that the support of parents and alumnae was crucial to the school's success, and she cultivated cooperation rather than the contention that had often characterized the relationship between different elements of the school community.

The Bryn Mawr School was perpetually short of funds. As the Depression drew to a close, however, Bryn Mawr seemed poised to achieve financial stability it had never known. The school had been raising money since the mid-1920s, and "planning committees" launched new fund-raising campaigns with increasing sophistication. In 1941, the school optimistically pledged to raise money to retire its remaining debt and begin new building projects: as McIntosh described it, "The psychology of expansion rather than the psychology of despair would be appealing." Accordingly, new fund-raising initiatives abounded. The school mailed appeals to parents, and families responded.[24] By 1943, Bryn Mawr had raised almost eight thousand dollars toward their goal of ten thousand dollars. In the late 1940s and 1950s, various Bryn Mawr School committees routinely planned for the future and raised money, focusing on needs ranging from expanding the school's music and art departments to building a new gymnasium, library, and study hall.[25] Participating in the institution-building boom of the 1950s, the Bryn Mawr School continued the building plans of the 1920s for its country campus.

As Bryn Mawr expanded and institutionalized its fund-raising activities, the participation of men in its management increased. The school embraced a perpetual philosophy of growth, and men's business experience and financial expertise seemed increasingly essential to the school's success. Whereas the Bryn Mawr School of the 1920s, still under Thomas's influence, had been careful to delineate the limits of male influence when it first formed the Men's Advisory Committee, that old reluctance to involve men was fading.[26]

In 1949, a woman agreed to head the school's latest fund-raising drive only on the condition that a man would serve as her co-chair and "that the men connected with the School would support her." A 1956 summary of Bryn Mawr's capital funds noted that "this report is the result of a number of discussions with men who are parents of girls now in the school," including "business men" and a "very prominent banker." In 1957, the Bryn Mawr School planned to appoint fathers to head fund-raising drives for each class. They could coordinate efforts and solicit funds from other fathers—apparently a more effective tact than mothers soliciting from other mothers. In fact, Bryn Mawr School alumnae—mirroring the concerns of female educators more than a century earlier—acknowledged the difficulties their school faced because women did not contribute financially to their institutions as generously as did men. In a 1953 fund-raising letter addressed to "Friends of the School and Business Men," Bryn Mawr School alumnae explained their dilemma: "Men traditionally give to boys' schools and men's colleges. Their wives can seldom contribute to their alma maters in proportion. To overcome this inequality, we are appealing to you to help us get our Fund started."[27]

Men also grew more prominent in direct management of the school. As late as 1928, Thomas had been fighting to ensure that her school's board remain exclusively female. At the country-day Bryn Mawr, however, that old prohibition—based on the fear that men could never truly appreciate quality female education and should not be entrusted with it—seemed old-fashioned and unreasonable. As early as 1941, the Bryn Mawr School was considering permitting men to serve as full members of its board. No immediate steps were taken, but a decade later, a committee rewriting the school's bylaws revisited the issue, proposing to abolish the old Men's Advisory Committee and instead elect four or five men to the school's regular board. In keeping with those suggestions, the Bryn Mawr School elected its first male board members—the president of Goucher College and the headmaster of Gilman School—in 1953. Later in the decade, more fathers of Bryn Mawr students were elected. By the late 1950s, men comprised approximately one-third of the school's managing board.[28]

The Bryn Mawr School founders might have understood these changes as a regression from their educational vision, but the modern Bryn Mawr understood its inclusion of male leadership as pragmatic and right. They harbored little of the earlier generation's fears about what male influence might mean for the education of girls in general and their institution in particular, and the positive benefits of welcoming male leadership within their school community seemed to far outweigh the old suspicions. The presence of men never did lead the Bryn Mawr School to relinquish its reliance on the leadership and abilities of exceptional women. Unlike many girls' schools and women's colleges that hired male headmasters and presidents in the mid-twentieth century, the Bryn Mawr School retained its tradition of having a headmistress and continued to elect women of notable achievement to its board. Of the eight women on the board in 1957, three were Bryn Mawr School alumnae who, as the top graduates of their classes, had won the school's annual scholarship to Bryn Mawr College.[29]

By the mid-1950s, the Bryn Mawr School was thriving, particularly in comparison with its situation during the difficult preceding decades. By 1952, Bryn Mawr had a waiting list in two classes. In 1953, the school was declared full with 446 students. By 1955, Bryn Mawr had so many more applicants than places that it considered changing its admission policy to include testing of all applicants. Rising numbers of applicants, combined with successful fund-raising and building expansions, signified the solidification of the school's position in Baltimore, both socially and financially.[30]

From Missionary to Establishment: Expectations, Academics, and Atmosphere

As the Bryn Mawr community institutionalized itself in the Baltimore suburbs, the school consciously refashioned its image. When its representatives spoke to parents and prospective students, they portrayed the country-day Bryn Mawr School very differently from the original school. Whereas catalogues from the early Bryn Mawr had emphatically asserted the school's curricular and examination requirements, country-day Bryn Mawr circulars emphasized the school's beautiful country surroundings and the broad, well-balanced education it offered to all girls. Rigorous college preparation no longer reigned as the school's overriding priority. To the contrary, Bryn Mawr seemed eager to reassure parents, especially in the early country-day phase, that the school's continuing college-preparatory requirement would interfere neither with their daughters' pleasures nor with the development of their well-adjusted personalities. Catalogues stressed that the Bryn Mawr School was devoted to much more than academics: its program was designed to "create a most favorable environment for a well-balanced school life—for mental and physical health, for appreciation and accomplishment in the arts," as well as "for academic work of high quality."[31]

Although such statements confidently advertised the country-day Bryn Mawr's approach to girls' education, the school sometimes seemed torn between its founders' academic vision and its newer philosophy. As its charter demanded, the Bryn Mawr School continued to require every student to prepare for college, although no longer always those colleges with the highest standards. The school also continued to offer a scholarship to Bryn Mawr College to the top student in each graduating class who showed "promise of academic distinction in college," but Mary Garrett's promise to pay four years of college expenses had dwindled to a token offering.[32] At the same time, the Bryn Mawr School openly appealed to parents who had no college aspirations for their daughters. As the school first publicly proclaimed in the 1930s, "The college preparatory course also gives a thorough and well-balanced education to the pupils who do not expect to go to college."[33] In catalogues from the late 1940s to 1959, Bryn Mawr still advertised that "the school offers a thorough and well balanced education to those who do not expect to go to college as well as to those who do."[34]

By the end of the Depression, however, college attendance was nearly universal among Bryn Mawr School graduates. In 1940, twenty-four of Bryn Mawr's twenty-six graduates enrolled in various colleges (while another began nurse's training). A few years later, twenty-two of twenty-seven students proceeded to college (with one choosing art school and two selecting business schools). In 1949, twenty-three of the school's twenty-six graduates entered college (while the remaining three chose art and secretarial courses).[35] But not all Bryn Mawr School graduates were attending colleges with the highest standards.

Once the Bryn Mawr School had primarily prepared girls for the Seven Sister colleges (and particularly Bryn Mawr College for its best students), but those eastern women's colleges were becoming more selective, and not all Bryn Mawr School graduates could realistically expect to be admitted. As Millicent Carey McIntosh (then headmistress of Brearley) confided to the Bryn Mawr School board in 1946, "I personally feel that having spent sixty-four years persuading every girl to go to college, the Brearley School must now educate its parents to the idea that the major colleges must be reserved for a highly selective group." Similarly, Katharine Van Bibber predicted that "it will be more and more difficult to get girls into the major colleges and the parents must be trained to be more broad-minded about college." Bryn Mawr's board concluded that "more stress should be put on what Bryn Mawr graduates accomplish," rather than emphasizing admission to particular colleges.[36]

In the 1930s and particularly the 1940s and 1950s, Bryn Mawr School graduates were continuing their education at a wider variety of institutions. In 1935, Bryn Mawr graduates attended colleges such as Swarthmore, the University of Maryland, and the University of Michigan, in addition to the traditional Smith, Vassar, Wellesley, and Bryn Mawr Colleges. Especially popular were women's colleges such as Hollins, Sweet Briar, Randolph-Macon, and the local Goucher. By 1950, only eight of Bryn Mawr's twenty-seven graduates planned to attend the "major" eastern women's colleges (Bryn Mawr College and Vassar), while the others chose a variety of southern women's colleges, junior colleges, or coeducational schools including Rochester, Wheaton, and Reed.[37] In the 1940s, art and secretarial courses were popular with some students, and the Bryn Mawr School counseled its weaker students to enter junior colleges. Indeed, in 1949, eight of Bryn Mawr's twenty-six graduates enrolled in junior colleges. In 1951,

Headmistress Van Bibber warned that the school's senior class was "weak" academically and that many of its members would be applying to junior colleges or not at all: "This is just as well," she concluded. And as late as 1957, only twenty-seven of thirty-seven graduates applied to four-year colleges, while the rest applied to junior colleges or secretarial courses or planned to marry instead.[38]

From its beginnings, of course, the Bryn Mawr School had educated girls with a variety of academic abilities and aspirations. Although the early Bryn Mawr had of necessity accepted students who did not embrace its academic vision, it had emphasized its goals of rigorous academic training for all and had refused to graduate students who ultimately failed its final examination requirement. The country-day Bryn Mawr gradually made more concessions toward accommodating its weaker students. It recruited and institutionalized a place for the "average" student.

Catalogues from the 1950s outlined the range of academic courses offered at Bryn Mawr. All students were required to study English, Latin, and French throughout their high school years. As in the past, Greek or German could be taken as substitutes for certain language or science classes or as electives. Students took four years of math (no specifications) and two of science (somewhat less than in the past). All students took the same history classes during all years but their final two, and those courses now placed less emphasis on the chronology of the history of civilizations and more on current events. Physical education was required for all students; music and art were required in all but a girl's final two years. A new "Bible" elective course was available to seniors.[39]

Curricular requirements listed in catalogues (with a few exceptions, such as the Bible elective) from the 1940s and 1950s varied remarkably little from those during the early twentieth century, but course titles are not very revealing about the kind of instruction that took place in actual classrooms. Discussions of student academic achievement in the minutes of Bryn Mawr School board meetings in the mid-twentieth century are suggestive, however. By the 1940s and 1950s, teachers and administrators routinely assessed the aptitudes, interests, and performance of their students. Worries about the "average" and "slow" student (whom the early Bryn Mawr School had merely tolerated) surfaced as never before. In a 1944 meeting, the Bryn Mawr board agreed upon the need for "remedial training" for such students and passed a resolution that "more attention be given to the extra curricular development of the average child." In a 1957 board meeting, the school formally opposed "sectioning by ability"—although it debated the merits of programs of "Acceleration" and "Enrichment"—and still claimed to demand college preparation of all its students. But the board agreed that Bryn Mawr teachers could develop different programs to meet the needs of both "the unusually brilliant girl" and the "Slow Student."[40]

Katharine Van Bibber even suggested, around 1960, near the end of her tenure as headmistress, that the Bryn Mawr School's most crucial role might not be its historic mission to prepare its best students for the most selective colleges but instead to prompt "average" students to achieve at higher levels than they might in other schools. At Bryn Mawr, she argued, "We are proud of our top girls, and we make it possible for them to go much farther intellectually than they could go if we had not had them." However, she continued, "They ... would get into college from any school." In contrast, the "next group" of students—"good but not outstanding"—required the extra attention that only a school like Bryn Mawr could provide. As a small, private institution, Van Bibber reasoned, the Bryn Mawr School was uniquely equipped to "prepare and send to college a fair-sized group of students of less than outstanding ability."[41]

According to Van Bibber, the prevailing feeling at the country-day Bryn Mawr was that the original school had been, "perhaps, a bit too Darwinian."[42] Both Van Bibber and Millicent Carey McIntosh—Bryn Mawr School "successes" who had thrived at Thomas's and Hamilton's Bryn Mawr and excelled in graduate school and their professions—believed that their old school had, at times, been unnecessarily harsh and insensitive to its less-talented or less-ambitious students. As McIntosh argued in 1939, "No girl, who is a good citizen and is able to do the senior work, should be humiliated and given a sense of failure because she is unable to acquire the necessary points [on the College Board examinations] for a School diploma." From her and Van Bibber's perspective, the Bryn Mawr School could maintain its standards and yet be a more compassionate institution. Even girls who did not meet the school's requirements "could be treated at commencement in the same manner as those receiving diplomas without violating the School charter." Bryn Mawr's practice of excluding girls who would be required to retake their examinations later was "medieval," suggested both Van Bibber and McIntosh, particularly given that the "modern tendency is getting away from disgracing a child in public."[43]

In contrast to the model school's rigid course and examination requirements, Van Bibber described the country-day school's curriculum in 1941 as "extremely elastic." "Each individual takes those courses that are suited to her own needs and gifts," and every student "is given special help in overcoming her difficulties." Again, according to Van Bibber in 1948, "The old hard and fast series of required courses that we followed, sometimes painfully, a generation ago" were being replaced with "greater emphasis on imagination, initiative, and logic" and "increased emphasis on the development of the individual."[44]

As college requirements and the College Board examinations themselves grew more flexible—and as Bryn Mawr's internal philosophy of the best ways of educating girls evolved—the school offered more and more elective classes. "Because the college requirements are so much more elastic," Van Bibber reported to the board in 1953, "the schedule can be adapted to the needs of each girl." When the College Board announced its plans to begin offering tests in humanities, music, and art appreciation, Bryn Mawr responded that "our curriculum already points in that direction and can easily be extended." New courses in the humanities, music and art appreciation, and Bible study were just a few of the popular classes added in the 1950s.[45] This wider variety of subjects—as well as the ability of students to choose and follow their own interests—helped the country-day Bryn Mawr offer its students a "well-rounded" education that developed the "whole person." The growth of elective courses and extracurricular activities also gave the school a means of responding to the board's assertion that "more stress should be put on what Bryn Mawr graduates accomplish."[46]

School activities and associations—growing even at the city Bryn Mawr in the second decade of the twentieth century—proliferated at the suburban campus. In keeping with the country-day philosophy, the Bryn Mawr School sought to offer a balance of participation in athletics and exposure to the arts. "As health is the first requisite for happiness and success, special attention is paid to sports and recreation," Bryn Mawr proclaimed in the mid-1930s. Students played hockey, basketball, lacrosse, and tennis, and improvements to the school's physical education programs were ongoing.[47] While Bryn Mawr students had long embraced athletics, the school's arts programs had sometimes lagged behind. But the school tried to correct that and encourage "culture." In 1944, the school's Curriculum Committee concluded that Bryn Mawr should offer more art and art history courses. Throughout the 1950s, interest in arts and dramatics grew. To encourage students' appreciation of culture in 1952, the Bryn Mawr School Parent-Teacher Association pledged tickets to the Baltimore symphony's Sunday afternoon concerts to two students every week. Students served on a Student Council and produced student publications.[48] According to Head-mistress Van Bibber in 1957, the Bryn Mawr School offered so many extracurricular activities—with "opportunity to enjoy and profit from athletics, art, music, dramatics, stage craft, etc."—that the school had to remember to honor the need for young girls to enjoy some free time with "no stress and strain."[49]

The atmosphere and expectations of the Bryn Mawr School also reflected America's national concerns in the 1940s and 1950s. Given the nation's preoccupation with the threats of totalitarianism during World War II and Communism in its aftermath, Bryn Mawr would try to shape an education appropriate for girls and their future roles in society. During World War II, the school community "sought, in our thinking and in our conversations, to discover what our duty may be and how we can help most constructively in this time of great emergency." Bryn Mawr offered First Aid, Red Cross, Nutrition, and Home Nursing courses; it raised money for the Red Cross and conducted air-raid drills.[50]

During the cold war, Bryn Mawr established emergency shelters, provided first-aid training for faculty, and stockpiled canned foods and medical supplies. Upon the demand of parents—"some of whom have been stirred up by several frantic mothers"—such activities would continue into the 1960s. In 1952, the Parent-Teacher Association purchased new American flags for the school because "'patriotism' or love of country, cannot be stressed too greatly in these days."[51] The curriculum was also updated to reflect the times. History courses incorporated new emphasis on civics and the development of European and American democracies, social science, current affairs, and citizenship.[52] As one board member expressed, "The present cold-war crisis" and "the rising nationalism in Africa and Asia and the breakdown in the Western alliance" meant that schools needed more than ever to train their students "for thoughtful participation in the electoral process."[53]

In this environment of defending democracy, the Bryn Mawr School became more overtly Christian than ever before, associating Christianity with society's best democratic impulses. The school supported a "Christian Association," formed at the request of four students in 1940, throughout the 1940s and 1950s.[54] Bryn Mawr had always been overwhelmingly Protestant. Students during Edith Hamilton's years had listened to Scripture readings and sung Christian hymns as part of their morning school-day rituals. And the Christian Association's volunteer activities—in 1964, for example, the association sponsored "volunteer work at various old age homes and children's hospitals in the city"—were certainly reminiscent of the Bryn Mawr School Alumnae League's charity work in the 1920s. The league had been more secular in orientation, however, although individual alumnae might have been motivated by Christian

impulses. This self-conscious public acknowledgment of the connections between the Bryn Mawr School and Christianity—Headmistress Van Bibber, for
instance, in outlining "The Aims and Purposes of the Bryn Mawr School," discussed the school's "spiritual aims" and noted how Bryn Mawr students were
"continually faced with the question of the relevance of Christ and His teaching
to their own individual lives"—was something new.[55]

The Bryn Mawr School took seriously its duty to train students for democracy, which could also mean instilling them with Christian values. Sometimes
this impulse resulted in what, from today's perspective, seem like irrational plans
and worries—such as advice to parents on how to protect girls from Commu-
nist agitators. At other times, the school's concerns bore marks of the earnest-
ness and seriousness of purpose that had characterized the founders' Bryn Mawr
School. Van Bibber pondered the higher purposes of a Bryn Mawr School education, seeking to cultivate a sense of responsibility and duty to society and others in her students. Like Bryn Mawr School leaders before her, Van Bibber
clearly believed in the power of education in general—and the Bryn Mawr
School in particular—to shape the lives of girls and the women they would become.

Once the Bryn Mawr School had challenged the prevailing culture, but the
school of the 1940s and 1950s most frequently reinforced existing social structures. As the school applauded American-style democracy and the U.S. way of
life, Bryn Mawr concurrently validated traditional places for girls and women
within society. The Bryn Mawr School perceived itself as less of the missionary
institution it had once been and more as a firm supporter of democratic America—and that usually included its ways of construing gender in society.

The Bryn Mawr School during the middle decades of the twentieth century
not only reflected the political concerns of the country but also acknowledged
the domestic roles of women celebrated in 1950s culture as never before. While
many Bryn Mawr School graduates went on to remarkable pursuits, most did
not defy traditional expectations for women of their class. Most, even after graduating from college, settled into lives of traditional domesticity in Baltimore.
This had clearly been the case from the school's earliest days, but the country-
day Bryn Mawr was growing more openly accepting of this pattern in its alumnae.

In 1953, the Bryn Mawr School Alumnae Association circulated a "Suggested
Letter to Friends of the School and Business Men." Alumnae, they proposed,
could encourage men to donate money to their school by pointing out the ben-

efits of a Bryn Mawr School education. Many men, they acknowledged, would wonder why they should support a school for girls when those girls would eventually just be homemakers. In answer, the alumnae essentially agreed that, while most Baltimore girls would not have careers, the Bryn Mawr School was valuable because it could make them especially good wives and community volunteers: "We wonder if you realize how many of the women in our community have gone to Bryn Mawr School and how many are civic leaders as well as homemakers. They are our best example in talking about the advantages of a private school education." The message was clear: the Bryn Mawr School deserved financial support not because it would open exceptional intellectual and career opportunities for its graduates but because it would benefit Baltimore's families and community. "Bryn Mawr," they argued, "has been particularly alert in giving its graduates a sense of responsibility for the larger needs of community life." No reference was made in the letter to the inherent rights of girls to an equal education, to their needs for serious college preparation, or to the careers and distinction that a Bryn Mawr education might make possible. Almost seven decades after its founding, the Bryn Mawr School seemed, more than ever, to be embracing the oldest of arguments for why girls should be educated. The Alumnae Association appeal justified a Bryn Mawr School education in light of the indirect influence women exerted on society through their associations with men and the family.[56]

In such an atmosphere, the country-day Bryn Mawr sometimes viewed its founding vision as a liability. A 1949 address to the Alumnae Association from a former student is instructive in the way it emphasized the superiority of the country-day model of education over the education the founders had worked so hard to institutionalize: "It is no longer thought necessary to introduce our children to wisdom in tile and mosaic mausoleums decorated exclusively with plaster casts of Greek deities and framed photographs of sepia monuments. Sunlight and air and cheerful surroundings have become the order of the day." Thankfully, she concluded, "aesthetics have come to stay" at the Bryn Mawr School.[57]

That alumna lauded the modern Bryn Mawr School for accepting, rather than challenging, traditional female roles. At the original Bryn Mawr, "aesthetics were frowned upon" and "glamour was definitely suspect." The old school had scoffed at training for domesticity:

Cooking, labeled "Domestic Science," was offered gingerly to those girls who were willing to admit they were morons and did not aspire to the ultimate Bryn Mawr ideal—a Bryn Mawr College degree, followed by a job in teaching or scientific research or at least in some field which would advance the sacred cause of Feminism and establish the superiority of woman over man. That a pupil should aspire to a profession as common as marriage, so crass as commerce, or so glamorous as motion pictures or the stage, was official heresy.

When once a top Bryn Mawr School graduate—winner of the school's scholarship to Bryn Mawr College—decided to marry rather than pursue higher education, it was remarked that it was "a pity" she "was going to waste her womanhood on a man." But, according to the alumna, the modern Bryn Mawr School understood better than to encourage students, teachers, and administrators alike to reject their femininity for the sake of "Feminism." Women could be both educated and traditionally feminine. To further this cause, the school planned to raise its teachers' salaries—signifying that "at long last the teaching profession seems about to be delivered from its coif-less nunhood." Henceforth, female teachers would be able to marry. "It would be good to teach even future headmistresses to cook palatably and serve glamorously a dinner," this alumna concluded.[58]

It would be unwise to construe one alumna's opinion as representative of the Bryn Mawr School. But echoes of her perspective could be found in many elements of Bryn Mawr by the mid-twentieth century. The school's connections to elite social circles were apparent, and, not surprisingly, Bryn Mawr's leaders shaped their institution to reflect the expected roles of women in affluent Baltimore society.

A School for Society Girls

At the modern Bryn Mawr, some aspects of the school's founding educational vision were rendered outdated, unfeminine, and unappealing. These changes reflected shifting educational philosophy and national culture. But the attitudes also mirrored changes in the school's constituency. In its earliest days, the Bryn Mawr School had attracted only modest numbers of students, often from families unusually interested in education or concerned about their daughters' future college and employment opportunities. Most Baltimore families—as evidenced by the school's lagging enrollments for several decades—had dismissed the Bryn Mawr School and its philosophy of educating girls as too radical. Throughout the decades, public perception of the Bryn Mawr School and its place in Baltimore had changed. By the mid-twentieth century, Bryn Mawr had evolved into an integral part of Baltimore's exclusive network of private schools. The school that had once challenged Baltimore's attitudes toward female education was now one of the choice schools for the daughters of its elite.

The early Bryn Mawr School had struggled to fill its classrooms—offering many tuition reductions as incentives to the daughters of Johns Hopkins University families and needy girls—but the country-day school attracted a steady stream of students from prominent Baltimore families. Francis Beirne, a 1950s observer of Baltimore's "Society with a Capital 'S,'" noted that social life and position in Baltimore revolved around "a mysterious compound of family, money, occupation, residence, membership in exclusive organizations and friends." Among those "exclusive organizations" were private schools like Bryn Mawr, where all the "right" families educated their children. "Newcomers from the North and West are shocked also to discover that a place in society demands attendance at a private, not a public, school."[59] From the perspective of the 1980s, a much later observer concurred on the interconnections between Baltimore "Society" and certain private schools: "A generation ago, the majority of Baltimore's prep schools were populated almost exclusively by scions of Baltimore's social register."[60] Friendships with other children from the "right" families formed at private schools like Bryn Mawr comprised a social network that continued far beyond a child's formal school years.

By the 1940s and 1950s, the Bryn Mawr School drew its students from a select segment of Baltimore society, making the school in many ways an insular institution. A 1959 graduate recalled that Bryn Mawr provided a "very sheltered environment," populated with girls from the same kinds of families living in the same kinds of neighborhoods. Bryn Mawr School students and their classmates rarely ventured beyond their secluded suburban campus or out of their affluent social circles.[61] The school's students—like its suburban environment—were exclusively white. As in the vast majority of private and public schools, segregation prevailed. Bryn Mawr students shared similar socioeconomic backgrounds, coming from affluent families who could afford private school tuition.

Students' lives—both in and out of school—reflected their social position. Francis Beirne observed that "when little girls in the private schools reach their early teens one fine day one of them will announce proudly to her fellow classmates that she is going to be presented to society at the Bachelors Cotillion." Many Bryn Mawr students were debutantes, and the Bryn Mawr School and its students frequently appeared on the society pages of Baltimore newspapers. The "Smart Set Magazine" (the society pages of a Baltimore newspaper) frequently featured photographs and descriptions of Bryn Mawr School debutantes—

"most of whom will make their bow to society this season"—and their social activities. Newspapers also covered events like a Bryn Mawr fashion show, noting that "the clothes will feature spring and summer wear for the debs and sub-debs."[62] And they announced the engagements and weddings of Bryn Mawr School students and alumnae.

The school's flourishing student culture reveals that most Bryn Mawr students enjoyed lives of rare privilege, often with interests—surely not atypical of teenage girls across the nation—revolving more around concerns about popularity, physical appearance, and the opposite sex than around academic achievement. Bryn Mawr School yearbooks (*Bryn Mawrtyrs*), particularly from the 1950s, provide a glimpse into the social culture of students. In 1956, graduating seniors reminisced about their school years—revealing a consumer culture enamored of female beauty, fancy possessions and pursuits, travel, and boys, boys, boys. Seniors recalled the "two-tone Ford convertible" and "yellow Chevy convertible." They reminisced about "Nassau," "spring vacation in Bermuda," and "Europe the summer of '56." Girls wanted to look good: various girls were associated with "divine clothes," "Chanel No. 5," "peach and cream complexion," "21-inch waist," and "hair that has that just washed, just curled look." Bryn Mawr girls consulted "that little blue calorie book" and reminded each other of "the diet that she promises to go on tomorrow." And they thought about boyfriends and marriage: "that good-looking brother and his MG," "Navy, Navy, Navy," "trying on Gilman rings for size," "modeling wedding dresses," "that beautiful ring," and "Betty Crocker's foremost competitor."[63] The school had an official "Posture Association" and voted for the girls who were the best dressed, most attractive, most feminine, and most domestic. They also chose the girl with the most personality and the classmate most likely to be married first. They even selected a "class babe."[64]

The school culture of the 1950s was far removed from the atmosphere of the founders' Bryn Mawr. Bryn Mawr School students were not influenced more by popular culture and its images of ideal womanhood than were most other middle- and upper-class teenagers of their time. Despite the school's founding mission to challenge traditional assumptions about womanhood, however, Bryn Mawr's students frequently embraced society's expectations for girls and women. Student and alumnae culture, as well as the country-day educational curriculum and ideals, made the Bryn Mawr School of the mid-twentieth century not easily distinguishable from a host of other schools for well-to-do girls. The Bryn Mawr School epitomized its times and its constituency.

CHAPTER FIVE

Challenging the Vision

Broadening the Independent School Philosophy
and Constituency

> A good many of our children, especially those raised in affluent suburbia,
> are actually underprivileged in the sense that they are being deprived of
> real experiences and opportunities for work, for service, and for making
> choices. — HEADMISTRESS DIANE HOWELL, 1968

The country-day Bryn Mawr School of the mid-twentieth century was very different from the model school envisioned by its founders in the 1880s. Although Baltimore's initial acceptance of the school had been limited, Bryn Mawr's embrace of its community would finally ensure the school a secure place in the elite world of private education in Baltimore and, indeed, the nation. Tensions in the school community, however, were evident, if not readily visible, and the decade of the 1950s contained the seeds of change that would, ultimately, crack the school's country-day facade.

The civil rights movement of the 1950s and 1960s—which addressed the reality of racial segregation first in the South and then across the nation—called into question the basic tenets of American society. It addressed the American educational system as one of the key arenas that had perpetuated—and could potentially ameliorate—racism. Issues of integration, racial equality, and equal opportunity would have a profound effect in shaping all schools—whether public or private—and determining the kinds of schools they would become in the later twentieth century. New activism on college campuses—marked by New Left students' organizations, civil rights demonstrations, and eventually anti-Vietnam protests—and the counterculture of the late 1960s and the 1970s transformed the landscape of higher education and changed the perceptions and expectations of both students and families about the future of American society. At the same time, the rush to domesticity that had characterized the post–World War II period was slowing—with rising marriage ages and falling birth rates—with yet unclear implications for women.[1]

Times were indeed changing. As the social turbulence of the 1960s called into question the values of the more complacent 1950s suburban ideal, the educational world—eventually in all places and at all levels—would have to adapt to new circumstances. For country-day schools like the Bryn Mawr School—which as private institutions serving the affluent were in many ways insulated from the social problems and upheaval of the larger culture—the influence of change was initially minimal. Gradually, however, a new spirit of questioning, at first tentative and then more urgent, would encourage the Bryn Mawr School to revisit its institutional foundations and missions. Along with other private schools that found themselves increasingly out of touch with the world beyond their immediate community, the Bryn Mawr School would embark on a new exploration of exactly the kind of school it wanted to be.

The Roots of Social Change

In contrast to the tremendous expansion of public education and the increasing numbers of American youth attending high schools during the second half of the nineteenth century and the first half of the twentieth century, private elementary and secondary education had declined steadily since the Civil War. In the mid-nineteenth century almost all secondary education had been private, but by the end of the 1930s, only 6.5 percent of students enrolled in high schools attended private schools. The 1950s, however, saw a short-term reversal of this decline: at the beginning of the decade, private secondary schools enrolled 10.5 percent of the students in high schools, and by 1960 they were enrolling 10.9 percent of the high school population. In Maryland—which had a strong tradition of both secular and parochial private schools—at least 20 percent of the total elementary and secondary school student population attended private schools in 1950.[2] The percentages were much higher in affluent social circles.

In many respects, the country-day model of education had suited the needs and desires of well-to-do private school circles for much of the twentieth century. The affluence of the post–World War II period, which gave a greater percentage of families income to spend on their children's education, and the demographic and economic changes remaking American cities, which encouraged the flight of the middle class to the suburbs and left the cities and their schools increasingly to the poor and disadvantaged, encouraged families of financial means to seek private or suburban education for their children. Private schools provided a refuge from urban change and, like the suburbs, seemed to provide an oasis of safety and stability in times of national tensions. Although boarding schools attracted some elite families (including those drawn by social prestige, those who lived in smaller communities and had no access to private day schools, and those with "problem" daughters for whom the discipline of boarding school life was thought to be beneficial), country-day schools proved extremely popular. Private day schools allowed families to protect their children from the perceived problems of public education, to shelter them from the "wrong" kinds of people, to help weaker students in need of extra attention, and to cultivate lifelong connections with prominent families. Particularly in older cities like Baltimore, where private schooling was a well-established tradition and children often attended the schools their parents and grandparents had attended, public education was never considered an option among certain classes. In this prosperous and receptive environment, many private schools could be complacent, seemingly assured of a steady flow of students.

In Baltimore, the Bryn Mawr School community debated how it should attract students and, in doing so, revealed significant differences in attitudes among its leaders and supporters. One group was confident in Bryn Mawr's position as the school of choice for a substantial proportion of the city's elite daughters and considered it beneath the school's dignity to reach out to families beyond its established clientele. In 1939, the school received criticism from within its community for contacting parents who might send their daughters to Bryn Mawr's Primary School, even though the practice was common at other Baltimore private schools. When Bryn Mawr, faced with further decreases in enrollment in 1940, attempted to recruit girls from other private primary schools for its upper division, the board tried to separate its recruiting from the official school, concluding that "it was felt more dignified for the members of the Board to go after children than for the Head Mistress to do so."[3]

Debates about the dignity of advertising and recruiting continued through the 1950s. Even when the school experienced declines in the numbers of applicants such as it had not seen in years, many individuals within the school community objected to Bryn Mawr openly recruiting new students. Headmistress

Katharine Van Bibber echoed the reluctance in 1958: "Any influence on a child's choice of school should be confined to friendship with the mothers" of those children. While an alumnae tea for potential students might be acceptable, "there should be no official act [of the Bryn Mawr School] as a group." Another board member asserted that "Bryn Mawr sells itself. It *would not* be wise to look for students; simply let it be known that the school is receptive to the application of good girls at any level."[4]

Other Bryn Mawr constituents questioned the school's reticence to advertise itself, wondering how they might reverse what they feared were declines in the school's reputation and popularity. An Admissions Policy Committee meeting in 1958 addressed the concerns. Some committee members worried that the Bryn Mawr School's old "air of being 'the best'" rendered the school dangerously complacent. Perhaps a "deep-seated alumnae prejudice that Bryn Mawr is still in its former position of preeminence" blinded many to changes in the school and the community, rendering them incapable of perceiving the school's real need to reevaluate itself and its relationship with Baltimore. As one board member succinctly concluded, "Times have changed."[5]

As recognition of this reality grew, the Bryn Mawr School, in conjunction with other schools—because the changing social context of the 1960s, 1970s, and 1980s would render some elements of private school culture inappropriate and unappealing to many families—would embark on a slow process of rethinking its institutional identity. After more than four decades of establishing itself as a country-day academy, the Bryn Mawr School would begin, for the second time in its history, a reevaluation of its ideals and its mission for the education of girls. As the school addressed key issues—including the value of accreditation by external agencies, the implications of the Supreme Court's ruling in *Brown v. Board of Education*, and the potential benefits of diversity and community outreach—Bryn Mawr would ultimately reinvent itself for modern American society.

The Accreditation Issue

Signs of a tentative new self-scrutiny at the Bryn Mawr School—about the kind of educational institution it was and wanted to be—surfaced in debates about whether the school should seek accreditation from outside educational organizations. In the nineteenth and early twentieth century, private schools had relied heavily on reputation, on the perceived quality of their programs and their students, both to attract families and to gain admittance to colleges and universities for their graduates. At the early Bryn Mawr School, the requirement that every student pass the Bryn Mawr College entrance examination had assured a certain level of accomplishment in all of its graduates. The educational community, particularly the most selective women's colleges, had readily recognized the school's academic quality and welcomed its graduates. But the educational world had broadened. As the number and variety of both public and private secondary schools proliferated, colleges and universities received more applicants than ever and came to rely more heavily on standardized measures of achievement. The colleges and universities wanted confirmation of the quality of the secondary schools their applicants had attended. Likewise, parents sought reassurance that their schools adhered to high standards acknowledged beyond their immediate communities. Parents wanted—and demanded—external validation of their private schools.

The issue of the Bryn Mawr School's accreditation first surfaced immediately after World War II. While few within the school community doubted the quality of a Bryn Mawr School education, some questioned why Bryn Mawr did not seek endorsement from the Middle States Association of Colleges and Secondary Schools. Although Millicent Carey McIntosh asserted in 1946 that "up to date we have not felt the need of the stamp of their approval," some parents worried whether the Bryn Mawr School's reputation alone would satisfy all colleges and universities where their daughters might seek admission. Van Bibber and McIntosh conceded that some of these concerns were justified. Van Bibber admitted that lack of accreditation might "work a hardship on the applicant from a private school" when applying to state schools, such as the University of Maryland, which required their students to have graduated from an accredited secondary school. McIntosh, too, acknowledged that, "if many more Junior Colleges turn down our weaker girls [because Bryn Mawr is not accredited], we may find it necessary" to seek accreditation.[6]

For the most part, however, the Bryn Mawr School leadership dismissed the worries of parents as ungrounded. Headmistress Van Bibber asserted in 1946 that "colleges knew Bryn Mawr School's standing and reputation for strict marking and judged accordingly." Bryn Mawr leaders viewed accreditation as primarily "intended to keep the country, as well as city, public schools up to a certain standard"—and, therefore, unnecessary for a suburban, private school of Bryn Mawr's quality. In other words, accreditation was for schools with lower standards, not for institutions like Bryn Mawr.[7] Debate continued in the 1950s.

Van Bibber reasoned that accreditation would require too much time and pa-
perwork—particularly troublesome because "women teachers have not so much
free time as the faculty of a boys' school, for, when we go home at the end of a
long school day, we have the house work still to do and dinner to get, as well as
our papers to read and mark."[8]

Essentially, the Bryn Mawr School argued that it was too good to need accreditation and could best evaluate and improve itself from within.[9] Confident
of "being 'the best,'" as one member of Bryn Mawr's Admissions Policy Committee had described it in 1958, the school would not seek accreditation by the
Middle Atlantic Association until 1978.[10] Bryn Mawr's eventual capitulation
stemmed largely from pragmatic necessity—namely, recognition that families,
colleges and universities, and potential sources of educational funding all demanded that their schools be accredited. Also, the Bryn Mawr School was gradually adopting a more critical stance toward itself. In this newer, more
questioning environment, Bryn Mawr acknowledged that the "extensive evaluation process" required for accreditation might encourage "self-scrutiny" that
could ultimately benefit the school.[11]

Civil Rights and Education: The Integration Debates

The U.S. Supreme Court's landmark decision in *Brown v. Board of Education
of Topeka* on 17 May 1954 had enormous ramifications for American society generally and for its educational system particularly. Reflecting the beliefs of civil
rights activists—and those of so many reformers before them—the decision
posited the educational arena as key in shaping the minds and lives of children
and, through them, the kind of society they would create as adults: in the Court's
words, schooling was "a principal instrument in awakening the child to cultural
values, in preparing him for later professional training, and in helping him to
adjust to his environment." The *Brown* ruling overturned the 1896 *Plessey v. Ferguson* decision, which had been used to justify "separate but equal" facilities in
public schools and elsewhere. In contrast to *Plessey v. Ferguson*, *Brown* interpreted "separate educational facilities" as "inherently unequal" and thus harmful to the children attending them.[12]

The impact of *Brown* on public schools (at least certain ones) was dramatic.
In the South, resistance was fierce. Images of the 1957 integration of Little Rock
High School, when the Arkansas National Guard blocked the entrance of nine
black students to the previously all-white school, ultimately provoking Presi-

dent Eisenhower to send federal troops to the city, shocked the country and remain rooted in the nation's memory.[13] The immediate impact of *Brown* on other cities—including Baltimore—was more muted.

In the month after the *Brown* decision, the Baltimore School Board accepted the ruling (and the board of the University of Maryland voted to accept black residents of the state for all levels of study).[14] The Baltimore school district opted for compliance to the *Brown* ruling with a "choice" plan, which gave students the option of choosing to attend any school with vacancies. "Choice" plans, more popular in many cities than more pro-active desegregation policies, had little effect on the status quo. Baltimore, like so much of America, was a very racially divided city in the 1950s. The flight of middle-class citizens had begun earlier in the century, leaving much of the central city to the poor, and neighborhoods within it evolved strictly differentiated by race. The vast majority of Baltimore students attended neighborhood schools that reflected segregated residential patterns both before and after *Brown*. As the Maryland Commission on Interracial Problems and Relations and the Baltimore Commission on Human Relations found in a study on desegregation in 1955, Baltimore city public schools had 86,624 white students and 57,064 "colored" ones. The city maintained sixty-one all-white schools, eighty all-black schools, and forty-eight schools that were primarily white. Only about 3 percent of African American students in Baltimore in 1955 attended integrated schools. A decade later, in 1964, 95 percent of African American children in Baltimore still attended schools that had over 95 percent African American enrollment.[15]

The early stirrings of the civil rights movement would not initially affect the rarified, private school atmosphere at the Bryn Mawr School or the students who learned within its sheltered walls. The *Brown* decision applied to public facilities, and private institutions like the Bryn Mawr School were excluded from its mandate. Yet no school was truly immune from the ramifications of desegregation. In Baltimore, as in many cities across the nation, private schools faced immediate pressure to make clear statements of their admission policies regarding race. The Baltimore area superintendent of Catholic schools declared his system's policy of following the *Brown* decision just a few months after the ruling, immediately after the Baltimore public schools (at least officially) accepted the desegregation mandate.[16] But secular private schools as a group made no such commitments.

From its beginnings, the Bryn Mawr School had been concerned about maintaining itself as an institution where its students would associate with the "right" kinds of people, though the nuances of "right" had shifted slightly over the years. The original school courted the Johns Hopkins families considered most likely to embrace college-preparatory education for their daughters, while the country-day Bryn Mawr had struggled to establish itself among the socially elite residents of Baltimore's fashionable suburbs. Despite subtle differences, the school had always catered to a relatively homogeneous segment of society—overwhelmingly white, Protestant, and affluent. Although the founders had accepted some scholarship students (deemed respectable as well as needy) and a few Jewish students, their vision had always primarily been about the education of girls from a very narrow segment of society.

While Bryn Mawr had thus in many ways epitomized "establishment" education, emerging social and cultural issues challenged the school. The integration issue would force Bryn Mawr, according to one board member at a 1956 meeting, "to have clear ideas about what kind of school the Bryn Mawr School is, its education, economic and social qualifications for students."[17] As public schools faced the mandate to integrate, private schools would have to define their place in the educational system much more clearly than before—whether they would follow the spirit of the *Brown* ruling or whether they, as institutions, would become places where families avoided integration.

The issue of school desegregation surfaced at the Bryn Mawr School immediately after *Brown*. Given its history and its social position in Baltimore—a city accustomed to strict racial divisions—the school's initial response to the Supreme Court decision was predictably negative. Minutes from a Bryn Mawr School board meeting in January 1955 succinctly—and not very revealingly—stated that "an interesting discussion on racial integration followed." The board noted that "the consensus of opinion was that the present policy on admission is unchanged and no definite action has been taken as there have been no Negro applicants." It was concluded that it would be best to "cross that bridge quietly" and that "no policy statement should be made public." When the first African American girls applied in 1955 to test the school's response to the ruling, Bryn Mawr denied them admission.[18]

The decision against integrating the school was not unanimously applauded within the school community. Growing awareness and agitation among Bryn Mawr administrators, alumnae, and parents generated heated discussions in both board meetings and school organizations. The board—mindful of the suspicions of some individuals that it might take action on the issue without regard to the opinions of the larger community—assured the Bryn Mawr community of its commitment to studying school integration carefully and with the input of a variety of individuals.[19]

Debates over integration were often tumultuous and frequently angry and ugly, as some Bryn Mawr School constituents expressed their determination to keep their school an exclusively white institution sheltered from the challenges and turmoil facing public schools. Such individuals asserted that, since the Bryn Mawr School was a private school, parents—who, after all, paid for their children's education—had the right to choose their children's schoolmates. As a private school, one faction argued, Bryn Mawr had no obligation to accept students it did not want, and parents' views on who they wanted their children's classmates to be should take primacy in admissions policy.[20]

Simultaneously, another voice—albeit initially less passionate and focused than that decrying racial integration—was being raised within the Bryn Mawr School community. This alternative perspective proposed that opening Bryn Mawr to the outside world—first by accepting minority students and then by reaching out to the community and bringing students into more direct contact with the realities of the larger world—could benefit the school and its constituency. Individuals embracing this perspective questioned the school's tendency to shelter its students in a homogeneous environment, suggesting that Bryn Mawr students should mix with people of different races and backgrounds. In board reports from 1955 and 1957, it was suggested that isolating girls with students from similar backgrounds—and embracing a "cradle to grave" philosophy that Bryn Mawr should favor students who spent their entire precollegiate years at that institution—was not in keeping with Bryn Mawr's goal of offering high-quality education. That the Bryn Mawr School might be "an ingrown school, so opposed to outside stimuli" was "appalling and frightening," they declared, and, hence, Bryn Mawr should recruit more diverse students, particularly to its upper grades.[21]

Still other members of the Bryn Mawr School community argued that integrating the school was simply the right thing to do—"kindly, generous, and liberal," according to one board member in 1955.[22] As a leader in the Baltimore community, it was argued, Bryn Mawr should set an example of responsible, Christian behavior by moving forward with integration. By responding to changing social conditions and making courageous decisions—rather than retrenching and retreating into its familiar, comfortable, and exclusive private school social circles—the Bryn Mawr School could assume its old position of leadership and prestige in Baltimore and the larger educational community.

The Bryn Mawr School remained divided, sometimes bitterly, on the issue of change. Discussions were numerous and progress slim as the school waffled, making vague statements and placating gestures about its intentions to study the subject of racial integration. Bryn Mawr's public statements on the issue revealed a desire to walk a thin line by attempting to appear progressive without actually admitting African American girls. In 1956, Bryn Mawr issued an ambiguous statement:

> The Board reaffirms the continuing responsibility and intention of the Bryn Mawr School to prepare its students for the world in which they will live. It has decided to make no change at this time in its admission's [*sic*] policy; to be guided in the future by continuing study of changing human relations in our society; and to make no change without ample notification.

Specifically, Bryn Mawr agreed to give its school community eighteen months notice before it might enroll an African American student.[23]

Nervous about angering parents and alumnae or losing students to other private schools that might remain exclusively white (one school survey estimated that parents and alumnae opposed integration by about two to one, although by far the largest percentage of respondents reported themselves as "equivocal" on the issue), Bryn Mawr discussed altering its policies in conjunction with other private schools. The Bryn Mawr board believed there could be safety in numbers if area private schools integrated simultaneously. Ultimately, Bryn Mawr would announce a desegregation policy in conjunction with the Roland Park Country School, its closest counterpart and primary competitor in Baltimore private school circles.[24]

In January 1962, the Bryn Mawr School board (with a vote of sixteen to four) resolved to accept all qualified applicants "without regard to color" and sent notification of the new policy, to begin in September 1963, to parents.[25] Although exactly how integration would proceed was still under debate, Bryn Mawr's administration had prevailed in its belief that the school was making a necessary decision that was not only morally right but also essential to the school's reputation and future success as a high-caliber educational institution.[26] Bryn Mawr's decision to integrate coincided with the retirement of longtime Headmistress Katharine Van Bibber (who had presided over the years of debate) and the welcoming of her successor, Diane Howell. In her remarks after the school's announcement of the new policy, Van Bibber emphasized that, by accepting integration, the Bryn Mawr School was living up to "the Judeo-Christian belief that every person of whatever race is a child of God and must be treated accordingly." Incoming Headmistress Howell declared herself "thrilled" with the board's decision to integrate: "In my opinion, this is the only right decision, the only possible decision, in fact, at this juncture in American history." The Bryn Mawr School board, she added, "couldn't give Miss Van Bibber a more welcome parting gift or me a better welcoming one."[27]

The decision to integrate made, the Bryn Mawr School had to explain and interpret its actions to its school community. Bryn Mawr sought to do so by portraying its modern decision as an extension of the school's revolutionary founding. For decades, the country-day Bryn Mawr had struggled against its original tenets as it established itself among the city's well-to-do suburban residents. Now Bryn Mawr drew on its heritage—select parts of it—to justify its actions. Headmistress Van Bibber portrayed the Bryn Mawr School's decision to integrate as "completely in harmony with the principles upon which this School was founded." As a "pioneer institution," Bryn Mawr had challenged prevailing gender stereotypes at its founding, asserting the rights of girls to an equal education, and now, she claimed, that same revolutionary impulse had led the school to embrace equal education for students of all races.[28] As a reformer seeking to justify to its larger community the changes at her institution, Van Bibber was portraying those alterations as wholly in keeping with the school's founding principles, seeking to portray as legitimate and gain support for what were undoubtedly controversial reforms. Headmistress Van Bibber linked the decision to integrate to Bryn Mawr's founding vision rather than to the country-day model of education. Reference to Bryn Mawr's "pioneering" history, rather than to its close connections to Baltimore's establishment more apparent in recent country-day years, suited newer times better.

Integration proceeded relatively quietly. New Headmistress Diane Howell reported, based on conversations with Katharine Van Bibber, "that there had, of course, been one or two protests, letters, phone calls, etc. of an unpleasant nature, but that on the whole the reaction had been positive or neutral." Although a few families abandoned Bryn Mawr, life at the school continued relatively unchanged.[29] There were no signs that the school intended to fight for racial equality—even to admit very many African Americans—or that it had begun to consider the difficulty of truly integrating minority students into its rarified environment. And although African Americans were the most obvious group barred from Bryn Mawr, the school's costly fees and its entrenchment among Baltimore's elite excluded even most white Baltimore families. Hence, the school, as one insightful member of the Bryn Mawr community understood in 1956, would have to consider its unstated "economic and social qualifications for students."[30] An important decision in the school's history had been made, but the process of redefinition was just beginning.

"Independent" Schools: Exclusive or Inclusive?

Katharine Van Bibber's retirement coincided with significant changes both in the Bryn Mawr School and in the larger nation. Van Bibber, a true Bryn Mawr School insider, had presided over the school during its growth as a country-day academy, and Diane Howell would lead the school during the markedly different decade of the 1960s. Although the decision to integrate took shape during Van Bibber's final years, it was Howell who would oversee the implementation of the new policy and the updating of a school and an educational philosophy that were not well suited to new times. For some years, the Bryn Mawr School had been engaging in a process of defining, as the board had realized as early as 1956, "what kind of school the Bryn Mawr School is."[31] Under the leadership of Howell, the school would rethink the education it provided and whether it should be extended to African American girls, and it would also reconsider its relationship with the community beyond its affluent suburban neighborhood.

A graduate of the Northfield School for Girls in Massachusetts and of Barnard College in 1944, Diane Howell served as a naval communications officer in the WAVES during World War II and worked briefly in advertising before beginning her career in the private school realm. Howell taught English and history at the Windsor School in Boston and then acted as assistant to the principal at the Milton Academy for Girls near Boston. Although Howell clearly had deep connections to the exclusive world of girls' schools, she did not have the explicit connections to the Bryn Mawr School and to Bryn Mawr College of most of the school's former headmistresses and administrators.

Howell's appointment as headmistress of the Bryn Mawr School came at a time when the school was being forced to reevaluate its policies and philosophy, and she pushed Bryn Mawr to change. Under her administration, Bryn Mawr began to comprehend and explore the impracticality and even impossibility of maintaining itself as a bastion for the daughters of Baltimore's elite, aloof from the problems and realities of modern society. Inevitably, the changes during Howell's years sometimes provoked controversy among alumnae and families who wanted their school to remain as it was.[32]

Howell called for a new sense of social responsibility within the Bryn Mawr School community, a theme that had some resonance in the school's history. Although most often the school had been consumed with establishing itself, looking inward and focusing on the needs of its own constituents, both Edith Hamilton's Alumnae League and the 1950s Christian Association had encouraged alumnae and students to undertake charitable activities among Baltimore's more unfortunate citizens. Some members of the Bryn Mawr community embraced the value of such social service for both themselves and others; others espoused an attitude tinged with an air of noblesse oblige. An internal report on school admissions from the 1950s epitomizes that attitude. A private school like Bryn Mawr, the memo explained, was in no way intended to be democratic like public schools. Instead, it was designed to provide "an aristocratic education for those who have good minds and characters and can be taught to use them for the benefit of the community." "Aristocratic" the memo defined as "superior to the rest of the community ... in intellect."[33] Although the statement represented only one perspective within the school community rather than official policy, it reflected the tenacity of old notions that would be hard to change.

In the atmosphere of the 1960s, with social and cultural upheaval that challenged the status quo, schools like Bryn Mawr had to reconsider their roles as private—which generally connoted privileged and exclusive—institutions. Headmistress Howell focused on developing new relationships between private schools and the larger public communities that encompassed them. Rejecting the inward-looking impulse of private schools, she argued, would be essential if schools like Bryn Mawr were to remain relevant to modern society. In keeping with Howell's philosophy, talk about the importance of encouraging students' interaction with the "real world"—through exposure to social problems and engagement in community service—proliferated in the school community of the 1960s. Although the country-day Bryn Mawr School of the mid-twentieth century had sought to shelter children from the harmful influences and undesirable populations of the urban environment, the modern school was beginning to question the merits of the isolated environment it had cultivated for decades.[34]

The motivations for the Bryn Mawr School's new questioning were multifaceted. Obviously, in the larger American culture, the mood of the 1960s stands in contrast to that of the 1950s. The tendency of the post–World War II years had been to retreat into domesticity and to encourage conformity to the suburban ideal. Young President John F. Kennedy symbolized changing times. His exuberance and challenge to Americans—"Ask not what your country can do for you; ask what you can do for your country"—sparked new enthusiasm and commitments, especially in young people. Movements for social change encouraged individuals to question and challenge rather than passively accept the status quo in their communities. The optimism of these movements, which encouraged involvement and held out hope that individuals could create a better society, excited and influenced educational leaders and families alike. The anger and frustration of later years—in the wake of the assassinations of the Kennedys and of Martin Luther King Jr., the escalation of the Vietnam War and antiwar protests, the "drop out" attitude of the counterculture, and fights over federally enforced busing policies—encouraged families to seek shelter from turbulent times in private education. In contrast, the early 1960s encouraged private schools to reshape themselves if they wanted to be seen as progressive institutions and continue to attract good students.

Private schools—both nationally and in Baltimore—faced unprecedented public relations problems in the 1960s. According to Howell, the popular perception was that private schools were "snob schools" where parents sent their children primarily to cultivate the right social connections. She conceded that private schools were partly to blame for such misconceptions because they "have been notably weak in explaining their purposes and programs to the public—even to their own patrons." If "independent" (the term that schools like Bryn Mawr now preferred, since the word "private" carried "undemocratic connotations") schools were to overcome these negative stereotypes and remain relevant and respected, they would have to change their fundamental attitude toward education. Primarily, they needed to encourage students to be involved in all aspects of society. Students had to be prepared to meet the challenges of modern life. In the face of "a frighteningly complex future," Howell suggested, "it is no longer possible to retreat into a niche and live a totally private uncommitted life." To do so "is certainly immoral for anyone who has received the benefits of education."[35]

While pragmatic necessity was responsible for some of the shifts within private school culture in the 1960s, many Bryn Mawr School leaders had a sincere commitment to instilling a sense of social responsibility in their students. Cultivating such sentiments would encourage students to fulfill their responsibilities to the community and could benefit the students, who were themselves deprived by being too disconnected from the real world. Expressing sentiments not unlike that of turn-of-the-century women such as Edith Hamilton in her establishment of the Bryn Mawr School Alumnae League, the modern Bryn Mawr

School asserted the value of bringing its privileged students into contact with the larger society—for the benefit of both.[36]

At the same time, the most savvy among school leaders clearly perceived the pragmatic necessity of promoting change within their school community. In the 1920s the popularity of the country-day movement had forced Bryn Mawr to transform itself. That philosophy of educating girls suited Baltimore and the larger American society of the 1920s, 1930s, 1940s, and 1950s, but whether it would continue to suit society was in doubt. In the 1960s—when fewer families, it seemed, were willing to pay for a private education they perceived as increasingly irrelevant or counter to modern society—the school again faced the need to adapt and reposition itself to suit changing social times.

"Let's Unplug Them and Wire Them into the World," Diane Howell argued in a 1965 article. "A good many of our children, especially those raised in affluent suburbia, are actually underprivileged in the sense that they are being deprived of real experiences and opportunities for work, for service, and for making choices." Students needed to confront the great issues of modern society: "poverty, war, racism, violence, and the moral and ethical dilemmas that spring from these problems and the recent rapid advances in science and technology." Ending the isolation that private schools had traditionally espoused—by exposing students to "real-world" situations, encouraging their participation in volunteer work, expanding their knowledge of career possibilities, and teaching them to cope with social problems such as racism and drug abuse—was critical to preparing students for the modern world.[37] If the Bryn Mawr School did not promote its relevancy to the real world, it would lose the respect and support of the most enlightened individuals within the educational community, gradually regressing into a school primarily for families seeking to remove their children from what they perceived as the negative social forces of the 1960s. Reformulating their philosophies and institutional identities were thus becoming essential to both ensuring the survival and preserving the quality of private schools like Bryn Mawr.

Although the Bryn Mawr School's students still came overwhelmingly from affluent families able to afford its substantial tuition and fees, the culture of the school showed signs of change by the mid-1960s. Whereas the catalogues of the original Bryn Mawr School had outlined its rigorous academic requirements and those of the country-day school had emphasized its well-rounded education offered in bucolic surroundings, those of the modern school described the purposes of its education in broader, more sweeping terms. Bryn Mawr's 1966–67 catalogue declared the school "equally concerned with a girl's ethical, moral, and spiritual development." A Bryn Mawr magazine of the 1960s declared that, "since the pursuit of education is not a selfish, personal quest, a girl must learn to give a portion of her time and talents toward helping others." A 1968 Bryn Mawr School yearbook touted "involvement" (in community volunteer work as well as in more traditional clubs) as a major theme of school life. That same year, the student president of the Bryn Mawr Self-government Association proclaimed the importance of student organizations making "students more aware of the needs of the community": a Bryn Mawr School education, she argued, should include what it sometimes lacked, "that part received only by giving and helping others."[38]

Just as the modern Bryn Mawr School had called on its past to explain its acceptance of integration, it portrayed its modern concern with community outreach as a logical extension of the school's history. A 1968 school magazine outlined Bryn Mawr's "Tradition in Service" by linking the Bryn Mawr School Alumnae League with current "individual opportunities and participation in serving the needs of others." The article described the Alumnae League as having served the community "long before the founding of such community service organizations as the Junior League, or even before the social service department of the Johns Hopkins Hospital was established." In both the past and the present, it argued, "an important aspect of the philosophy of The Bryn Mawr School is the effort to train and equip the individual student to develop her own skills and talents for service to others."[39]

The Bryn Mawr School's acceptance of integration and its interest in promoting the community involvement of its students did not revolutionize the still extremely sheltered institution or the education of the girls within it. Accepting (as opposed to actively pursuing) desegregation and encouraging engagement with society's problems (while still protecting students from the realities of troubled public schools most students experienced) could not render what was still a private school "real world" in the sense that school leaders discussed. Still, it would be a mistake to dismiss the school's new concerns as mere fads, too shallow to last. Although real change was often slow and uneven, the Bryn Mawr School of the 1970s and 1980s first gradually and later with gaining momentum would explore these themes as it struggled to define itself as a leader in the education of girls. The Bryn Mawr School was learning that it could simultaneously promote socially conscious values in its students and enhance its image in the larger community.

The 1970s: Curriculum and the Limits of Change

In the early 1970s, Blair Stambaugh replaced Dianne Howell as Bryn Mawr's headmistress. Bryn Mawr had looked in new directions—and away from the country-day model of education—during the 1960s, but the pace of change seemed to slow during the 1970s. Certainly, things happened at the school. Its campus had expanded as a result of campaigns in the 1960s: a library and Science-Mathematics Center opened in 1969, and a new Lower School followed in 1972. Course offerings grew. In 1976, the school enrolled 531 students.[40] On the whole, however, the school's policies, stated missions, and curriculum remained relatively static during 1970s.

The 1970s saw some continuation of the new emphasis on community involvement and diversity, although catalogues and viewbooks from the decade did not emphasize that aspect of the school to prospective parents. Bryn Mawr's magazine, in a retrospective of Stambaugh's accomplishments at the school, recalled that "Blair always took a stand on financial aid that may have been unpopular with some" and "always insisted that some portion of the operating budget be committed to financial aid, as a statement of the School community's commitment to economic diversity in the student body."[41] In 1978, scholarships were established "to broaden the pool of qualified applicants, to allow Bryn Mawr to reach out farther into the community, and to make possible a Bryn Mawr education for some highly able students whose families have not thought to seek such an opportunity for their children." Despite such financial aid, the Bryn Mawr board reported in 1983 that the school had "a black enrollment of 9%" by the early 1970s. By the end of the decade, "that had dropped to 4%."[42]

Perhaps the most notable change in the 1970s—and that with the greatest implications for the school in the late twentieth century—was the program of "coordination" with the Gilman School for boys. Bryn Mawr's campus was located adjacent to the all-boys school with which it had long-standing informal ties, and in 1973, the two schools began offering classes together. Although administrators and teachers found burdensome the process of coordinating two different curricula, class schedules, faculties, and school traditions, the program appealed strongly to students and parents. As a result of this coordination, Bryn Mawr's curriculum would change more than it had throughout most of the twentieth century. The expansion of the program was gradual, but coordination meant that the range of advanced courses and electives for students would grow continuously. For the first time in the school's history, Bryn Mawr students would experience coeducational classrooms (a topic addressed further in ch. 6).

By the 1960s and 1970s, the emphasis in Bryn Mawr's curriculum had shifted somewhat, and requirements were fewer. In 1966, minimum graduation requirements were four years of English, one year of American history, two years each of two foreign languages (or three years of one language), one year of algebra, one year of geometry, and one laboratory science course. History requirements (in contrast to the sequence of ancient, Western, and American history taught to all students earlier in the century) were substantially reduced, and language requirements were also (students had heretofore taken both Latin and French throughout their course of study). In the 1970s, Spanish was added, and more advanced courses in science and mathematics were offered to, though not required of, older students. Overall, 1970s students had more choice of electives, and senior independent projects encouraged them to pursue their own interests.[43]

Extracurricular activities at the school of the 1960s and 1970s continued to be strong. Athletics dominated. In the 1970s, catalogues included more detailed lists of sports programs than of academic courses and electives. Students could choose from varsity and intramural programs in "hockey, badminton, basketball, lacrosse, tennis." They could take "jogging, gymnastics, general first aid, softball and volleyball," in addition to regular gym classes, which included instruction in "European country dancing, rhythmic exercises and game skills." Figure skating, ballet, yoga, or horseback riding taken outside of school hours could fulfill a physical education requirement. The school also sponsored a choir and strings ensemble, literary publications, afternoon art classes, student government, and dramatics, photography, and cinema clubs.[44]

Ironies: Redefining Private Education and New Diversity after the 1960s

In the 1970s, many aspects of the Bryn Mawr School still operated under the country-day model of education. Changes had been made in the 1960s, but they were not always consistent and were not without ironies on several fronts. This was most evident with respect to the issue of diversity. In the years after Bryn Mawr's initial integration, the number of African American students enrolled at the school dropped, highlighting the reality that a policy of admitting students regardless of color and the actual promotion of integration were not necessarily the same thing. The school's emphasis on community involvement in the 1970s coincided with a kind of retrenchment in the larger culture in which private schools were viewed in a more favorable light by many families. Just as leading private schools were trying to become "real world," families actually may have been attracted to them specifically because they were not. By the 1970s, many families viewed private schools as positive retreats from the culture in general and from public education in particular.

If the spirit of the early 1960s had been hopeful, frustration and even violence characterized the later years of the decade. The optimism and progress of the early civil rights movement gave way to racial turmoil and division, and anti–Vietnam War protests angered and divided Americans. Student protests and the "hippie" counterculture, with its connections to free love and drugs, transformed America's college campuses and their students—or at least a highly publicized segment of them—and scared many parents. In many communities, federal busing policies precipitated flight from public schools—and a new kind of retreat into private ones. And so, ironically, schools like Bryn Mawr were seeking connections with the larger community at the same time that much of the larger community sought these schools as a kind of buffer from the outside forces affecting their children. Given this situation—with families torn between wanting to protect their children from society and public education and yet wanting them prepared for the "real world"—the pressure continually to redefine the relevancy of private education would continue.

Clearly, issues of race and integration—or, to use later educational jargon, the promotion of diversity—would be central to any redefinitions. Although *Brown v. Board of Education* had technically mandated an end to "separate but equal" schooling for black and white students, most American children continued to attend largely segregated schools. By the early 1970s, a new approach to achieving racial integration and providing equal opportunity to students of different races had emerged. Busing was intended to address the continuing reality of de facto segregation by integrating children in schools located away from their immediate neighborhoods, and, in 1971, the Supreme Court, in *Swann v. Charlotte-Mecklenburg Board of Education*, supported the policy as a tool for promoting racial integration and providing equal educational opportunities to children from disadvantaged backgrounds. The policy generated heated controversy, with unanticipated and often unintended long-term implications for both public and private schools.[45]

162   *A Vision for Girls*

In Baltimore, although a decade of school board policy had granted students regardless of race the right to enroll in the public school of their choice, the vast majority of students still attended segregated schools at the end of the 1960s. In an era of pro-active government policy designed to desegregate schools, Baltimore and its surrounding suburban counties experimented with policies to promote "racial mixing." In 1970, busing was introduced in Baltimore City and nearby Prince George's County (the tenth largest school district in the country). The impact was dramatic—much more so than in the wake of school freedom of choice policies introduced in 1954—and not necessarily as expected. Within a decade, the proportion of white students in Baltimore City public schools declined to 20 percent. In Prince George's public schools, the proportion of white children enrolled in public schools fell from 80 percent to 45 percent.[46] The redistribution of students in Baltimore—the so-called "white flight" that left city school systems primarily to the poor and minorities—mirrored the fate of public schools in cities across the nation.

While many families fled busing policies by moving to suburban areas with only small minority populations, other families explored private schools as an alternative to public education. This was a new clientele for independent schools, one that did not necessarily have long traditions of private schooling in their families (or loyalty to particular institutions). From the perspective of these families, private schools protected their children from busing specifically and from the perceived breakdown of order and values in society generally. Private schools promised structure, discipline, and individualized attention—all seen as missing in public schools. More and more middle-class families abandoned public schools, leaving them with lower tax bases, poorer populations, and deteriorating conditions. Even some families who in theory supported the justice of integrating public institutions were discouraged by the state of public schools and retreated. Many parents who seemed increasingly anxious about their children's future—in contrast to the Bryn Mawr School's country-day years, when families seemed to take for granted the social position their daughters would eventually occupy—turned to independent schools as part of their strategy for ensuring their children's future success.

Obviously, private schools were poised to benefit from the influx of new families. But they also faced difficult decisions. Some private schools might become shelters against busing, places where students could continue to mix exclusively with their "own kind." But other private schools took different paths, striving to bring openness and diversity to their institutions.

By the early 1980s, the National Association of Independent Schools (NAIS)—a coalition of coeducational and single-sex day and boarding schools that represents more than one thousand leading independent schools today— had embraced the goal of broadening the constituency and increasing the diversity of the students of its member schools. Separating themselves from private schools that appealed to families wanting to avoid contact with different kinds of people, these private schools (like leading American colleges and universities) promoted diversity as a priority and a positive advantage. The organization required nondiscriminatory policies of its members and encouraged a multicultural approach to education. At the Bryn Mawr School, which wanted to retain its preeminence within Baltimore and the larger independent school community, rejection of the isolation and social snobbery often associated with private education was the only real choice. In conjunction with other private schools both in Baltimore and nationally, Bryn Mawr embraced NAIS goals and continued to reshape itself.[47]

Not much progress on this front had been made in the 1970s, when the enrollment of minorities had dropped from late-1960s levels. In the 1980s, however, redefining the Bryn Mawr School took on a new urgency. Bryn Mawr would build upon the changes initiated in the 1960s and, in keeping with changing educational models in the world of higher education and in private school circles, implement significant new ones. In 1980, Barbara Landis Chase assumed leadership of the school. A graduate of Brown University (who earned a masters of liberal arts degree from Johns Hopkins University while serving as Bryn Mawr's headmistress), Chase came to Baltimore after serving as the dean of admissions at the Wheeler School in Providence, Rhode Island. When interviewed about her new position, Chase outlined directions for her administration. She emphasized her priorities as recruiting a greater diversity of students, cultivating a closer relationship between the school and its city, and emphasizing the importance of family, particularly in an era that stressed women's pursuit of careers.[48] During Chase's administration, the policies and goals of the National Association of Independent Schools figured prominently in Bryn Mawr's internal discussions and decisions.

Reflecting NAIS goals, Chase emphasized the themes of diversity and community involvement at the Bryn Mawr School, and her leadership in these areas would be significant. Describing what she called "education of the heart," Chase spoke of "the courage to go beyond just the academics and to see the school as a social agent beyond the three 'Rs.'" Chase's innovations would include the expansion of volunteer opportunities for Bryn Mawr students and the founding of summer camps to expose inner city girls to computers and literature. She organized a national conference in the early 1990s to discuss ways that private schools could help at-risk children. She founded the Baltimore Education Scholarship Trust, a recruiting program that placed and counseled minority students in area private schools, and she was a leader in the Baltimore Consortium for the Teaching of History, which brought together private and public schools with museums and universities for exchange projects to the benefit of all.[49]

Headmistress Chase emphasized as a top priority the goal of increasing Bryn Mawr's visibility in the Baltimore community beyond exclusive private school circles. In 1978, the Bryn Mawr School—which had traditionally secluded itself on its country campus—had recommended that inviting "outside groups" to use the school's facilities would be a good public relations strategy.[50] In the 1980s, the school instituted educational programs designed to draw individuals to the school. "Evenings at the Bryn Mawr School" (with minicourses on subjects ranging from archeology and computers to jewelry-making and CPR) brought many adults to the campus. "Readers' Camp" and "Summertech" science and computer courses targeted underprivileged students and their teachers, who could benefit from Bryn Mawr's resources.[51] And measures such as refashioning the school's lecture series into a community-wide (rather than just a schoolwide) event potentially attracted a greater diversity of people to the Bryn Mawr School.[52] In addition, by the 1980s, participation in service projects had become mandatory for Bryn Mawr students.[53]

The school faced an even greater challenge in changing the composition of its student body. Although official acceptance of racial integration, both at Bryn Mawr and in all NAIS schools, signified a major hurdle overcome, it had still not transformed the overall racial or economic profile of most independent school students. Powerful factors—including economic realities that essentially reserved expensive private schools for affluent families and lingering prejudices about who would "fit in"—continued to make schools like Bryn Mawr institutions comprised overwhelmingly of affluent white children. By the 1980s, however, many independent schools were making unprecedented commitments to recruiting and retaining students of different racial, ethnic, and socioeconomic backgrounds.

For decades the Bryn Mawr School had been "populated almost exclusively by scions of Baltimore's social register," as one modern Baltimore magazine observed. In attempts to combat the image of private schools as "undemocratic," Diane Howell had argued that private schools like Bryn Mawr—which deliberately sought to enroll students from different backgrounds—were actually likely to be more diverse and less homogeneous than many suburban schools that drew exclusively from one neighborhood. Despite the rhetoric of exposing students to "the real world," "bringing the outside world to BMS," and seeking "increased diversity and access," however, the school remained predominantly white and affluent.[54]

The shift from its founding vision to the country-day philosophy had marked a significant change in the mentality and mission of the Bryn Mawr School. By the 1980s, Bryn Mawr had embraced a third paradigm—one that championed real-world experiences, community service, and diversity. Although the Bryn Mawr School had made initial attempts to diversify, it had had mixed success in recruiting and retaining minority students in the 1960s and 1970s. School officials in the 1980s, led by Chase, were committed to changing Bryn Mawr's culture to achieve the goal of diversity. The school faced a complex challenge. How could a private school—exclusive by its very nature because families were required to pay high tuition and fees for their children's education—be democratic and diverse? How could private schools open their doors to less affluent families and remain financially viable? School leaders seemed to appreciate that only a broad, multifaceted strategy could create a Bryn Mawr School culture that welcomed diversity. They also understood that substantially increased financial aid would be essential to attracting diverse families.

A "multicultural" approach to education—as was coming into vogue at many of the nation's top colleges and universities—gave essentially elite independent schools a way to address, if not really solve, the dilemma. Multiculturalism proposed incorporating into the academic curriculum the study of different racial, ethnic, and religious groups from their own perspectives and including in school life the celebration of diverse cultural traditions. The new model offered private schools the opportunity to sensitize their traditional students to the experiences of minority groups and to welcome the diverse student populations the schools were trying to attract. At Bryn Mawr, multiculturalism offered a model for the more open, diverse, and relevant institution the school had been struggling to become. And it helped change the school in concrete ways that Bryn Mawr leaders of former generations—even those who had championed racial integration—would never have imagined.

In real terms, increases in the ethnic and racial diversity of Bryn Mawr School students in the 1980s were dramatic, a result of the efforts of Bryn Mawr's leaders to attract and retain diverse students. At the end of the 1970s, the school had had an African American enrollment of 4 percent. By the late 1980s, Bryn Mawr had an African American enrollment of about 10 percent, with a total minority enrollment of about 20 percent. The change in Bryn Mawr's student body mirrored changes at other NAIS schools across the country. In Baltimore, area independent schools enrolled, on average, 16 percent minority students.[55]

As it increased the diversity of its students, Bryn Mawr simultaneously revised its curriculum in keeping with the multicultural philosophy. As Barbara Chase explained in 1985, "The process of defining a liberal education" was a major area of "concern and challenge" for the school.[56] Bryn Mawr leaders like Chase wanted to promote a culture of diversity at the school, and more diverse students themselves wanted new electives. Independent preparatory schools and colleges and universities across the country were beginning to update their academic offerings to reflect modern concerns, and Bryn Mawr joined them.

At the beginning of the 1980s, Bryn Mawr catalogues described students taking courses in English, U.S. and European history, art history and music appreciation, economics, and science and mathematics. Language studies included French, German, Spanish, Latin, and Greek. Bryn Mawr students could choose independent senior projects and enjoyed a new senior elective in women's history, but most liberal arts courses focused on fairly traditional offerings in European and American history and literature.[57]

By the 1990s, the school's curriculum had been transformed. An emphasis on knowledge and appreciation of non-Western peoples and cultures shaped new course offerings. Bryn Mawr students could choose from a dizzying array of courses in history, literature, and cultural studies.[58] Bryn Mawr "viewbooks"— designed to attract potential students and their families—explained the school's curriculum. In a section entitled "Appreciating Differences," Bryn Mawr explained that its course offerings were "carefully designed to celebrate diversity and to enable students from various ethnic groups to share information about their cultures through class projects and discussions." The school boasted a wide range of multicultural courses for its high school students, including "Literature of the Other America," "African and Caribbean Literature," "South African History and Literature," "The Asian Experience," "Native American Studies," "Black History," "Chinese Studies: Behind the Bamboo Curtain," and

"History of the Modern Middle East." School viewbooks also emphasized how Bryn Mawr's diverse students—including Hindus, Koreans, and African Americans—enjoyed the opportunity to study "Third World issues" in the classroom.[59]

Simultaneously, the Bryn Mawr School focused on what could be broadly categorized as "values education"—an exploration of contemporary issues, social problems, and ethics.[60] In the 1980s, the Bryn Mawr community frequently reflected on the need to expose students to political and social problems—and to link their awareness directly with school classes and activities.[61] Schools, Headmistress Chase emphasized, had the responsibility (once assumed largely by families and religious organizations) to teach children ethics and social responsibility, encouraging them to contemplate critical issues such as world peace and nuclear politics.[62] And so, again, the school's curriculum and culture came to reflect society's concerns. Bryn Mawr experimented with such courses as "Comparative Religion," "Metropolitan Issues," "Moral Dilemmas," and "Ethics and Contemporary Issues."[63] The school encouraged the formation of student clubs and interest groups focused on contemporary social concerns ranging from "diplomacy" to "human sexuality."[64]

With its active pursuit of diversity, the modern Bryn Mawr School was clearly a very different place from the country-day academy that its supporters had struggled so hard to create in the 1920s and 1930s. As the school more and more sought to reflect and expose students to the "real world" and all its diversity, it was sure to alienate some of its traditional supporters who still viewed private schools as places to shelter their children. Overall, however, the school's embrace of diversity did not negatively affect enrollment (as some opponents of racial integration in the 1950s and 1960s had feared). To the contrary, during the 1980s, Bryn Mawr's applications for admission rose 40 percent, including significant increases in minority applicants. As the number of students seeking admission rose dramatically, Bryn Mawr—whose lagging enrollments had once forced the school to accept students with poor academic records and few educational aspirations—could concurrently raise the academic standards it required for admission. The Bryn Mawr School had confirmed that embracing diversity was both attractive from a philosophical point of view and compatible with (perhaps even partially responsible for) the school's increasing popularity.[65]

But Bryn Mawr still faced the paradox of being a private school that wanted to be democratic. Despite the school's considerable efforts to overcome its negative image in the community, Bryn Mawr's own research revealed that the larger Baltimore community still harbored impressions of the school as elitist. One marketing study commissioned by the school asserted that Baltimore's perception of Bryn Mawr as a snobbish and elitist school with high tuition was "troublesome and atypical," even compared to perceptions of other independent schools in the area. Such negative images, the report concluded, were more pervasive among the public than any positive images.[66]

Despite its efforts, how "real world" an independent school like Bryn Mawr could be was debatable. A Baltimore magazine observed the difficulties experienced by some minority students adjusting to private school culture. Those from less affluent households expressed their feelings of living in two very different and incongruous worlds—their beautiful, sheltered suburban school campuses versus their own home neighborhoods. The atmosphere at a private school like Bryn Mawr was certainly far removed from the educational experiences of many students at public schools in Baltimore and other cities across the nation. Bryn Mawr students might take a variety of courses exploring different ethnic traditions and contemporary social problems, but they never had to deal with the turmoil and harsh realities—such as low academic standards, overcrowded and decaying facilities, undertrained faculty, and safety concerns—that too many children in public schools endured daily.[67]

The Bryn Mawr School's efforts to diversify were genuine and often successful. But there remained a fundamental paradox faced by independent schools wanting to be open and diverse while simultaneously being private and thus reserved for only a lucky few. The new paradigm of multiculturalism promised to help such schools think about themselves and their missions in new ways, but it could be dangerous, too. Without continued introspection and self-awareness, independent schools could tout their diversity without considering all the implications—and ironies—inherent in their institutions and their place in American education.

The Bryn Mawr School's modern redefinition of itself for contemporary American society was not unique. While Bryn Mawr embraced the movement to open and diversify private preparatory schools, the school made most of its new commitments—from racial integration to modern multiculturalism—concurrently with other Baltimore private schools and in keeping with the stated goals of the National Association of Independent Schools. Indeed, emphasizing their progressiveness and relevance to modern American society, leading independent schools were in a sense engaging in both local and national campaigns to market themselves to new generations of students, parents, donors, and institutions of higher education. Given the nearly 17 percent growth the NAIS reported in its member schools during the 1990s, those efforts seem to have been successful.[68]

CHAPTER SIX

Reinventing the Vision

A School for Girls

> No matter what the state of research on gender, we feel affirmed in our
> status as a single sex institution.
> — HEADMISTRESS BARBARA CHASE, 1985

As the Bryn Mawr School initially molded a new school culture for modern
times, questions of gender rarely informed its redefinition of itself and the education it offered to girls. On one level, this omission seems surprising. After all,
the Bryn Mawr School had been founded with specific ideas about the relationship between girls' education and the roles women would later assume in the social order. The rhetoric of the original school had been full of references to the
unique circumstances and needs of girls and women. As the school embraced the
country-day educational model, however, it had gradually shed much of its self-
consciousness about what, exactly, it meant to be an institution devoted specifically to girls' education. A sense of gender injustice had motivated the Bryn
Mawr School founders, but later leaders proved more ambivalent in their attitudes toward the prevailing social expectations for females. With the increasing
social desirability of higher education for women, they had lost the old sense of
urgency to challenge the norm in the education of girls.

Even as late as the 1960s, the decade when Bryn Mawr (in conjunction with
other independent schools) began reevaluating its relevance to modern society,
the school often implicitly accepted the stereotypes its founders had been com-

mitted to overcoming. The very headmistress who urged Bryn Mawr to respond positively to modern social forces—urging the school to move forward with racial integration, to shed its old aloofness, and to engage its students in social issues and community service—did not extend her critique to gender issues. Diane Howell, still operating within the country-day framework (which generally enforced reigning gender norms), justified a Bryn Mawr School education for girls using old arguments of social expediency. Essentially, she (like so many before her) linked the importance of quality education for girls to their roles as mothers: "The future lies in the minds, bodies, hearts, and hands of girls as well as boys—in some ways more so for it is women who are largely responsible for shaping the attitudes of children and thus ensuring the future of our society."[1]

That argument may have reflected the attitudes of her audience more than personal convictions. When asked in a 1962 interview about her attitudes toward teaching "home management," she had responded that girls could learn that at home: "To teach sewing or cooking in school would be at the expense of an academic activity," she asserted.[2] But the old rhetoric about girls and women and their education that M. Carey Thomas and her fellow school founders had fought proved incredibly tenacious and resilient, retaining its currency at the school almost a century after its establishment.

While the Bryn Mawr School discussed the importance of exposing girls to society in all its forms and with all its problems, the school engaged in no concurrent debates about how women, specifically, would participate in that society. The school's renewed emphasis on community service probably reinforced old assumptions that the primary influence of many affluent women on their community beyond the home would stem from their charitable volunteer activities rather than from the professional, remunerated careers Bryn Mawr's founders had supported. Seldom did the school question why, if real world experience was so valuable, the Bryn Mawr School should continue educating girls apart from boys. The tradition of single-sex education at Bryn Mawr and in the larger Baltimore community was well established, and few seemed to consider the implications—either positive or negative—of Bryn Mawr's single-sex factor. The Bryn Mawr School was for girls largely because of tradition.

As the "right" and "proper" roles for women in modern American society came into question with increasing frequency and fury in upcoming decades, the Bryn Mawr School would not—and could not—ignore the implications of the trends. As challenges to women's places in families, in schools, in the workplace and professions, in politics, and across society proliferated, the expectations and aspirations of the girls and women whom Bryn Mawr traditionally served would change. The Bryn Mawr School—as a specifically female school—would have to respond, reexamining its attitudes, in this case, toward the education of girls and the school's status as a single-sex institution.

The Second Women's Movement and the Onslaught of Coeducation

The onset of the second women's movement had profound implications for women across a wide spectrum of American society. The movement encompassed individuals and philosophies ranging from young radicals sparked by their experiences in the 1960s movements for greater social justice to experienced professionals lobbying for legislative change in the U.S. Congress. During the 1960s and early 1970s, Americans of both sexes rethought roles of women and men that were commonly taken for granted. A host of issues—including legal inequalities, discriminatory employment practices, equal pay for equal work, quality child care, the roles of men and women in the family, and access to safe abortions—gained national attention as women and men questioned traditional cultural assumptions about gender.

Not surprisingly, the issue of education played a key role in the debates. Sharing a national faith in the power of education to mold children and the adults they would become, reformers on behalf of women had for almost two centuries seen schools as key to challenging deeply ingrained attitudes about the places of women and men in society. Like many early reformers, feminists in the modern women's movement called both for increased access to education and for a rethinking of the nature and shape of that education. In the realm of higher education, they introduced the study of women—or women's studies—into the college curriculum, and they reinvigorated women's collegiate athletics. Noting that, as late as 1970, only 8.9 percent of physicians and 4.7 percent of lawyers were women despite the fact that women had comprised almost half of all college undergraduates since the 1920s, they demanded equal access to graduate training and to the professions beyond it. Finally, they lobbied for women to be admitted to the nation's remaining male-only institutions of higher education.[3]

In 1890—just a few years after the founding of the Bryn Mawr School—there were 1,082 colleges in the United States. Of those, 37 percent were for men only, 20 percent were for women only, and 43 percent were coeducational. By 1957, of 1,326 colleges, 74 percent were coeducational, with 13 percent for men only and 13 percent for women only.[4] Despite the clear trend to coeducation, many of the nation's most prestigious educational institutions remained single sex. From the perspective of reformers, the remaining male-only institutions were bastions of male privilege and power. Securing women's access to those prestigious colleges and universities was crucial to women's ability to enter the powerful networks that extended from the collegiate years into business, professional, and political circles.

One educational barrier after another fell. By 1981, of the 1,928 colleges and universities in the United States, 92 percent were coeducational, with 3 percent for men only and 5 percent for women only. In the early 1970s, prestigious universities including Yale, Princeton, and the University of Virginia opened their doors to women for the first time, and by the time Columbia University admitted women as undergraduates in 1983, only a few all-male colleges remained. The goal of opening all-male institutions to women had largely been met. But what had not been anticipated was the effect on all-female institutions.[5]

Having enjoyed secure and prestigious positions as the preferred colleges for many affluent young women throughout the previous century, many women's colleges watched in shock and dismay as their traditional constituency flocked to coeducational schools. The Ivy League seemed to hold more appeal for many modern young women than the Seven Sister colleges. The phenomenon extended to women's colleges in other regions as well. Girls' schools like the Bryn Mawr School—which had once expected a large number of their graduates to attend women's colleges (and which, in the case of the Bryn Mawr School, had particular ties with a specific women's college)—witnessed the changing aspirations of their students. In 1980, Bryn Mawr's assistant headmistress noted that, "with the growing movement toward coeducation, there have been fewer students going to [Bryn Mawr] College, perhaps five or six every decade ... Typically only two or three students from each graduating class attend a women's college." Finally, she added that "this year's class, like their predecessors, are almost unanimous in their desire to attend four-year, liberal arts coeducational colleges."[6]

Remaining all-female institutions and their supporters were distressed by the negative associations that single-sex education frequently evoked. Not atypical was one high school girl's query to an admissions director at Barnard College: "Aren't women's colleges unnatural?"[7] In earlier decades, when much of society had embraced an understanding of the sexes as fundamentally different, educating young women and men together (even though the norm in precollegiate and public schools) had often been viewed suspiciously. By the 1970s, however, many women and men viewed women's institutions as relics of the past that were increasingly irrelevant in a society striving to treat women and men equally. Segregating the sexes appeared artificial and unhealthy to many modern women and men. Coeducation seemed the more progressive option.

Changing circumstances placed women's colleges on the defensive. Forced by declining applications and negative publicity to rethink their traditional positions, these institutions struggled to adapt to changing attitudes and, indeed, to survive. For institutions with long histories, deep traditions, and loyal faculty and alumnae, the process of reevaluating their institutional identities and accommodating the preferences of the modern educational landscape was difficult and sometimes agonizing. Different institutions made different decisions. Some women's colleges (like Vassar) began accepting male students. Others (like Wellesley, Smith, Mount Holyoke, and Bryn Mawr Colleges) remained single sex yet accommodated educational trends by cultivating relationships with nearby coeducational schools. Although some women's colleges survived as single-sex institutions, the change in the landscape of higher education for women was marked: in 1960, there were 298 women's colleges. By 1970, half of those schools had either become coeducational or closed their doors. From 1966 to 1986, the number of all-female colleges dropped from 231 to 102. By 1980, only 2.3 percent of college women were attending all-female institutions. By 1992, only 84 women's colleges remained.[8]

The fate of single-sex institutions in American higher education was shared at the precollegiate level.[9] Both girls' and boys' schools—which included many of the most prestigious college-preparatory schools in the nation—faced an overwhelming preference for coeducation at all levels among students and their families. Hard choices were inevitable as institutions with long histories had to reshape their identities fundamentally. Many girls' schools merged with nearby boys' schools; others closed. In the mid-1960s, more than 60 percent of schools in the National Association of Independent Schools were single sex; a decade later, that proportion had dropped to less than 30 percent. From 1964 to 1976, 180 NAIS single-sex schools became coeducational. During those same years, the percentage of coeducational schools in NAIS rose from 38 percent to 70 percent. By 1986, only 12 percent of NAIS schools were for girls only.[10]

Although some independent schools retained their single-sex status, their position could no longer be as secure as it had been in the past. Accommodation to the popularity of coeducation became essential. "Coordination" provided an alternative to merger with an all-male institution at several women's colleges and girls' schools. At the Bryn Mawr School, the new program of coordination with the Gilman School introduced in 1973 helped assure families that their daughters would not be "unnaturally" separated from the opposite sex. The opportunity for students to mix in some classes, as well as in extracurricular activities, appealed to students and parents enormously. The coordination program expanded greatly throughout the 1970s and 1980s (eventually including a second girls' school, Roland Park Country School). The presence of boys became more common on Bryn Mawr's campus and in its classrooms, and trips to Gilman became a frequent, even daily, routine for Bryn Mawr Upper School students. Coordination gradually evolved into an essential element of Bryn Mawr's identity and its ability to survive in a society skeptical about too completely segregating girls and boys, men and women.[11]

If accommodation to coeducation seemed inevitable, why did institutions like the Bryn Mawr School remain single sex? What was the role of a school exclusively for girls in light of the overwhelming acceptance of coeducation as the norm in American society? Undoubtedly, history and tradition were powerful factors. Administrators and faculty members who had devoted their professional lives to their schools and alumnae who treasured their educational experiences surely found the possibility of losing their institutions painful. Resisting the trend to coeducation must have seemed the only option to many supporters, but how could girls' schools—in a society where even most girls at single-sex schools planned to attend coeducational colleges and universities—continue to attract new families and students? After enjoying decades of loyal patronage from affluent families, girls' schools—in danger of becoming relics—would be called upon as never before to justify their existence, redefine their mission, and prove their relevance for the future.

The Larger Picture: Education and Women's Places

The girls' schools that found themselves in crisis in the 1970s operated in relatively narrow, independent school circles that prepared students for a cluster of selective colleges and universities, but they existed against the backdrop of public education. And that education was in crisis, too, although a crisis of a very different nature. In 1967, the National Education Association chose Baltimore to symbolize the problems—including increasing percentages of disadvantaged children and children with special needs, underpaid teachers, deteriorating buildings, and shrinking tax bases—facing American urban school systems. During the 1950s and 1960s, approximately ten thousand white and middle-class African American children had left Baltimore City schools and enrolled in suburban schools—abandoning city schools largely to the poor and underprivileged. By 1978, two-thirds of Baltimore public school children were African American.[12]

The ramifications of the real and perceived decline of public education on private schools were notable. In the mid-1970s, private schools that had only recently declined in popularity were beginning to see their enrollments climb. Perceived negatively as elitist and antidemocratic in the 1960s, private schools by the 1970s were beginning to be seen as calm havens from the problems of alcoholism, drugs, and violence perceived to be ravaging public schools. Promises of small class size and individual attention, emphasis on discipline and moral values, and dedicated teachers and high academic expectations appealed to many concerned parents. There was also the unacknowledged but certain reality that private schools provided a means of avoiding the court-ordered desegregation and subsequent busing policies that had changed the racial and socioeconomic character of neighborhood public schools.[13]

The National Association of Independent Schools reported a 19.4 percent growth in its member schools during the 1990s.[14] Surely, problems in public education, as well as independent schools' successes in addressing the concerns of parents, played a powerful role in their growth, particularly among populations that had not traditionally supported private schools. Parents, ever more worried about their children's future achievements, perceived private preparatory schooling as a powerful first step in launching their children into the "right" colleges and universities, graduate schools, and business and professional circles. During the Bryn Mawr School's country-day years, families had seemed to take their children's future position in society more for granted, but modern families feared that an increasingly competitive marketplace would make it difficult for children to achieve or exceed their parents' status. This anxiety—combined with keen competition for places at the nation's most selective colleges and universities—fueled the renewed popularity of private precollegiate education.

Whether single-sex institutions—particularly girls' schools—would play a significant role in this resurgence of interest in private schools was not clear in the 1970s. Changes in women's places in society in the wake of the women's movement had raised the expectations of both parents and their daughters. By 1980, over half of all adult women were employed outside the home even after they married and had children, including, by 1985, 53.4 percent of women with preschool children. Unlike a majority of female college graduates only a generation earlier, most young women expected to work outside the home. Working women for the most part still found themselves in traditionally female jobs, however. In 1973, almost half of all working women were employed in clerical and service work, and over half of all female professionals remained teachers and nurses. At the same time, however, opportunities for women—particularly for highly educated ones—had increased in advanced education, the professions, and political life, which had traditionally been dominated by men.[15]

For families with daughters, the stakes were high. Families considering independent preparatory schools wanted for their daughters what they had always wanted for their sons—the best access to higher education and professional life beyond. Girls had new, visible female role models—politicians, doctors, judges, businesswomen—and they had high expectations for their futures. Independent schools that vied for the opportunity to educate modern girls would have to convince families that they were the best institutions to prepare those girls to occupy places in society where not very long before few women had ventured. The sharp declines in single-sex schools during the 1970s—the very decade when private schools in general began their resurgence—did not bode well for their ability to respond to new demands and perceptions. Given the skepticism about female educational institutions that had their roots in the days when many male institutions excluded girls and women, whether girls' schools would—or could—play a significant role in training girls to enter traditionally male realms of society seemed dubious.

The Emergence of a New Paradigm: "Difference"

In contrast to the emphasis on equality and the push to coeducation in the 1960s and 1970s, a new group of feminists and educational theorists were reevaluating the notion of female difference and the value of single-sex education by the 1980s and 1990s. Arguing that the emphasis on the similarities between the sexes and women's rush to emulate men were forcing women to lose much that was special, they championed the need to nurture women's different "ways of knowing," in the words of a 1986 book that popularized the new theories.[16] Claiming innate differences in the natures of females and males, they proposed that only institutions that acknowledged and appreciated those differences could offer girls and women the quality education they deserved.

This new "difference" coalition centered around the work of Harvard University Professor Carol Gilligan. In her 1982 landmark study, *In a Different Voice: Psychological Theory and Women's Development*, Gilligan argued that women's experiences give them a distinct moral and intellectual perspective. Because society has always accepted the male perspective as the norm, women's special "ethic of care"—which encourages nurturing and a sense of connectedness between individuals—has been devalued. Living in a society (both in schools and beyond) that values the male sense of justice, autonomy, and competitiveness above the female ethic of care, girls find their feelings and ways of viewing the world neglected. Judged by male norms, they suffer loss of confidence and self-esteem. Gilligan proposed that devaluation of the female "different voice" not only is detrimental to individual girls and women but also deprives the entire society of an important and potentially beneficial perspective.[17]

Gilligan garnered a loyal following—among scholars, educators, and feminists. Her theories spawned a new generation of works (both scholarly and popular) on feminine difference that had influence beyond the academic realm.[18] But her theories—and the school of difference feminism it fostered—sparked substantial controversy, too. Critics questioned the legitimacy of some arguments about female difference and their implications for women. In a 1986 forum in *Signs*, an interdisciplinary journal of women's studies, several scholars critiqued Gilligan's work, suggesting that, although her theories were presented in a compelling style, they were not supported with empirical evidence. Others criticized her research methods, particularly her reliance on students in a class on moral development at Harvard University as a basis for generalizations about the population as a whole.[19]

Women's historian Linda Kerber questioned whether "different voice" theory romanticizes and oversimplifies women. Even within the women's movement, she pointed out, women have proven that they can be as selfish and racist as men. Kerber also warned of the inherent danger of resurrecting the old "separate spheres" specter. Recollecting how past arguments about women's superiority—their more moral, pious, peaceful, and domestic natures—have often been turned against them and used to bar women from positions of power and equality, she cautioned that contemporary talk of female difference carries with it clear "risks."[20]

In less sympathetic tones, Christopher Lasch accused Gilligan of romanticizing women, ignoring the reality that the "nurturing" sex could act cruelly and abuse power just like men. Carol Tavris, in 1992's *The Mismeasure of Woman: Why Women Are Not the Better Sex, the Inferior Sex, or the Opposite Sex*, outlined the work of researchers who have found no evidence of substantial differences in the moral reasoning of women and men. Yet, as Howard University psychologist Martha Mednick noted in the *Signs* forum, "the belief in a 'different voice' persists; it appears to be a symbol for a cluster of widely held social beliefs that argue for women's difference, for reasons that are quite independent of scientific merit."[21]

Despite such vocal criticism of difference theory, proponents of single-sex education were drawn to the implications of new research on female difference. In the world of girls' schools—struggling to define their place against the tide of coeducation—Gilligan became something of a star and a prophet. At a 1983 meeting (just a year after the publication of *In a Different Voice*), the National Association of Principals of Schools for Girls featured Carol Gilligan as its speaker. The Bryn Mawr School's Headmistress Barbara Chase, who attended the meeting, in turn discussed the implications of Gilligan's work for girls' education with the Bryn Mawr School board.[22]

Gilligan's work and the research it sparked provided a new paradigm by which girls' schools could define their mission. Girls' schools began to draw liberally on theories of female difference (or, at least, select parts of them) as powerful justification for their important role in the lives of girls in particular and in the modern educational landscape in general. From the perspective of difference theory, girls' schools could be seen as potentially important preserves of female difference—institutions that, in the absence of males, could nurture the unique voices of their female students instead of the "male" voices upheld as the standard in coeducational schools. Institutions that longed to maintain their traditional single-sex status in what had become an increasingly unreceptive environment embraced the new paradigm enthusiastically.

Certainly, this proved to be the case at Bryn Mawr. During the 1970s, the school had made some adjustments precipitated by the women's movement. Bryn Mawr alumnae instituted "career days" in the late 1970s. In 1977, the school announced its intention to operate a preschool targeted at working mothers: "The Bryn Mawr School which has always provided a rigorous academic program for girls of Baltimore, with the implicit assumption that they would *use* this education, today seeks to help women combine careers and responsible parenthood through the establishment of an early childhood center known as the Little School." In another effort to meet the needs of modern women, Bryn Mawr established financial planning symposia that advised women on money management.[23]

When interviewed in 1980, incoming Headmistress Barbara Landis Chase asserted her commitment to increasing the school's diversity and encouraging community involvement—both goals embraced by previous administrations. But Chase also emphasized helping girls understand the choice of combining a career and a family, as she herself did. "We have to impress girls with the possibility of that choice," remarked Chase. "I see myself as a role model for that point of view."[24] Under Chase's leadership and in response to emerging national debates, the Bryn Mawr School would evidence a renewed self-consciousness about exactly what it meant to be a school for girls only. More than it had since its founding decades, Bryn Mawr would revisit the central issue of the relationships between gender and education and the status of women in society far beyond the classroom.

According to Chase, "gender in education" was one of the major "areas of concern and challenge" the school faced in the future.[25] Bryn Mawr's headmistress was encouraging the school to revitalize itself, partially by harkening to the school's past as a place devoted to exceptional academic rigor and female achievement and, simultaneously (and some might say paradoxically, given the founders' sentiments), by encouraging an exploration of difference theory. As Chase, a respected and well-loved figure at Bryn Mawr and in the community beyond, urged the school to explore the implications of its single-sex status in a new light, subtle changes in the school's emphasis and self–image would become evident. The Bryn Mawr School was shedding lingering remnants of the country-day philosophy as it embraced theories of female difference. This new paradigm, along with that of multiculturalism, would come to serve as its guiding educational models.

Bryn Mawr began to advertise itself as uniquely suited to addressing the needs of adolescent girls. New emphasis on helping girls in what it called the "confidence-crumbling" middle school years appeared in school literature throughout the 1980s and 1990s. According to Chase, "It's critical to provide young women with experiences that will lead them toward a growing sense of identity and confidence."[26] Bryn Mawr and Chase referred directly to Carol Gilligan's theories. As an article in Bryn Mawr's magazine explained it, Gilligan "concluded that age 11 'is the point in a woman's life at which she has the most self-esteem and the surest knowledge of herself and the rest of the world.'" As girls develop, "this self-confidence and clarity begin to seem so out of sync with what society says about girls that they become adrift in a sea of doubt ... Research suggests that young women have a more difficult time holding on to self-esteem, as society tries to influence the way they look, think and behave." Gilligan's research, the article concluded, "tends to support the desirability of girls-only schools."[27] Bryn Mawr thus defined itself as a place with a special ability to address girls' critical problems.

This emphasis, of course, was new. In the early 1960s, Bryn Mawr had considered merging its middle grades with those of Gilman—with no concerns about the potentially negative effects of coeducation on girls' psychological development.[28] Both schools were in need of new facilities, and the Bryn Mawr board appointed a committee to consider combining Bryn Mawr girls and Gilman boys in grades four through eight. Headmistress Van Bibber had opposed the proposal, arguing that girls and boys developed at different stages and thus held each other back in their schoolwork. By the 1980s, however, Bryn Mawr had clearly redefined its special mission to adolescent girls.

The Bryn Mawr School responded to the emerging discourse on difference in concert with other girls' schools that had survived the downturn in single-sex education in the 1960s, 1970s, and early 1980s. In the late 1980s, a group of girls' boarding schools, worried about their declining enrollments, pooled their resources to hire an educational consultant to conduct a marketing research project. By the early 1990s, girls' day schools were also joining together to conduct their own surveys. The schools' efforts coincided with the growth of research on feminine difference and the potential advantages of single-sex education for girls and women, and the schools hoped to capitalize on those academic findings. In November 1991, fifty-six girls' boarding and day schools formed the National Coalition of Girls' Schools (NCGS), designed as an advocacy group to promote and publicize single-sex education for girls. NCGS's mission was to market girls' schools and increase interest in and enrollment at member institutions.[29]

In the early 1990s NCGS described itself as "an organization of seventy-five girls' boarding and day, private and public schools from across the United States with affiliates in Canada and Australia." "While differing in history, tradition, location, academic rigor, extracurriculars, religious affiliation, size, and philosophy," NCGS explained, "coalition members share a commitment to the values and advantages of all-girls schools." To explore, explain, and promote those advantages, NCGS (again in its own words) "collected and conducted research on

gender issues; surveyed member school alumnae, parents, and prospective families; sponsored national forums for leading girls' and women's groups; gathered
comparative institutional data."[30] By 1997, NCGS had eighty-eight member
schools and reported that its schools' enrollments in 1997 were up 11.6 percent
since 1991. The Bryn Mawr School is one of NCGS's largest members.

Allusions to Gilligan's "different voice" and "women's ways of knowing" proliferated in NCGS promotional and recruiting literature. NCGS advertised that
"recent research has revealed that the way girls learn, the way they act and interact, is different from boys" and that "girls' schools offer girls the opportunity
to learn *their* way, with courses and teaching strategies specifically designed for
how girls learn best." NCGS quoted Gilligan on the importance of preserving
the female voice: "Girls must … hold on to their own ways of hearing and seeing." Experts such as sociologist David Riesman contributed arguments as to the
potential benefits of girls' schools for all schools and both their male and female
students: "Girls' schools provide an environment that not only is good in and of
itself, but that in its redefinition of competitiveness and collaboration, of autonomy and connectedness, presents a model that other schools do well to emulate." The headmistress of a girls' school reported her experiences at a single-sex
institution: "When the student body is female and more than half the teachers
are women, there is an unspoken validation of female norms and their consequences."[31]

NCGS literature enthusiastically promoted the advantages of single-sex
education for girls. In doing so, the coalition called not only on Gilligan-style
difference arguments but also on several related theories and research findings—or, at least, generalized interpretations of them. Together they composed
a mosaic portrait of why all-girls' schools might provide the best environment
in which to educate girls. The resulting hybrid arguments—a mix-and-match of
various theories—tend to vary according to the setting, audience, and purpose
of the moment. Sometimes they are inconsistent; other times, they overlap and
interconnect. But they have proven remarkably useful to girls' schools in defining themselves for the modern world.

The New Dialogue: Self-esteem, Science, Achievement, and Success

In the early 1990s, the American Association of University Women
(AAUW)—respected for its advocacy, research, and financial support of

women's endeavors in higher education and society—entered the debate. Established as the Association of Collegiate Alumna (ACA) in 1882, the organization had published its first report on women and education in 1885 as a refutation of the claims by Edward Clarke that higher education was detrimental to women's health. In the early 1900s, M. Carey Thomas had served as the chair of the ACA Publications Committee and had spoken at several ACA conventions. A century later, the AAUW Educational Foundation commissioned a study on girls' education to be researched by the Wellesley College Center for Research on Women (a division of a women's college facing similar pressures to redefine its mission and assert its own relevance as a single-sex institution).[32]

Carol Gilligan's work had painted with broad strokes a picture of the female "different voice"; the 1992 *How Schools Shortchance Girls—the AAUW Report: A Study of Major Findings on Girls and Education* outlined what it called "a problem of national proportion and consequence." It alleged that the American educational system routinely and systematically discriminates against girls. According to AAUW Educational Foundation President Alice Ann Leidel, there is "disturbing evidence that girls are not receiving the same quality, or even quantity, of education as their brothers." The AAUW charged that, although girls and boys entered school "roughly equal in measured ability" (girls, in fact, ahead of boys in some areas), girls soon fell behind boys "in key areas such as higher-level mathematics and measures of self-esteem." To make matters worse, public debate—"rather than acknowledging and exploring the links among sex, gender, and academic performance"—"ignores them."[33]

The AAUW and Wellesley College Center for Research on Women were not alone in making these claims. Myra and David Sadker's widely publicized 1994 *Failing at Fairness: How Our Schools Cheat Girls* contributed to the popularization of what it described as the persistent if largely unobserved "educational sexism" in American schools. Like the AAUW, the Sadkers portrayed girls as "second-class educational citizens." They condemned the patterns of coeducation, where girls suffer from "uneven distribution of teacher time, energy, attention, and talent," as well as "a curriculum of sexist school lessons." Such sexism in schools, whether conscious or not, precipitates "loss of self-esteem, decline in achievement, and elimination of career options" for girls.[34]

Coeducation was accused of causing undue suffering among girls on several fronts. The AAUW report based many of its claims on the notion that young girls rapidly lose their self-confidence as they approach adolescence—the same argument beginning to appear in Bryn Mawr literature by the early 1990s. The report relied on studies that included the comments of Carol Gilligan (along with Lyn Mikel Brown and Annie Rogers) on how the "striking capacities for self-confidence" and "courage and resistance to harmful norms of feminine behavior" in very young girls give way to the "more tentative and conflicted" voices of female adolescence. It viewed loss of self-esteem not as a problem of adolescence in general but of *female* adolescence in particular. "Moving from 'young girl' to 'young woman' involves meeting unique demands in a culture that both idealizes and exploits the sexuality of young women while assigning them roles that are clearly less valued than male roles." Moreover, girls who mature physically earlier than their male counterparts suffer from painful awkwardness, at best, and severe eating problems and depression, at worst. As the confidence of earliest childhood dissolves into self-doubt and uncertainty, girls are vulnerable to "declining self–esteem, negative body image, and depression." As a result of such suffering, girls become passive followers in schools, while boys are active leaders and "doers"—both in the classroom and in extracurricular activities. Often unknowingly, teachers, including female ones, perpetuate these patterns.[35]

The AAUW report asserted that peer pressure, low teacher expectations, and a scarcity of female role models in traditionally male fields result in the "gender tracking" of girls into the arts and humanities. These factors, combined with the prevalence of "male" teaching methods—which are geared toward the way boys, rather than girls, learn—cause girls to lag behind boys academically and professionally, especially in the fields of mathematics and the sciences. Contemporary studies popularized the phenomenon known as the "gender gap" between male and female performance, particularly in math and science. The NCGS, for example, argued that SAT and ACT scores reveal the "gender gap." The AAUW report was somewhat more cautious, acknowledging that math test scores have been "found to underpredict women's achievement." The AAUW report did, however, emphasize that "gender differences in science achievement are not decreasing and may be increasing" (although admitting that girls seemed to be closing the gap in mathematics and that achievement levels of females and males may vary in different racial and ethnic groups). And, continued the AAUW, "more discouraging still, even girls who take the same mathematics and science courses as boys and perform equally well on tests are much less apt to pursue scientific or technological careers than are their male classmates."[36]

Even the U.S. Department of Education entered the dialogue. In a 1992 report that NCGS frequently cited, the department registered its concern:

The continuing under-representation of women in mathematics-related and scientific careers has led many earlier proponents of gender-neutrality to consider rethinking how US society educates women and encourages their pursuit in such careers ... We conclude there is empirical support for the view that single-sex schools may accrue positive outcomes particularly for young women.[37]

This endorsement from the U.S. government validated the popular new theories.

Girls' schools and the NCGS touted these studies and reports that highlighted what they, too, believed were the disadvantages of coeducation and the unique advantages their students enjoyed. According to the NCGS in pamphlets with titles such as "What Every Girl Needs to Know," "Schools have been short-changing girls all across America. The messages in newspapers, on TV, in Doonesbury cartoons, and even from Barbie herself can be discouraging for girls." Coeducational schools (which mirror, it is assumed, the patterns of the larger society)—in which girls receive "less attention from teachers," "fewer chances to participate in class discussions," "lower teacher expectations," "little encouragement in areas like math and science," "inadequate sports offerings and facilities," "the absence of female perspectives," "limited access to leadership positions," and "too few teachers who really understand the ways girls learn"— were to blame. Girls also suffer from a "chilly classroom climate" and "subtle signs of second-class citizenship," retarding both their intellectual and psychological development. "Unlike their male counterparts, [girls] tend to lose rather than gain in confidence, have diminished educational aspirations ... as they progress through their school years. All too often they are listeners rather than doers."[38]

In contrast, NCGS literature painted a glowing picture of all-girls schools where girls "are always at center stage." In the absence of boys—and, thus, the pressure to defer to them and their male norms—girls hold on to their self-esteem. They become more active participants in their education—nurtured and supported by their teachers as rarely happens in coeducational classrooms— and they develop confidence and leadership skills. According to NCGS, "the top scholars, the team captains, the yearbook editors, the leads in the school play—they're all girls. Girls are the ones with their hands up, using the microphone, seeking the teacher's attention, being heard." As a result of these single-sex educational experiences, girls' school "graduates are confident learners, critical thinkers and self-starters."[39]

NCGS emphasized how the students in girls' schools did not follow national trends. Pamphlets advertised that "close to 100% of girls' school students take four years of math." Quoting a *Boston Globe* article, NCGS argued that, "compared to their counterparts at other schools, girls in all-girls schools take math and science courses at double the national average, do well in physics, and, according to a study by Hunter College, outperform girls in coed schools on the Advanced Placement calculus exam."[40] Moreover, girls' schools encouraged excellence by employing "teaching strategies that make learning and achieving in math and science the standard expectation." NCGS claimed that "graduates of girls' schools pursue careers in math, science, and technology four times more often than their peers from other schools."[41]

The modern Bryn Mawr School epitomizes the integration of theories arguing for the value of girls' schools into school dialogue and marketing. Bryn Mawr's 1995 viewbook—designed to recruit prospective students and their families—illustrates how girls' schools incorporate a hybrid of theories about the advantages of single-sex institutions into their sense of mission and identity. In contrast to earlier catalogues—often virtually silent on what made Bryn Mawr as a girls' school unique—the modern school stresses its commitment to meeting girls' special needs. "Using research on how girls learn and develop, Bryn Mawr creates opportunities that build and strengthen self-confidence." Bryn Mawr promotes its nurturing environment, "an atmosphere of encouragement and support in the classroom." As a result, the viewbook argues, "young women feel comfortable asking questions and contributing answers. They do not hesitate to voice their opinions on a wide range of topics and issues." Bryn Mawr also publicizes the fact that its students routinely take four years of math and science in secondary school and participate widely in sports and extracurricular activities.[42]

Girls' schools emphasized their special ability to encourage girls to achieve in traditionally male subjects. NCGS sponsored symposia on "Math and Science for Girls" and "Girls and the Physical Sciences." The Bryn Mawr School offered lectures and workshops on the phenomenon of "math anxiety." Reflecting both a sincere desire to increase girls' achievement and the pragmatic realization of the strategic value of realigning their priorities, the Bryn Mawr School pledged to strengthen its math and science programs in the 1980s. "As a girls' school, Bryn Mawr has a special commitment to addressing the phenomenon of 'math anxiety'"—that is, the "tendency among girls to avoid mathematics," the school claimed. Because it offered "special encouragement and nurturing in mathematics ... there is perhaps no better setting for this process than an all-girls' school like Bryn Mawr, which couples a century-long concern for the advancement of women with a cadre of math teachers who are sensitive to this special problem."[43]

Recollecting its own historic mission, the Bryn Mawr School cited recent works that found that "the great majority of women achievers in nontraditional fields for women have at some stage in their lives, either high school or college, attended a single-sex institution." Bryn Mawr encouraged these perceptions, initiating new "mentoring" programs designed to introduce students to women working in technical fields, as well as offering summer computer and science programs for underprivileged girls. The school emphasized that the "Summertech" programs were "designed especially for girls": "Bryn Mawr has always been a place in which girls are encouraged to stretch and grow even in fields that have not been associated with women." Summertech also sought to foster self-esteem in adolescent girls, as well as expand the school's community outreach.[44]

The message that students at girls' schools performed better in mathematics and science was becoming more and more overt in Bryn Mawr School literature as the school advertised this advantage to prospective students and their families. The cover of a 1980–81 Bryn Mawr marketing and informational brochure featured a girl absorbed in a science experiment, and Bryn Mawr's Middle School highlighted its science requirements for girls in every grade. Educators in girls' schools believed that they could help girls overcome the "gender gap" in math and science achievement—and that seemed compelling and good business sense. To families concerned about their daughters' future academic and professional achievements, the promise of success in subjects that could lead to lucrative employment (much higher paying than traditional feminine careers in teaching, nursing, or social work) in the fields of science, engineering, and technology was powerful endorsement for the value of single-sex education for girls.

Debates about girls' achievements (or lack thereof) in mathematics and the sciences are an area where the concerns of the modern Bryn Mawr School and the early school coincide. Just as the school's founders rejected traditionally "feminine" education in favor of "male" models that emphasized classical languages and laboratory sciences, today's Bryn Mawr defines high achievement in mathematics and the sciences as a key component of its curriculum. During Bryn Mawr's country-day years, in contrast, the school often emphasized the humanities rather than mathematics or sciences. In the 1950s, when the College Board began offering separate achievement examinations in the humanities, social studies, and natural sciences, Bryn Mawr noted that most of its students would not take the science examination because adequate preparation would come at the expense of language studies. Similarly, Bryn Mawr offered Advanced Placement courses and examinations for students to earn college credits in French, English, and history—but not in mathematics or any of the sciences. Not until the late 1950s did one Bryn Mawr student take an Advanced Placement examination in mathematics "purely as an experiment." As late as the 1960s—with the school's science laboratories desperately in need of improvement—Bryn Mawr's Headmistress Diane Howell, while joking that "Bryn Mawr may yet produce an astro-physicist!" resorted to the argument that science was good for girls because "a girl may not become an astro-physicist herself, but she may very well become the wife or mother of one." Howell also noted that "it is hardly necessary to say that a knowledge of science is essential for intelligent citizenship in the future." As voters, women "will increasingly be called on to make political decisions influenced by scientific developments."[45]

In contrast, modern girls' schools touted their success in encouraging students to explore and expand their future career options. But they cited statistics on their graduates' successes without comparative data on the achievements and expectations of girls at coeducational schools with similar academic standards and without reference to the socioeconomic, racial, or ethnic background of students, making it difficult to evaluate their claims. NCGS advertised that girls' school graduates "demonstrate higher educational aspirations, spend more time on homework, and are more likely to achieve later in their careers" than their counterparts at coeducational schools. At girls' schools, moreover, "98% of the seniors expect to have full-time careers and four out of five say they will attend graduate school." NCGS and member girls' schools proudly pointed to the achievements of their alumnae—which they claimed were significantly higher than those of women in the country at large. "Close to three-quarters of alumnae in one survey report working full or part-time; 77% of these women are professionals or hold executive positions in business and believe that single-sex schooling helped prepare them for balancing their professional and personal lives." Again, "almost 80% of the recent alumnae surveyed cite their single-sex school experience as pivotal in preparing them for productive personal and professional lives."[46]

Surely M. Carey Thomas would have been pleased. When she and her compatriots founded the Bryn Mawr School, they did so with the explicit desire to increase women's participation in the professions. Believing that, as Thomas remarked in reference to Bryn Mawr College, "Our failures only marry," the founders had envisioned their model school as enabling its graduates to move beyond the constraints of traditional female domesticity to become active participants in the public sphere.[47] Although Bryn Mawr had downplayed this component of its legacy in its country-day years, as it adapted to the more traditional expectations of its constituency, the modern Bryn Mawr School felt no reticence in once again emphasizing its commitment to preparing young women for the contemporary workplace—and not just in traditionally "female" areas.

The Bryn Mawr School's renewed commitment to career education coincided with changing attitudes toward and real increases in the numbers of women working outside the home—and particularly the visibility of professional women. By the 1980s, more and more Bryn Mawr School families expected that their daughters would pursue careers and that they would continue them after they married. Certainly, young women enjoyed more opportunities. In 1972, Congress's Higher Education Act included Title IX, a provision that "no person in the United States shall, on the basis of sex, be excluded from participation in, be denied the benefits of, or be subjected to discrimination under any education program or activity receiving federal assistance." In the wake of Title IX and the modern women's movement, the numbers of women in professional schools rose dramatically. In 1970, women were less than 9 percent of all medical school graduates, but that proportion rose to 23 percent by 1979 and to close to 50 percent by the end of the 1990s. Similarly, the percentage of female law students rose from 8 percent in 1970 to 31 percent by the end of the decade and had increased to almost 50 percent by the end of the 1990s. Although women's participation in fields such as engineering and the sciences and their representation in the higher levels of their professions and in corporate America continued to lag behind men's, the rising expectations of young women for careers were great.[48]

For the first time in the 1980s, the Bryn Mawr School itself was led by a headmistress who was combining her career with marriage and a family. Barbara Chase was the first in the Bryn Mawr School's long line of headmistresses to be married and have children (her two daughters attended the Bryn Mawr School while she was headmistress). A married headmistress—and particularly one whose husband quit his job to move to Baltimore with her—was enough of a novelty in 1980 that it was a topic of discussion in Baltimore and in the Bryn

Mawr School community. One newspaper article introducing the new head-mistress and her plans for the school titled its discussion, "She Got a Better Job: Family Moved for Bryn Mawr Headmistress's Career." Another article noted that, "indeed, David Chase's support of his wife is a bit unusual even in this age of the Equal Rights Amendment and women's liberation," and a prominent Bryn Mawr School leader was quoted as remarking that Chase "has the backing of a husband, which can make a real difference in this situation." "I believe—ob-viously—it's possible for a woman to combine having a career with having a fam-ily," Chase responded.[49]

Just as Chase mirrored changing attitudes toward women and work, so did the institution she headed. Once the Bryn Mawr School had accepted that only a few of its more exceptional graduates would pursue careers, but now the school increasingly came to view career preparation as the norm. Bryn Mawr's new perspective reflected the changed aspirations of students and families. A century ago, many Baltimore parents had questioned the practicality—even propriety—of a Bryn Mawr School education that seemed more suited to prepa-ration for "masculine" careers than the "feminine" pursuits to which they as-sumed their daughters should aspire. Even as late as the 1960s, Bryn Mawr sometimes still justified the education of girls in terms of making them better wives and mothers. But modern families believed their daughters would work outside the home, and they wanted to provide them with all possible advantages. Bryn Mawr School literature emphasized that, "since 90% of girls now in school will probably work for a living at some stage of their lives," entering college and the workplace "with the strong educational background, self-confidence, and sense of responsibility that a school like Bryn Mawr can provide" was increas-ingly important. The school marketed itself to families who wanted to invest in their daughters' futures.[50]

With the help of the media and NCGS, girls' schools were successfully spreading the word about recent research on single-sex education and their own successes. Distinct changes in the public perception of all-female institutions re-sulted. A 1994 *Newsweek* article explained that "single-sex education has made a comeback and even become E.C.—educationally correct." While "sisterhood," "feminism," and single-sex institutions had been "out" as recently as the early 1980s, women's colleges and girls' schools—"far from the days of white-gloved socials and busloads of prospective hubbies on the weekends"—have made a comeback. "Young women are flocking to women's colleges and girls' schools because they are single sex." According to a 1994 *New York Times* article, "The women's coalition appeals to what it says is a growing awareness that the opportunities for girls are better in single-sex settings." The same year, the *New York Times* confirmed the trend: "Women's colleges and girls' schools are seeing a resurgence in applications unprecedented in the last 20 years, even as applications to private, coed institutions have remained stagnant." In the early 1990s, NCGS reported that two-thirds of their schools had seen applications increase by 37 percent. And in 1995, NCGS reported that "member schools have enjoyed an 8.1 percent increase in enrollment since 1991." Increases in the Bryn Mawr School's enrollment paralleled—even surpassed—those national trends. In 1980, Bryn Mawr enrolled 542 students; by 1993, it had 757 students in grades K–12.[51]

As the popularity of girls' schools soared, so did alumnae interest in and financial contributions to their schools. According to NCGS, "In a recent sampling of member schools, 92% reported an increase in giving among their alumnae during 1994." Financial instability had always plagued the Bryn Mawr School. Despite repeated efforts though the decades, the school had no significant endowment until recent decades. During the 1980s and early 1990s, however, Bryn Mawr's endowment rose from one million to seven million dollars. By the late 1990s, the endowment stood at around sixteen million dollars. At the same time, the school launched an extensive building campaign, making needed improvements to its campus. Yet the Bryn Mawr School's endowment—mirroring its often troubled financial past—still lagged behind that of comparable schools, both single sex and coeducational. In 2000, the Bryn Mawr School reported an endowment of approximately $17.5 million; in contrast, the neighboring Roland Park Country School for girls had an endowment of around $42.2 million, and the Gilman School for boys has an endowment of more than $47.2 million.[52]

Recent successes in enrollment and fund-raising have correlated with proclamations from groups such as the NCGS about the superiority of single-sex education for girls. The Bryn Mawr School linked the "dramatic increase in alumnae donations" to "recent reports showing that girls in single-gender schools have higher self-esteem and achieve more than girls in coeducational schools." A 1994 Bryn Mawr publication suggested that "alumnae philanthropy" was perhaps "a form of empowerment of the institutions that have made a difference in their lives." Seemingly, the modern conversation on the advantages of girls' schools was not only prompting more parents to consider single-sex education for their daughters but also encouraging alumnae to reevaluate their experiences at all-female institutions.[53]

In 1985, the Bryn Mawr School celebrated its one hundredth anniversary. Symbolizing its commitment to exploring issues of gender and education—particularly girls' and single-sex education—the Bryn Mawr School chose to highlight this milestone by sponsoring a conference on "The Education of Girls: An Agenda for the Future." As the school proclaimed, "In celebration of its Centennial year and its pioneering role in the education of girls, The Bryn Mawr School invites public and private school educators to attend a one-day conference with leading scholars and researchers who will address critical areas of concern in girls education." Asserting its leadership in the modern movement, Bryn Mawr brought together scholars to explore the now familiar issues ranging from girls' different development to math anxiety. As Headmistress Chase asserted in her lecture at the Centennial Conference, "There are tremendous advantages in learning and leadership for girls in their own environment." Reflecting the new sense of mission the Bryn Mawr School had gained from recent research on female difference and the advantages of all-girls education, she asserted that "no matter what the state of research on gender, we feel affirmed in our status as a single sex institution."[54]

Critics

According to some admirers, statistics proved the success of girls' schools. But did they make the case for the superiority of single-sex education? Not everyone thought so. Some skeptics wondered whether the impressive achievements of girls' school graduates—in mathematics and the sciences, graduate and professional education, leadership, and careers—were solely attributable to the absence of boys in their schools. Was gender composition the only—or even the most important—factor responsible for such notable successes? How many of those student achievements could be directly attributed to the single-sex factor, and how many of them were, in fact, the result of the privileged position of private schools and their constituencies? In other words, do girls at private girls' schools achieve at higher rates than girls in coeducational schools because their schools are single-sex or because they come from families with high academic expectations and attend private schools with selective admissions policies and high academic standards? Was it really fair for NCGS and its member schools to compare the achievements of their private school students and alumnae to those of the general population? Comparing the achievements of girls at all-girls schools with girls at equally prestigious, competitive, and affluent coeducational private schools (or even public high schools with students from similar socioeconomic backgrounds) would seem more fair.

At Bryn Mawr, how much of the school's growth in recent decades could be directly linked to its single-sex factor and how much could be attributed to the rising popularity of private schools in general is less than clear. As worries about the perceived declining quality of public education consumed parents, quality private schools have enjoyed a receptive marketplace. Girls' schools that had successfully weathered the trends to coeducation of the 1960s and 1970s would, by the 1980s, find themselves in an environment receptive to all kinds of private education. Strong academic curriculum, successful college placement, broad extracurricular programs, and emphasis on achievement both in and outside the classroom, as well as a safe and supportive environment, are among parents' most critical criteria in selecting schools for both their daughters and their sons. Indeed, some evidence suggests that the "single-sex" factor may not be the primary appeal of all-girls schools and may even be a source of concern for some families.

NCGS emphasizes to prospective families that girls' schools offer girls "the best of both worlds"—that they are in no way "anti-male" and allow girls plenty of time to interact with the opposite sex. A survey commissioned by the Bryn Mawr School in the late 1980s found that, although families appreciated some advantages of the school being for girls only, they did not chose to send their daughters to Bryn Mawr *because* it was a girls' school. To the contrary, parents claimed that they selected Bryn Mawr because of its overall academic reputation rather than its all-girls status. Additionally, parents reported that they wanted Bryn Mawr to strengthen its program of "coordination" in both academics and extracurricular activities with the Gilman School. Families wanted their daughters—especially in the upper grades—to spend more time interacting with boys. The consultants who conducted the marketing study for Bryn Mawr urged the school to promote itself as offering the "best of both worlds," and they stressed the importance of Bryn Mawr strengthening its relationship with Gilman. If Bryn Mawr backed away from coordination, they warned, families would go to other schools—especially to the neighboring Roland Park Country School, which also coordinated classes with Gilman.[55]

This strong support for "coordination" stemmed from the acknowledgment by both families and girls' schools themselves that the overwhelming majority of girls' school students will choose coeducational colleges. An appreciation of single-sex education at the elementary or secondary school level does not necessarily translate into support for single-sex higher education. Indeed, many girls' school constituents view the segregation of male and female college-aged students as unnatural and limiting both academically and socially for young women and men. Some families who like single-sex education at the precollegiate level express reservations about women's colleges, which they perceive as too "feminist," anti-male, or lesbian. Girls' schools may be partners with women's colleges in defining the value of single-sex education up to a point, but girls' schools—which need to attract families who prefer coeducational higher education—are careful to draw distinctions between their missions. Girls' schools balance their embrace of single-sex education with support of coeducation, too.

While girls' schools carefully negotiated their position, some critics attacked the new dialogue that had proved so helpful to them in defining their relevance for the modern world. Carol Gilligan's theories had undergone much scrutiny, and the AAUW's report on the hazards of coeducation for girls would endure the same. In 1994's *Who Stole Feminism? How Women Have Betrayed Women*, Christina Hoff Sommers challenged the conclusions of the AAUW report and the motives of its authors. Sommers—a self-defined "equity" feminist in contrast to "difference" feminists—accused the report's authors of poor research techniques and misleading assertions constructed to support their political agenda. Relying on the work of other researchers, Sommers questioned whether girls really suffer from lower self-esteem than boys. Some research indicated that higher dropout and suicide rates among boys suggest that boys suffer disproportionately from low self-esteem. Furthermore, correlations between self-esteem (an ephemeral concept at best) and success in school were unclear. Studies might report that white girls had low confidence levels, yet they received among the best grades and had the highest college attendance rates of any group of students. On the other hand, African American girls reported higher self-esteem scores than either white girls or boys, yet theirs was among the lowest academic performance.[56]

Sommers also criticized reports on the alleged gender bias in coeducational classrooms and the gender gap in academic achievement. Attacking the motives and methods of researchers like Myra and David Sadker, she accused them of "seeing" only the evidence of discrimination for which they were looking. Even if teachers did call on boys more often than girls, she suggested, there was no clear evidence that girls have suffered as a result: "Girls are getting the better grades, they like school better, they drop out less, and more of them go to college."[57] Ultimately, Sommers concurred that the educational system has discriminated against women in the past. Nor did she deny that girls might still have some special needs that should be addressed. While she acknowledged some differences in math and science performance between boys and girls, however, she accused the AAUW and their sympathizers of exaggerating gender disparities in achievement and overlooking what she argued was the real "crisis"—namely, how poorly both American girls and boys perform in relation to their Asian, European, and Canadian peers. From Sommers's perspective, girls and women have made impressive gains in education and in American society in general, and the issue of gender bias in education is largely a false one that draws critical attention and funds away from more pressing problems preventing both girls and boys from receiving quality education.[58]

Sommers's attacks on the "gender feminists" were provocative and, not surprisingly, generated their own critics—particularly among the diverse supporters of "difference" feminism and theory in its various shapes. Her sharp criticisms made it easy for her opponents to dismiss her as hostile and adversarial. But the shifting stance of the AAUW—which had been a central player in popularizing the "difference" dialogue and its implications for female education—would present a new challenge to supporters of girls' schools. While the AAUW's 1995 report had strongly emphasized the disadvantages of coeducation, by 1998, the AAUW had publicly refuted many of its own earlier claims about the superiority of single-sex education.

The AAUW's 1998 report, *Separated by Sex: A Critical Look at Single-Sex Education for Girls*, asserted that "there is no evidence that single-sex education in general 'works' or is 'better' than coeducation." Based on a review of literature and papers presented at a 1997 AAUW forum, the report, while acknowledging that "single-sex educational programs produce positive results for some students in some settings," stressed that "good education" is not in general correlated with the gender composition of classes. Research on single-sex education—primarily on independent and parochial girls' schools—provided data too limited to warrant broad conclusions about the desirability of girls-only education. Furthermore, the AAUW acknowledged that, because single-sex educational programs come in many forms, they could, depending on the orientation of particular programs, foster as well as challenge stereotypes about women's place in society. Many of the AAUW's cautions about single-sex programs stem from applications of the "single-sex factor" in public education (subject to the dubious motives of policy makers) and within coeducational schools (and thus disruptive of the larger educational setting). The report concluded less with assertions about single-sex education than with calls for more research.[59]

The tenor of the debate had shifted. Certainly, the AAUW report did not detract from the achievements of particular girls' schools and their students. The report acknowledged the effectiveness of some single-sex programs, as well the preference for all-girls classes expressed by some girls and their families. But the AAUW had moved away from assertions of the victimization of girls in coeducational classrooms and polarized arguments about the merits of single-sex versus coeducational settings to acknowledgment of the need for more nuanced discussions about the relationship between gender and education. For girls' schools, this may signal a changed context in which to define their identities, one that encompasses a lesser—or at least more qualified—emphasis on female "difference" as a key to why some single-sex schools make such good places for girls to learn.

Today at the Bryn Mawr School, the future seems bright. The school is proud to be an institution devoted to girls' education. Students, families, teachers, and administrators seem happy to be at a school for girls, and they seem pleased with the balance between single-sex and coeducational status that coordination with a boys' and another girls' school has given them. In a society where issues of female equality and difference and questions about the nature of the relationships among women, men, education, work, and the family—the very debates that engaged the Bryn Mawr School founders in the 1880s—are still on the table, however, defining a role for single-sex schools for girls in the educational landscape of the twenty-first century will remain challenging. The Bryn Mawr School has been defining what, exactly, it means to be a school for girls for over a century, and the process will continue.

Conclusion

Much has changed over the decades at the Bryn Mawr School. When Edith Hamilton became Bryn Mawr's headmistress in 1896, Mary Garrett's city building housed sixty-four students. Today, the school educates almost eight hundred girls, from prekindergarten through twelfth grade. Through coordination with two other schools, Bryn Mawr Upper School students attend many classes with boys, both on their own campus and on neighboring campuses. Facilities on Bryn Mawr's bucolic twenty-six-acre campus have expanded significantly in recent decades, including new centers for drama and music and for science, new facilities for the Edith Hamilton Library, and a new Lower School, as well as upgraded computer and technology facilities. The school's endowment has risen to more than $17 million in 2000.[1]

The Bryn Mawr School's recent popularity and strength exist within the context of a society searching for a solution to what it perceives as the declining quality of public education. For many parents, that solution is found in private schools. The National Association of Independent Schools (NAIS), which represents approximately twelve hundred schools today (83% coeducational, 9% all-girls, and 8% all-boys), reports that enrollment in its schools is up 19.4 per-

cent over the last decade. The National Center for Education Statistics estimates that about 11.5 percent of the nation's children today attend private
schools, although proportions vary significantly in different regions.[2]

Across the country, applications to private schools are on the rise. Schools
and parents report a variety of factors—from the importance of smaller class size
and more individualized attention to the increasing competitiveness of college
admissions—as responsible for the increases. A Stanford University professor of
political science asserted that "the No. 1 consideration by far is [parents'] assessment of the performance of public schools and their assessment of whether
private school is better." Other observers note that parents see preparatory
schools as offering superior access to the nation's most prestigious colleges and
universities. Prominent preparatory schools boast their college placement
records (Bryn Mawr advertises its college admissions statistics prominently) and
are ranked accordingly. One former NAIS school head noted that the "almost
constant preparation for admission to one of about 20 or 25 American universities" constituted a "dark side" of elite private school culture.[3]

The popularity of independent schools has meant increasing competition for
places at those schools. According to the NAIS, 61 percent of those who applied
to independent schools in the late 1980s were accepted. In 1998–99, only 50
percent of applicants were admitted. At the most competitive NAIS schools,
percentages of applicants admitted are much lower. As one NAIS headmaster
noted, "It's like being in a seller's market."[4]

Tuition fees are on the rise, as well. According to the NAIS, the average tuition for private day schools for ninth grade is $14,735 for the 2001–2 school
year—up 31 percent since 1991. At the Bryn Mawr School, 2002 tuition was
$15,660 per year for kindergarten through fifth grades and $16,725 per year for
ninth through twelfth grades. Private schools attribute increases to a variety of
factors, including competition for teachers, the need to update technology and
physical facilities, and soaring financial aid costs. A NAIS spokesman acknowledged that "schools are totally worried about" the increased costs but that "there
is not enough support from outside sources to make the things that need to happen, such as increasing teacher pay, actually happen effectively without increasing tuition." While rising tuition costs have not affected the numbers of
applicants, some observers think they will threaten the efforts of the past two
decades to diversify private institutions. As costs rise, less financial aid may be
available for low-income students.[5]

Nonetheless, the NAIS pledges its commitment to increasing "choice in education," "affordability," and "access" to its member schools. Although close to 90 percent of the nation's children attend public schools—and access to private schools is, despite the efforts of many schools to diversify, subject to families' ability to pay substantial tuition fees—private schools view themselves as serving a purpose greater than the education of an elite segment of society. The NAIS articulates what it argues is a "public purpose" for private education. According to the NAIS, "Independent schools make up an extraordinary demonstration library of educational philosophies, pedagogies, and effective instructional strategies. As a result, these schools are uniquely positioned to make a powerful difference for our nation—not just the children they educate, but for all America's children."[6]

M. Carey Thomas and her fellow founders had hoped that their school would provide a model for the education of girls that could be emulated across the nation: according to Mary Garrett, the Bryn Mawr School might "prove the possibility of the existence of such schools and so be indirectly the means of the creation of similar ones in other places."[7] In many ways, the school's founding and survival foreshadowed and helped sustain the changing opportunities available to girls and women. The Bryn Mawr School is a working institution, with a history reflecting successes as well as flaws. Its history is suggestive of the shifting and interrelated ways that gender, schools, and society have operated in the past and continue to operate today.

The story of the Bryn Mawr School deserves recognition in the history of women and of education in American society not because it offers comprehensive explanations or solutions to ongoing struggles to educate young women, but because it encourages us to understand the texture of education through the decades of the late nineteenth and twentieth centuries. By demonstrating how one prominent girls' school has defined and redefined itself in relationship to the position of girls and women in society, the history of the Bryn Mawr School offers insight on modern educational debates and dilemmas. By exploring how debates about the nature of girls and women and the kinds of education they deserve have evolved over time—in response to the ideas and efforts of individuals, as well as to changes in the larger culture and society—the history of the Bryn Mawr School can help us refine our understandings of the kinds of education we want for girls—and for all children—today.

Notes

Preface

1. Rosamund Randall Beirne, *Let's Pick the Daisies: The History of the Bryn Mawr School, 1884–1967* (Baltimore: Bryn Mawr School, 1970).
2. Mike Bowler, "Bryn Mawr Closed Book on Career, Historian Says," *Baltimore Sun,* 2 Apr. 2002; Jennifer K. Ruark, "The History That May Never Be Read," *Chronicle of Higher Education,* 26 Apr. 2002; Mike Bowler, "Historians Sign on to Petition Bryn Mawr on Quashed Book," *Baltimore Sun,* 13 May 2002; "Girls School at Center of Book Flap," Associated Press wire story, 13 May 2002; "Practice What You Teach," *Baltimore Sun,* 15 May 2002; Mike Bowler, "Bryn Mawr to Allow Book on Its History: Board of Trustees Relents after Being Petitioned by Historians, Other Scholars," *Baltimore Sun,* 22 May 2002.

Introduction

Epigraph. M. Carey Thomas, "Education for Women and for Men," reprinted in Barbara M. Cross, *The Educated Woman in America,* Classics in Education no. 25 (New York: Teachers College Press, 1965), 147–48.
1. Helen Lefkowitz Horowitz, *Alma Mater: Design and Experience in the Women's Colleges from Their Nineteenth-Century Beginnings to the 1930s* (New York: Alfred A. Knopf, 1984), offers a rich comparison of the different founding visions of the Seven Sister colleges.

ONE: The Bryn Mawr Vision

1. "Republican motherhood" is analyzed in Linda K. Kerber, *Women of the Republic: Intellect and Ideology in Revolutionary America* (Chapel Hill: University of North Carolina Press, 1980).
2. Barbara Miller Solomon, *In the Company of Educated Women: A History of Women and Higher Education in America* (New Haven: Yale University Press, 1985), 15–16.
3. The female academy movement has been well studied. Solomon provides a concise summary of the female seminary movement (*In the Company of Educated Women,* 14–26). Thomas Woody, "The Expansion of the Seminary Movement," in *A History of Women's Education in the United States* (New York: Science Press, 1929), vol. 2, offers a more detailed survey of women's academies and their curricula. Willystine Goodsell, *Pioneers of Women's Education in the United States* (New York: Macmillan, 1931), reprints selected

writings of pioneers Emma Willard, Catharine Beecher, and Mary Lyon, outlining their criticisms of existing female academies and suggestions for their improvement. Also, Nancy F. Cott, *The Bonds of Womanhood: "Woman's Sphere" in New England, 1780–1835* (New Haven: Yale University Press, 1977), and Mary P. Ryan, *The Cradle of the Middle Class: The Family in Oneida County, New York, 1790–1865* (Cambridge: Cambridge University Press, 1981), discuss the emerging relationships among women's education, the separate spheres, and middle-class culture and status. Helen Lefkowitz Horowitz, *Alma Mater: Design and Experience in the Women's Colleges from their Nineteenth-Century Beginnings to the 1930s* (New York: Alfred A. Knopf, 1984), 11, points out that many female "academies" adapted the alternative term *seminary*, employed by institutions training ministers, to emphasize the seriousness of their mission to train teachers.

4. Solomon, *In the Company of Educated Women*, 18; Anne Firor Scott, "The Ever-Widening Circle: The Diffusion of Feminist Values from the Troy Seminary, 1822–1872," *History of Education Quarterly* 19 (1979): 16–17; Anne Firor Scott, "What, Then, Is the American: This New Woman?" *Journal of American History* 65 (Dec. 1978): 679–703. Kathryn Kish Sklar's biography *Catharine Beecher: A Study in Domesticity* (New Haven: Yale University Press, 1973) provides a detailed account of Beecher's role in the feminization of the teaching profession specifically and of her philosophy, career, and personal life more generally.

5. Horowitz, *Alma Mater*, ch. 1, esp. p. 11, presents a detailed analysis of Mary Lyon's vision and the system of education developed at Mt. Holyoke. Also see Kathryn Kish Sklar, "The Founding of Mount Holyoke College," in *Women of America: A History*, ed. Carol Ruth Berkin and Mary Beth Norton (Boston: Houghton Mifflin, 1979), 177–98.

6. Goodsell, *Pioneers of Women's Education*, 67, 76–79; Catharine Beecher, "An Address on Female Suffrage," given in Boston in 1870, reprinted in ibid., 189. The scholarly literature on nineteenth-century womanhood, domesticity, and the separate spheres is extensive. Seminal works include Barbara Welter, "The Cult of True Womanhood, 1820–1860," *American Quarterly* 18 (1966): 151–74; Nancy Cott, *The Bonds of Womanhood*; and Sklar, *Catharine Beecher*.

7. Christie Anne Farnham, *The Education of the Southern Belle: Higher Education and Student Socialization in the Anthebellum South* (New York: New York University Press, 1994), 28, 32, 186.

8. David Tyack and Elizabeth Hansot, *Learning Together: A History of Coeducation in American Public Schools* (New York: Russell Sage Foundation, 1992), 79, 128.

9. Ibid., 114, 136–37. On the ambiguity of the term *high school*, 121–22.

10. Ibid., 187, 164, 137.

11. Solomon, *In the Company of Educated Women*, 50–58.

12. Ibid., table on p. 44. In 1890, there were 1,082 institutions of higher education in the United States: 43% coeducational, 37% for men only, and 20% for women only. In 1910, 58% of the nation's 1,083 institutions were coeducational; 15% served women only. By 1930, 69% of the nation's 1,322 institutions were coeducational.

13. Horowitz's *Alma Mater* offers detailed histories of the foundings of the Seven Sister colleges, highlighting their similarities and differences. For a brief overview, see Solomon, *In the Company of Educated Women*, 47–49. On southern women's colleges, see Farnham, *Education of the Southern Belle*, 185–86. Although many female institutions called themselves "colleges," as late as 1917 the Association of Colleges and Secondary

Schools of the Southern States recognized only seven of those institutions (among them Sophie Newcomb and Baltimore's Goucher) as deserving the title "college."

14. Roberta Frankfort, *Collegiate Women: Domesticity and Career in Turn-of-the-Century America* (New York: New York University Press, 1977), table on p. 50. Even as late as 1904–8, 64% of Bryn Mawr College students had been educated at private schools, although notably the percentage of students trained at public high schools had risen to 22%.

15. Sherry Olson, *Baltimore: The Building of an American City* (Baltimore: Johns Hopkins University Press, 1980), 235; James B. Crooks, *Politics and Progress: The Rise of Urban Progressivism in Baltimore, 1895–1911* (Baton Rouge: Louisiana State University Press, 1968), ix. Also, see Crooks on political reform, 43; on city beautification and planning, 127–28; on improving social services, 155–56; and on the social standing of reformers, 197–98.

16. Marion E. Warren and Mame Warren, *Baltimore: When She Was What She Used to Be, 1850–1930* (Baltimore: Johns Hopkins University Press, 1983). This book of photographs depicts the establishment of Baltimore's intellectual and cultural institutions, including the Peabody Institute (with its library, music academy, art gallery, and endowed lecture series), Johns Hopkins University (1876), Enoch Pratt Free Library (1886), Walters Art Gallery (1909), and Baltimore Symphony Orchestra (with its first performance in 1916).

17. Anna Heubeck Knipp and Thaddeus P. Thomas, *The History of Goucher College* (Baltimore: Goucher College, 1938), 3, 27–28. Lilian Welsh is commenting on M. Carey Thomas's speech of 3 Dec. 1912, on the occasion of a college women's rally at Goucher (p. 201).

18. Helen Lefkowitz Horowitz, *The Power and Passion of M. Carey Thomas* (New York: Alfred A. Knopf, 1994). Horowitz's detailed biography is by far the best source of information on Thomas's life. For a discussion of Thomas's experiences at Johns Hopkins University, see 74–75.

19. Elizabeth Fee, Linda Shopes, and Linda Zeidman, eds., *The Baltimore Book: New Views of Local History* (Philadelphia: Temple University Press, 1991), 21.

20. Ibid., 27.

21. According to Horowitz, *Power and Passion*, 90–91, almost no descriptions of Mary Garrett exist, and Thomas seems to have been the only person ever to describe Garrett as appealing. For a description of Garrett's health problems, see 209–10. See 228–29 for discussion of Garrett's responsibilities in directing the new school.

22. Ibid., 92, 294. Rosamond Randall Beirne, *Let's Pick the Daisies: The History of the Bryn Mawr School, 1884–1967* (Baltimore: Bryn Mawr School, 1970), 2–4, also discusses the backgrounds of the five founders.

23. Horowitz, *Power and Passion*, 75–78, 89.

24. Ibid., 286–91. Carroll Smith Rosenberg's landmark "The Female World of Love and Ritual: Relations between Women in Nineteenth-Century America," *Signs: Journal of Women in Culture and Society* 1 (Autumn 1975): 1–29, provides a valuable perspective for interpreting intimate relationships between women on a continuum between pure heterosexuality and homosexuality.

25. For a discussion of the friend's involvement in the founding of the Johns Hopkins medical school, see Beatrice S. Levin, "Reaching for the Stars: Those Remarkable Johns

Hopkins Women," in *Women and Medicine* (Metuchen, N.J.: Scarecrow Press, 1980), 114–25.

26. M. Carey Thomas to Mary Garrett, 26 Apr. 1884, quoted in Horowitz, *Power and Passion*, 210.

27. Horowitz, *Power and Passion*, 288.

28. On separate-sex public schools, see Tyack and Hansot, *Learning Together*, 79; on Baltimore's private schools, see Allen Kerr Bond, *When the Hopkins Came to Baltimore* (Baltimore: Pegasus Press, 1927), 83; Doris Fielding Reid, *Edith Hamilton: An Intimate Portrait* (New York: W. W. Norton, 1967), 38.

29. Catalogue announcing the opening of the Bryn Mawr School (BMS) on 21 Sept. 1885, BMS Archives.

30. M. Carey Thomas to "Fellow Members of the Board and Dear Caroline and Helen," 2 Jan. 1928, box 2, BMS Archives; Mary Garrett to Mamie Gwinn, undated, Correspondence, BMS Archives.

31. Barbara J. Harris, *Beyond Her Sphere: Women and the Professions in American History* (Westport, Conn.: Greenwood Press, 1978), 101.

32. Ibid., tables on pp. 56 and 60; Solomon, *In the Company of Educated Women*, table 6 on p. 133.

33. Harris, *Beyond Her Sphere*, 56–60; Solomon, *In the Company of Educated Women*, 131–32; Julie Matthaei, *An Economic History of Women in America: Women's Work, the Sexual Division of Labor, and the Development of Capitalism* (New York: Schocken Books, 1982), table on p. 206. Solomon notes that, although law schools (becoming the primary avenue to law practice between 1870 and 1920) began to admit women—such as St. Louis University (1869), Michigan (1870), Yale (1886), Cornell (1887), and Stanford (1895)—law degrees did not keep states from excluding women from the bar. Most women who practiced law did so by working in their fathers' or husbands' firms or by using their training to further the cause of women (such as female lawyers Florence Kelley and Alice Paul).

34. For Gilman's quotation, see M. Carey Thomas, "A Brief Account of the Founding and Early Years of the Bryn Mawr School," *Bryn Mawrtyr*, 1931 BMS Yearbook, 84–88. Mrs. Ruskin McIntosh, transcript of speech from BMS's Seventy-fifth Anniversary Celebration, 4 Nov. 1960, reprinted in *Bryn Mawr School Bulletin* 17, no. 1 (1960–61): 6–7, in BMS Archives.

35. Marion Talbot to M. Carey Thomas, 12 Jan. 1885, Correspondence, BMS Archives. For a discussion of Marion Talbot, see Rosalind Rosenberg, *Beyond Separate Spheres: Intellectual Roots of Modern Feminism* (New Haven: Yale University Press, 1982), esp. 18–27.

36. Helen M. Barrett to Miss Rogers, 12 Jan. 1885, box 1, M. Carey Thomas Papers; Louisa Holman Richardson to BMS Committee, 22 Jan. 1885; Anna Minraher (unclear) to Julia Rogers, undated, box 1, M. Carey Thomas Papers; Louisa Richardson to BMS Committee, 2 June 1887, box 1, M. Carey Thomas Papers, all in BMS Archives.

37. Unreferenced newspaper clippings announcing BMS's 1885 opening, in box XI; Bessie King to M. Carey Thomas, Nov. 1892, in box 1, M. Carey Thomas Papers, both in BMS Archives; Beirne, *Let's Pick the Daisies*, 20.

38. M. Carey Thomas, quoted in International Federation of University Women, bulletin no. 1 (Report of the First Conference, July 1920), 56–57, cited in Tyack and Hansot, *Learning Together*, 117.

39. John D. Philbrick, "Coeducation of the Sexes," American Institute of Instruction *Lectures and Proceedings, 1880*, 122, 124, cited in Tyack and Hansot, *Learning Together*, 79.

40. BMS 1896 catalogue, BMS Archives.

41. First catalogue announcing the Bryn Mawr School's opening on 21 Sept. 1885, in BMS Archives.

42. Ibid.; article on M. Carey Thomas's address on BMS's aims and goals at its first commencement, *Baltimore Sun*, 9 June 1893, in BMS Archives.

43. *Baltimore Sun*, 9 June 1893; Millicent Carey McIntosh, unreferenced manuscript, probably an article or speech, box RG1, both in BMS Archives.

44. Mamie Gwinn to Mary Garrett, 18 Feb. 1895, Correspondence; Mary Garrett to "Dear Girls," 7 Dec. 1894, both in BMS Archives.

45. BMS 1885, 1886, 1891–92, and 1896 catalogues.

46. First catalogue announcing BMS's opening on 21 Sept. 1885.

47. *Bryn Mawrtyr*, 1931 Yearbook, 82.

48. Series of letters between Miss Abbot and the BMS Committee, Summer 1893, Correspondence, BMS Archives.

49. M. Carey Thomas to Editor of *Jewish Exponent*, 25 Nov. 1890, Correspondence 1889–1918; reprinted in *Baltimore American*, clipping in Correspondence, both in BMS Archives.

50. Unreferenced newspaper clippings in box XI, BMS Archives (one article dated 14 Jan. 1889); Mary Colvin to M. Carey Thomas, 1892, box 1, M. Carey Thomas papers; first catalogue announcing BMS's opening on 21 Sept. 1885; BMS 1896 catalogue.

51. Beirne, *Let's Pick the Daisies*, 11, 21–22.

52. Marion Talbot to M. Carey Thomas, 12 Jan. 1885, Correspondence 1885–89; Thomas to potential math teacher Mrs. Edgerton, 1885, BMS Archives; Beirne, *Let's Pick the Daisies*, 10, 22.

53. BMS 1900 catalogue.

54. Sklar outlines her interpretations of and cures for women's health problems in "Protective Customs, 1855," in *Catharine Beecher*.

55. Mary Colvin to M. Carey Thomas, 18 May 1890 or 1891 (unclear), Correspondence, BMS Archives.

56. Edward H. Clarke, *Sex in Education; or, a Fair Chance for the Girls* (1873), cited in Solomon, *In the Company of Educated Women*, 56, 53. For a much more detailed discussion of the emerging scientific literature and the influence of Charles Darwin, Herbert Spencer, and Edward Clarke, see Rosenberg, *Beyond Separate Spheres*, 5–12.

57. Rosenberg, *Beyond Separate Spheres*, xv; M. Carey Thomas, "Present Tendencies in Women's College and University Education," *Educational Review* 24 (1908): 68, quoted in Rosenberg, *Beyond Separate Spheres*, 12.

58. "Kirkus" to BMS Committee, 19 June 1885; Mary Colvin to M. Carey Thomas, 18 May 1890 or 1891 (unclear); Ellen Hyde to BMS Secretary Miss Andrews, 19 Oct. 1885, all in Correspondence, BMS Archives; Reid, *Edith Hamilton*, 39.

59. Beirne, *Let's Pick the Daisies*, 8–14; Horowitz, *Power and Passion*, 233.

60. Unreferenced clipping, 14 Jan. 1889, in box XI; Kate Campbell Hurd to M. Carey Thomas, 29 Apr. 1889; Hurd to Thomas, 2 June 1889, discussing lessons she is taking from Dr. Passee; Dudley Allen Sargent to Thomas, 17 May 1889, in which Sargent agrees to accept Hurd into his class; Hurd to Mary Garrett, 14 Nov. 1889; Hurd to Thomas, 16 Dec. 1889, all in Correspondence, BMS Archives.

61. A description of BMS's gymnasium facilities is included in an announcement for the 1889 opening of the new school building, box 6, BMS Archives. See also M. Carey Thomas to Kate Campbell Hurd, 2 Jan. 1890, and correspondence between Thomas and Dudley Allen Sargent, such as 4 Jan. 1890 and 31 Jan. 1890, Correspondence. Announcement for the 1889 opening of BMS's new school building, box 6, BMS Archives.

62. Horowitz, *Power and Passion*, 228–33, 252.

63. Beirne, *Let's Pick the Daisies*, 8–14; Horowitz, *Power and Passion*, 233.

64. Announcement for the 1889 opening of BMS's new school building, box 6, BMS Archives; Horowitz, *Alma Mater*, 119.

65. Miss Mary H. Cadwalader, unreferenced editorial by early BMS graduate in *Baltimore Evening Sun*, box RG1, BMS Archives.

66. Clipping from the *Critic*, 3 Dec. 1894, 398, BMS Archives. This article, describing a reception held for the Association of Colleges and Preparatory Schools of the Middle States and Maryland at BMS on 30 Nov. 1894, offers one of the most detailed descriptions of the BMS building.

67. Cadwalader, editorial in *Baltimore Evening Sun*.

68. Mary Marshall Morgan, *Bryn Mawr School Alumnae Association Bulletin* 1, no. 1 (Apr. 1941): 6–7, in BMS Archives. Morgan was a 1920 graduate of BMS.

69. Cadwalader, editorial in *Baltimore Evening Sun*.

70. E.g., Thomas protested in letters to BMS Headmistress Edith Hamilton that Bryn Mawr's longtime servant, Lee, was "sulky," "insolent," "neglectful," and dangerous. In contrast, Hamilton defended Lee as a "valuable" and loyal servant who deserved the good will of the school. Edith Hamilton to M. Carey Thomas, 29 May 1919, and Thomas to Edith Hamilton, labeled "STRICTLY CONFIDENTIAL," 22 June 1919, Correspondence, BMS Archives.

71. Horowitz, *Power and Passion*, 231–32.

72. Mary Colvin to M. Carey Thomas, undated, Correspondence; Thomas to Editor of *Jewish Exponent*, 25 Nov. 1890, BMS Archives. Thomas's letter of denial also appeared in the *Baltimore American*, a clipping of which is in Correspondence, BMS Archives.

73. In another incident reported in Horowitz's biography, Thomas refused to hire a teacher, who was a friend of BMS Headmistress Edith Hamilton, because she was Jewish.

74. [Unclear] to Mary Colvin, 1891, Correspondence, BMS Archives.

75. Essay by "ASH," *Book of Bryn Mawr School Themes of the Main School, 1893–1894*; French teacher Matilda de Maltehya Gouraszewska (surnames unclear) to "Madam," May 1885; Mary Augusta Scott to Julia Rogers, 3 Aug. 1889, Correspondence, all in BMS Archives.

76. Mary Garrett to "Girls," 23 Oct. 1894, box 2, M. Carey Thomas papers, BMS Archives.

77. M. Carey Thomas to Miss Bracket, 23 Jan. 1889, Correspondence; see box labeled "Background Checks"; Thomas to Edith Hamilton, 26 Sept. 1913, Correspondence, BMS Archives.

78. Thomas to Edith Hamilton, 3 Oct. 1907; Thomas to Hamilton, 26 Sept. 1913; Mary Colvin to Thomas, 6 Mar. 1893; Mamie Gwinn to Rosine Melle, 16 Mar. 1893; Melle to Gwinn, 17 Mar. 1893.

79. M. Carey Thomas to Miss Bracket, 23 Jan. 1889.

80. Unreferenced clipping from the *Kitchen Magazine*, Chicago, Apr. 1889, in BMS Archives.

T W O : Implementing the Vision

1. For a discussion of the personal relationships and conflicts among the five founders of the Bryn Mawr School (BMS), see Helen Lefkowitz Horowitz, *The Power and Passion of M. Carey Thomas* (New York: Alfred A. Knopf, 1994), 229–33, 283–85, 366–67, 369.
2. See ibid. for discussions of Thomas's and Garrett's activities.
3. See, e.g., Thomas's letter to Marion Talbot seeking recommendations for potential headmistresses: Marion Talbot to M. Carey Thomas, 12 Jan. 1885, Correspondence, BMS Archives.
4. Millicent Carey McIntosh, quoted in Doris Fielding Reid, *Edith Hamilton: An Intimate Portrait* (New York: W. W. Norton, 1967), 40.
5. In the BMS archives, boxes of correspondence between Thomas and Garrett and BMS's various secretaries (all but Buckingham), particularly the extensive correspondence with Headmistress Edith Hamilton, reveal the administrative history of the school. According to Rosamond Randall Beirne, *Let's Pick the Daisies: The History of the Bryn Mawr School, 1884–1967* (Baltimore: Bryn Mawr School, 1970), 20, BMS's first secretaries were Eleanor A. Andrews, Mary Noyes Colvin, Mary Buckingham, and Ida Wood. As just one of many examples of conflict between the board and the secretary over who was responsible for decisions at BMS, consider the conflicts between Headmistress Colvin and Thomas concerning the public scandal over BMS's admission of Jewish students, discussed in ch. 1.
6. "BMS Notes," 18 Jan. 1895, M. Carey Thomas Papers; unsigned memo (probably from M. Carey Thomas, since the writer refers to "Mamie and I"), 18 Jan. 1895, Correspondence, both in BMS Archives.
7. M. Carey Thomas described her philosophy (which she applied at Bryn Mawr College as well) of hiring inexperienced new teachers for low pay in a letter to Edith Hamilton, 2 Apr. 1914, Correspondence, BMS Archives.
8. Mamie Gwinn to Mary Garrett, 2 May 1895, Correspondence, BMS Archives. In this letter, Gwinn specifically argued that BMS should waive the usual school fees for its French teacher's daughter.
9. Mamie Gwinn reported Thomas's decision in a letter to Mary Garrett, 18 Feb. 1895, Correspondence, BMS Archives.
10. Edith Hamilton to Miss Reilly, 2 Feb. 1917, Correspondence; BMS Board Meeting Minutes, 9 Nov. 1923, both in BMS Archives.
11. Louise L. Sloan, *Communique* (BMS magazine) 1977: 16; unreferenced four-page report, probably from the late 1920s, discussing BMS's plans for moving to the country, BMS Papers, both in BMS Archives; Mary Bartlett Dixon Cullen, "Looking Back," *Bryn Mawrtyr,* 1931 Yearbook, 98–99.
12. Barbara Miller Solomon, "Who Went to College?" in *In the Company of Educated Women: A History of Women and Higher Education in America* (New Haven: Yale University Press, 1985), esp. 63–65.
13. Barbara Sicherman, *Alice Hamilton: A Life in Letters* (Cambridge: Harvard University Press, 1984), 14, 34.

14. Louise L. Sloan, *Communique* 1977: 16.
15. Andrews to BMS Committee, 6 Feb. 1888, Correspondence; letter to BMS Committee, 1 Aug. 1893, box 2, M. Carey Thomas Papers; Mamie Gwinn to Mary Garrett, 2 May 1895, Correspondence, all in BMS Archives.
16. Reid, *Edith Hamilton*, 41.
17. Ira Remsen to Julia Rogers, 11 June 1889; Mamie Gwinn to Mary Garrett, 27 Mar. 1895, Correspondence, BMS Archives. Gwinn was relaying a report from BMS Secretary Miss Woods.
18. Olga Schroeder to M. Carey Thomas, 13 Oct. 1887, Correspondence; Mary Bartlett Dixon Cullen, "Looking Back," *Bryn Mawrtyr,* 1931 Yearbook, 98–99; Mrs. Francis F. Beirne (a.k.a. Rosamond Randall Beirne), address given at BMS's Seventy-fifth Anniversary Celebration, reprinted in *Bryn Mawr School Bulletin* 17, no. 1 (1960–61): 5, BMS Archives.
19. Francis F. Beirne, *The Amiable Baltimoreans* (New York: E. P. Dutton, 1951), 284–85. Francis Beirne's wife, Rosalind Randall Beirne, chronicled the Bryn Mawr School's history in *Let's Pick the Daisies.*
20. "The Girls of Bryn Mawr School," *Bryn Mawrtyr,* 1892 Yearbook.
21. The primary recollection of Hamilton's life and career is found in Doris Reid's *Edith Hamilton.* Reid was a pupil of Hamilton's at the Bryn Mawr School, and, after Hamilton left BMS, the two women lived together for forty years. The account is certainly not objective, but it does provide a significant perspective. Sicherman's *Alice Hamilton,* a collection of the correspondence of Edith Hamilton's sister, includes helpful discussions of the Hamilton family and sisters and contains some letters from Alice to Edith and from Alice to other family members discussing Edith.
22. Sicherman, *Alice Hamilton,* 13.
23. Reid, *Edith Hamilton,* 31; Sicherman, *Alice Hamilton,* 20; Reid, *Edith Hamilton,* 33.
24. Reid, *Edith Hamilton,* 33, 35, 37; Sicherman, *Alice Hamilton,* 89.
25. Reid, *Edith Hamilton,* 37; Sicherman, *Alice Hamilton,* 136.
26. Sicherman, *Alice Hamilton,* 12.
27. Edith Hamilton to M. Carey Thomas, 27 May 1915, Correspondence, BMS Archives.
28. Thomas to Edith Hamilton, 12 Oct. 1909, BMS Papers, Correspondence; Reid, *Edith Hamilton,* 44.
29. BMS 1917–18 catalogue, BMS Archives.
30. Edith Hamilton to Thomas, 5 Feb. 1915, Correspondence, BMS Archives.
31. Hamilton to Thomas, 10 Nov. 1920.
32. Hamilton to Thomas, 5 Feb. 1915.
33. Hamilton to Thomas, 24 Feb. 1915.
34. Hamilton to Mary Garrett, 16 May 1913.
35. Thomas to Edith Hamilton, 1 Feb. 1915; Hamilton to Thomas, 5 Feb. 1915.
36. Hamilton to Thomas, 5 Feb. 1915.
37. Ibid.
38. Edith Hamilton to Thomas, 23 Nov. 1920, 2 Oct. 1913; Thomas to Hamilton, 20 May 1914.
39. Margaret Hamilton to Thomas, 16 Mar. 1916; Edith Hamilton to Miss Reilly, Feb. 1917.
40. Reid, *Edith Hamilton,* 41–42.

41. Edith Hamilton to Thomas, 16 Mar. 1914.

42. M. Carey Thomas, quoted in Solomon, *In the Company of Educated Women*, 84.

43. Reid, *Edith Hamilton*, 45.

44. Solomon, *In the Company of Educated Women*, 110.

45. Sicherman, *Alice Hamilton*, 182.

46. Edith Hamilton to Mary Garrett, 1 Nov. 1913, Correspondence; *Bryn Mawrtyr*, 1910 Yearbook. A 1917 pamphlet on the BMS Alumnae League describes the activities of the association. All in BMS Archives.

47. Edith Hamilton to Mary Garrett, 1 Nov. 1913; Hamilton to Thomas, 9 June 1913, Correspondence, BMS Archives; Horowitz, *Power and Passion*, 407–8.

48. Thomas to Edith Hamilton, 17 Mar. 1915, Correspondence, BMS Archives.

49. Edith Hamilton to Thomas, 23 Nov. 1920.

50. Correspondence between Edith Hamilton and Clara Murray Eager, June 1919, in BMS Archives. Also, Beirne, *Let's Pick the Daisies*, 35.

51. BMS Board Meeting Minutes, 12 June 1919; letter attached to and BMS Board Meeting Minutes, 9 Nov. 1920; Edith Hamilton to Thomas, 23 Nov. 1920, Correspondence. All in BMS Archives.

52. BMS Board Meeting Minutes, 12 June 1919; Thomas to Clara Eager, BMS Board Meeting Minutes, 12 June 1919; Edith Hamilton to Thomas, 23 Nov. 1920, Correspondence; BMS Board Meeting Minutes, 9 Nov. 1920.

53. Thomas to Edith Hamilton, 24 June 1919; BMS Board Meeting Minutes, 9 Nov. 1920; Hamilton to Thomas, 23 Nov. 1920.

54. Evidence of teacher discontent is expressed in the correspondence of teachers cited in following paragraphs.

55. Mary Augusta Scott to Julia Rogers, 28 Oct. 1889; letter of 13 Oct. 1889 also catalogues the problems she saw with BMS's management; series of letters to the BMS Committee by teacher with illegible signature, dated 9, 11, and 15 Mar. (no year cited). All in Correspondence, BMS Archives.

56. BMS Correspondence contains exchanges between board members and at least four fired teachers: Charlotte Smith to Julia Rogers, 14 May 1887; Alice Goddard to Thomas, 8 Mar. 1888; Rosine Melle to Mamie Gwinn, 15 Mar. 1893; Elizabeth E. Bickford (last name unclear) to Mary Garrett, 8 June 1893.

57. Charlotte Smith to Julia Rogers, 14 May 1887.

58. Thomas to Edith Hamilton, 2 Apr., 7 Apr. 1914.

59. Edith Hamilton to Mary Garrett, 13 Feb. 1913; Hamilton to Thomas, 5 Mar. 1914.

60. Edith Hamilton to Thomas, 13 Feb. 1913, 30 Apr. 1915.

61. Mary Garrett to Thomas, 6 Dec. 1897; series of letters between M. Carey Thomas and Edith Hamilton concerning the management and duties of BMS's servants: Thomas to Hamilton, 26 Sept. 1914, Hamilton to Thomas, 3 Oct. 1914, Thomas to Hamilton, 5 Oct. 1914, Hamilton to Thomas, 17 Oct. 1914, Thomas to Hamilton, 19 Oct. 1914, 21 Oct. 1914; refreshments discussed in Thomas to Hamilton, 28 May 1914. All in Correspondence, BMS Archives.

62. Mary Garrett to Edith Hamilton, 22 Sept. 1908, 9 Apr. 1910, 25 Feb. 1910; Hamilton to M. Carey Thomas, 25 Sept. 1914; Thomas to Hamilton, 27 Oct. 1914.

63. Edith Hamilton to Thomas, 29 May 1919, and Thomas to Hamilton, labeled "STRICTLY CONFIDENTIAL," 22 June 1919.

64. Edith Hamilton to Mary Garrett, 6 June 1912, 19 Oct. 1913.

65. M. Carey Thomas to Mr. Edward W. Boker, 28 Feb. 1912.

66. Thomas to Edith Hamilton, 26 Jan. 1914, Correspondence, BMS Archives; Sicherman, *Alice Hamilton*, 11–12, 252; Alice Hamilton to Margaret Hamilton, 9 Feb. 1922, reprinted in Sicherman, *Alice Hamilton*, 252, 257–58.

67. Edith Hamilton to M. Carey Thomas, 27 May 1915, Correspondence, BMS Archives.

68. Horowitz, *Power and Passion*, 429, 424–25.

69. For details of the conflict between Thomas and the Bryn Mawr College faculty, see ibid., 412, and ch. 22, "A Knockdown Blow," 407–21.

70. BMS Board Meeting Minutes, 29 Oct. 1919, 30 Oct. 1920, 21 Feb. 1922.

71. Memo reprinting the fathers' resolution, undated but with clear reference to Hamilton's resignation as BMS's headmistress, in BMS Papers. Resolution reprinted in BMS Board Meeting Minutes, 20 Mar. 1922. BMS Archives.

72. Box XI in BMS Archives contains newspaper clippings about Edith Hamilton's resignation and ensuing conflicts. Unreferenced newspaper clipping, "Dr. Thomas Threatened to Close School, Charge Fathers of Students in Baltimore Institution," *Philadelphia Evening Public Ledger,* 21 Mar. 1922; *Baltimore American,* 22 Mar. 1922.

73. William Ingle (president of Baltimore Trust Co.), quoted in newspaper clipping from *Baltimore American,* 22 Mar. 1922; George L. Irvin, quoted in unreferenced newspaper clipping, both in box XI, BMS Archives.

74. Newspaper clipping from *Baltimore American,* 22 Mar. 1922, in box XI, BMS Archives.

75. M. Carey Thomas to "Fellow Members of the Board and Dear Caroline and Helen," 2 Jan. 1928, box 2, Correspondence, BMS Archives.

76. Newspaper clipping, 22 Mar. 1922, box XI, BMS Archives.

77. Edith Hamilton's report in BMS Board Meeting Minutes, 3 Apr. 1922.

78. M. Carey Thomas to "Teachers and Staff," 10 May 1922.

79. Sicherman, *Alice Hamilton*, 252.

80. Beirne, *Let's Pick the Daisies*, 45, notes Reid's graduation date from BMS. Sicherman, *Alice Hamilton*, 214, 257–58.

81. Sicherman, *Alice Hamilton*, 257.

82. Ibid., 256, 260.

83. Ibid., 261.

84. Ibid., 407–8.

85. Grace Branham, "A Tribute," quoted in Reid, *Edith Hamilton*, 46.

86. M. Carey Thomas to "Teachers and Staff," 10 May 1922, BMS Archives.

THREE: Transforming the Vision

1. Particularly helpful discussions of changes in women's status in U.S. society are found in Sara Evans, "Women and Modernity, 1890–1920" and "Flappers, Freudians, and All That Jazz," in *Born for Liberty: A History of Women in America* (New York: Free Press, 1989), 145–96.

2. Amy Kelly, *Eleanor of Aquitaine and the Four Kings* (Cambridge: Harvard University Press, 1974).

3. Amy Kelly to M. Carey Thomas, 16 Feb. 1924, Correspondence, BMS Archives.

4. John L. Rury, *Education and Women's Work: Female Schooling and the Division of Labor in Urban America, 1870–1930* (Albany: State University of New York Press, 1991), 17.

5. Harvey Kantor and David B. Tyack, eds., *Work, Youth, and Schooling: Historical Perspectives on Vocationalism in American Education* (Stanford: Stanford University Press, 1982), 248.

6. For an in-depth discussion of the subject, see David Tyack and Elizabeth Hansot, "Differentiating the High School: The 'Boy Problem,'" in *Learning Together: A History of Coeducation in American Public Schools* (New York: Russell Sage Foundation, 1990), ch. 7.

7. Rury, *Education and Women's Work*, 17–18, 158–59.

8. Helen Lefkowitz Horowitz, *Alma Mater: Design and Experience in the Women's Colleges from Their Nineteenth-Century Beginnings to the 1930s* (New York: Alfred A. Knopf, 1984), 297.

9. Barbara Miller Solomon, *In the Company of Educated Women: A History of Women and Higher Education in America* (New Haven: Yale University Press, 1985), 62–63; Lynn Gordon, *Gender and Higher Education in the Progressive Era* (New Haven: Yale University Press, 1990), 43; Mabel Newcomber, *A Century of Higher Education for American Women* (New York: Harper, 1959), 46. Solomon notes that, "despite the endless discussions about college education for women, more and more parents and daughters became convinced of its desirability … The female proportion of the total college population rose from 21.0 percent in 1870 to 39.6 percent in 1910 and 47.3 percent in 1920." She also cautions that this shift occurred when most Americans still did not even graduate from high school (Solomon, *In the Company of Educated Women*, 62–63). Lynn Gordon, *Gender and Higher Education*, 43 and chs. 2 and 3, compares the experiences of women at different kinds of institutions (coeducation and single-sex institutions, private and public, in different regions) and concludes that female coeducational students suffered "backlash" that led male administrators to segregate women in certain academic departments and activities.

10. Dorothy Waldo, "College or Not," in *The Education of the Modern Girl* (Boston: Houghton Mifflin, 1929), 90. This collection contains essays written by a host of women educators (mostly heads of girls' schools), with an introduction by the president of Smith College, William Allan Neilson. Dorothy Waldo was headmistress of the girls' school Dana Hall.

11. Barbara J. Harris, *Beyond Her Sphere: Women and the Professions in American History* (Westport, Conn.: Greenwood Press, 1978), 104, 117; Kantor and Tyack, *Work, Youth, and Schooling*, 224; Julie Matthaei, *An Economic History of Women in America: Women's Work, the Sexual Division of Labor, and the Development of Capitalism* (New York: Schocken Books, 1982), 257.

12. On the legal profession, see Solomon, *In the Company of Educated Women*, 131. On the medical profession, see Anne Hendry Morrison, *Women and Their Careers: A Study of 306 Women in Business and the Professions* (New York: National Federation of Business and Professional Women's Clubs, 1934), 129, and Solomon, *In the Company of Educated Women*, 132. In 1876, the American Medical Association began accepting women as members, and increasing numbers of medical schools and hospitals began opening their doors to women. The 1870 census listed 527 women physicians and surgeons; by 1920, the census counted 17,784 female physicians and surgeons. Although women enrolled in medical schools (including Michigan and Johns Hopkins) made up as much as 10% of their classes in the 1880s and 1890s, their proportion dropped by as much as half by 1910.

According to Harris, *Beyond Her Sphere*, 138, during the first two decades of the twentieth century, more and more medical schools began limiting their number of female students. In 1925, U.S. medical schools imposed a general 5% quota on female students (a
quota that remained in place until 1945, when World War II created a shortage of doctors). For a discussion of female professors, see Harris, *Beyond Her Sphere*, 113–15.

13. Harris, *Beyond Her Sphere*, 104. According to Kantor and Tyack, *Work, Youth, and
Schooling*, 260, "Every census from 1900 to the present shows most female workers in oc-
cupations where most of their fellow workers (frequently 70–80%) are women."
Matthaei, *Economic History of Women in America*, 285–86.

14. Mabel Louise Robinson in *The Curriculum of the Women's College*, Bureau of Education Bulletin no. 6 (Washington, D.C., 1918), 120, quoted in Kantor and Tyack, *Work,
Youth, and Schooling*, 256–57.

15. Kantor and Tyack, *Work, Youth, and Schooling*, 256–57.

16. On nursing, see Morrison, *Women and Their Careers*, 129. On social work, see
Harris, *Beyond Her Sphere*, 118–19, 258; Matthaei, *Economic History of Women in America*,
206. Alice Parsons is quoted in Harris, *Beyond Her Sphere*, 257. On attitudes of women's
magazines, see ibid., 137–38.

17. James B. Crooks, *Politics and Progress: The Rise of Urban Progressivism in Baltimore,
1895–1911* (Baton Rouge: Louisiana State University Press, 1968), 155, 6; Sherry H.
Olson, *Baltimore: The Building of an American City* (Baltimore: Johns Hopkins University
Press, 1980), 135.

18. For examples, see Marion E. and Mame Warren, *Baltimore When She Was What
She Used to Be, 1850–1930* (Baltimore: Johns Hopkins University Press, 1983), 142.

19. Crooks, *Politics and Progress*, 14, 24, 127–28, 155, 157, 159, 162–63, 179, 182;
Olson, *Baltimore*, 266–68; Warren, *Baltimore When She Was*, 142.

20. Abraham Flexner and Frank P. Bachman, *Public Education in Maryland* (New York:
General Education Board, 1916), 87–88; George H. Callcott, *Maryland and America,
1940 to 1980* (Baltimore: Johns Hopkins University Press, 1985), 238.

21. Elizabeth Fee, Linda Shopes, and Linda Zeidman, eds., *The Baltimore Book: New
Views of Local History* (Philadelphia: Temple University Press, 1991), 32–33; Crooks, *Politics and Progress* 137; Olson, *Baltimore*, 212–13, 255.

22. Olson, *Baltimore*, 303–4; Fee et al., *The Baltimore Book*, 32–33.

23. Olson, *Baltimore*, 325; Fee et al., *The Baltimore Book*, 32–33.

24. Olson, *Baltimore*, 304; Warren, *Baltimore When She Was*, 147.

25. Bradford McE. Jacobs, *Gilman Walls Will Echo the Story of the Gilman Country
School, 1897–1947* (Baltimore: Waverly Press, 1947), 1, 5, 6, 9–10, 17, 21–22.

26. Frank S. Hackett (headmaster of Riverdale Country School, New York), *New York
Evening Post*, 2 Sept. 1911, reprinted in Jacobs, *Gilman Walls Will Echo*, 51–52; Otto F.
Krauschaar, *American Nonpublic Schools: Patterns of Diversity* (Baltimore: Johns Hopkins
University Press, 1972), 76–77.

27. Kraushaar, *American Nonpublic Schools*, table on p. 14; Rury, *Education and Women's
Work*, 160.

28. Four-page report from the late 1920s, citing BMS's reasons for moving to a new
country property, BMS papers; notice of meeting on "Choosing the College," 1929, in
box 2, BMS Archives.

29. Edith Hamilton to M. Carey Thomas, 5 Feb. 1915, 23 Nov. 1920, Correspondence, BMS Archives.

30. Kantor and Tyack, *Work, Youth, and Schooling*, 256.
31. Anna Heubeck Knipp and Thaddeus P. Thomas, *The History of Goucher College* (Baltimore: Goucher College, 1938), 200–201.
32. Discussion of changing college admission standards and their effects on BMS are scattered throughout BMS board meeting minutes. E.g., in minutes of 25 Oct. 1924, Headmistress Kelly reported on the difficulties of students preparing for and taking dual sets of examinations. Minutes of 31 Oct. 1925 report that Smith, in addition to Vassar, was now refusing to substitute Bryn Mawr College examinations for College Board examinations. Rosamund Randall Beirne also discusses the changing admission policies and their effect on BMS in *Let's Pick the Daisies: The History of the Bryn Mawr School, 1884–1967* (Baltimore: Bryn Mawr School, 1970), 72.
33. M. Carey Thomas to Margaret Hamilton, 11 Jan. 1916, Correspondence; undated letter from Thomas explaining her support for maintaining the requirement that all BMS students take the Bryn Mawr College entrance examination, box 2; Amy Kelly's report in BMS Board Meeting Minutes, 10 Jan. 1925, all in BMS Archives.
34. Amy Kelly's report in BMS Board Meeting Minutes, 10 Jan. 1925.
35. Amy Kelly to M. Carey Thomas, 28 June 1926, Correspondence, BMS Archives.
36. BMS Board Meeting Minutes, 24 Mar. 1926. A 1929 notice of a meeting "Choosing the College," in box 2, BMS Archives, reported that "it is most advantageous to know in advance which college is to be chosen so that the courses may be properly planned to insure the required credits."
37. Amy Kelly to M. Carey Thomas, 28 June 1926, Correspondence, BMS Archives.
38. Edith Hamilton to Mrs. Ingle, 3 June 1911, Correspondence; undated report detailing reasons and plans for BMS's move to a county location, in the late 1920s, both in BMS Archives.
39. Beirne, *Let's Pick the Daisies*, 57–60, documents the shift in physical education at the school. Board meetings during the 1920s continually debated problems of satisfying the demand for outdoor activities and athletics. See, e.g., Amy Kelly's report in BMS Board Meeting Minutes, 9 Nov. 1923.
40. Edith Hamilton to Mrs. Ingle, 3 June 1911; Hamilton to M. Carey Thomas, 1 Dec. 1914, 2 Dec. 1914, Correspondence; BMS 1917–18 catalogue, BMS Archives. Jacobs, *Gilman Walls Will Echo*, 48–49.
41. BMS 1917–18 catalogue. BMS board meeting minutes from 1917 to 1919 refer continually to the school's use of Montebello. See esp. BMS Board Meeting Minutes, 29 Oct. 1919.
42. Francis F. Beirne, *The Amiable Baltimoreans* (New York: E. P. Dutton, 1951), 266; *Bryn Mawrtyr*, 1929 Yearbook, BMS Archives.
43. Edith Hamilton to M. Carey Thomas, 25 Sept. 1914, Correspondence. Hamilton, e.g., reported to Thomas that BMS students did not have enough space to practice for their basketball games. BMS 1910 catalogue, BMS Archives.
44. BMS Board Meeting Minutes, 29 Feb. 1924, discuss the problems with relying on Montebello for BMS's athletic program. Amy Kelly's report in BMS Board Meeting Minutes, 9 Nov. 1923, notes that BMS was renting hockey fields from the City Athletic League. Kelly reported in BMS Board Meeting Minutes, 14 May 1927, that the athletic fields BMS was renting at Mt. Washington were unsatisfactory because of poor conditions in the locker house. The BMS board subsequently approved an agreement that BMS would continue to rent those fields for five years if the club would make appropri-

ate repairs. An unsigned letter (probably from the Buckler family) to Mrs. Carey, 5 Oct. 1922 (in box 2, BMS Archives), offered the use of the family's Evergreen estate.

45. Amy Kelly's report in BMS Board Meeting Minutes, 9 Nov. 1923. BMS Board Meeting Minutes, 29 Feb. 1924, also include a discussion of the possibilities for improving sports facilities, including the need for a hockey field and a second gymnasium for indoor sports.

46. Correspondence, board meeting minutes, and catalogues from 1880s–1920s show a gradual increase in extracurricular activities, as well as the incorporation of art and music into daily school routines. Bryn Mawr first experimented with afternoon classes (separate from the academic day) with a variety of extracurricular offerings. See BMS 1915 and 1917–18 catalogues; Edith Hamilton to Mrs. Ingle, 3 June 1911; M. Carey Thomas to Hamilton, 28 Dec. 1911; BMS Board Meeting Minutes, 23 May 1922.

47. BMS 1915 and 1917–18 catalogues; Edith Hamilton to Mrs. Ingle, 3 June 1911, and M. Carey Thomas to Hamilton, 28 Dec. 1911, Correspondence, BMS Archives.

48. BMS Board Meeting Minutes, 23 May 1922.

49. Report in BMS Board Meeting Minutes, 28 Oct. 1922.

50. Undated report on BMS's music program; BMS Board Meeting Minutes, 5 May 1923, 12 Apr. 1924, 14 Mar. 1927.

51. Unsigned letter to Dr. Sabin and Miss Reilly, 21 Nov. 1922, box 2, Correspondence, BMS Archives. The letter appears to be written by Headmistress Amy Kelly as a report to the BMS board on the administrative and scheduling problems she faced at BMS.

52. Undated, typed article labeled "Newspaper," probably from late 1920s or early 1930s, in BMS Archives.

53. Edith Hamilton to Mary Garrett, 16 May 1913; Margaret Hamilton to M. Carey Thomas, 19 Feb. 1916, Correspondence, BMS Archives.

54. Margaret Hamilton to M. Carey Thomas, 16 Mar. 1916; Amy Kelly to M. Carey Thomas, 31 May 1923.

55. Amy Kelly's report on competition from Roland Park Country School in BMS Board Meeting Minutes, 9 Nov. 1923. BMS Board Meeting Minutes, 29 Feb. 1924, noted Kelly's visit to Roland Park School. Memo on BMS stationary marked "Attention is called to the following clipped from a Baltimore daily about June 12." Attached to the memo is an undated newspaper article titled "Roland Park School to Build Additions." Amy Kelly to M. Carey Thomas, 28 June 1926, Correspondence. BMS Archives.

56. Beirne, *Let's Pick the Daisies*, 74; notice of Parents' Association meeting, 7 Mar. 1928; BMS Board Meeting Minutes, 14 Feb. 1928.

57. Beirne, *Let's Pick the Daisies*, 77; BMS Board Meeting Minutes, 1 May 1928, 17 Nov. 1928; Amy Kelly to [Mr.] Palmer, 1 Aug. 1929, box 2, BMS Archives. Palmer was the architect who designed BMS's country campus.

58. "The Bryn Mawr School: Its New Country Site and Its Financial Needs" (1928); "The Bryn Mawr School: A Frank, Business-like Statement of Its Financial Need for $300,000" (undated), both in BMS Archives.

59. M. Carey Thomas to "Fellow Members of the Board and Dear Caroline and Helen," 2 Jan. 1928, box 2, BMS Archives; Beirne, *Let's Pick the Daisies*, 76–77.

60. Plans for the new campus explicitly linked country-day ideals with "un-

institutional," "country" architectural types. See, e.g., undated report in BMS Archives, probably from late 1930 or early 1931, describing BMS's development of its country property.

61. Palmer to Amy Kelly, 19 Mar. 1929, box 2; unreferenced report, probably from late 1930 or early 1931, describing BMS's development of its country property; *Bulletin* (May 1931), all in BMS Archives.

62. Unsigned letter to Palmer, 4 Apr. 1929, BMS Archives.

63. *Bulletin* (May 1933), BMS Archives.

64. Unsigned letter to Palmer, 4 Apr. 1929, BMS Archives.

65. In 1937, the BMS board agreed to sell four "bas-reliefs" to Garrison Forest, noting that, although "there is great sentiment attached to these relics of the past, … we will never be able to use all of them." BMS Board Meeting Minutes, 19 Mar. 1937. BMS loaned its Parthenon friezes to the Roland Park Country School for ten years, even assuming the cost of moving the statuary to the school. BMS also donated one cast to Roland Park. In 1947, BMS sold the friezes to the Roland Park Country School. Other statues still remained in storage. By the late 1940s, the BMS board (which was paying $72 per year in storage fees and, hence, resolved to "advertise these casts" for sale) agreed to split the proceeds of selling "as many of the busts and casts as possible on a fifty-fifty basis" with the Bryn Mawr Club. But when their advertisements of the busts and casts for sale generated little interest, the board resolved to give away all remaining items rather than continue to pay for their storage. In 1954, nearby St. Mary's College or Seminary (board minutes do not specify) volunteered to take all of the remaining statuary and to pay transportation costs. BMS Board Meeting Minutes, 18 Mar. 1938, 28 Mar. 1947, 23 May 1947, 17 Oct. 1947, 19 Mar. 1949, 12 May 1954.

66. M. Carey Thomas to "Miss Kelly and other members of the Board of Managers," 11 Dec. 1927, BMS Archives.

67. Thomas to "Fellow Members of the Board and Dear Caroline and Helen," 2 Jan. 1928, box 2, BMS Archives.

68. Memo labeled "Points discussed and agreement reached by Mrs. Gibson and Miss Thomas during Mrs. Gibson's visit of 24 hours to Miss Thomas, Jan. 10 and 11, 1928"; Thomas to "Fellow Members of the Board," 2 Jan. 1928, both in box 2, BMS Archives.

69. BMS Board Meeting Minutes, 9 May 1929, 1 May 1928.

70. See, e.g., Amy Kelly to M. Carey Thomas, 12 Feb. 1932, Correspondence, BMS Archives.

71. BMS Board Meeting Minutes, 1 May 1928.

72. Beirne, *Let's Pick the Daisies*, 78, notes that the Men's Advisory Committee "advised strongly" against new construction until the school's city property was sold. But "it was hard for an enthusiastic group of women, bent on a quick move to the country, to take this advice cheerfully. They paid no heed to the gloomy predictions of a few business men." Olson, *Baltimore*, 333.

73. Olson, *Baltimore*, 333.

74. Announcement of Kelly's resignation in BMS Board Meeting Minutes, 4 Dec. 1934.

75. Unsigned letter (probably Elizabeth Thomas) to Amy Kelly, 20 Apr. 1933; Kelly to Elizabeth Thomas, 22 Apr. 1933; probably Elizabeth Thomas to Kelly, 2 May 1933.

Although several letters are unsigned, I reconstructed a series of exchanges in 1932 and 1933 and believe the letters can be attributed to Elizabeth Thomas, who was directing BMS's Upper School during Kelly's absense.

76. Amy Kelly to BMS accountants, 14 Sept. and 26 Sept. 1937; Kelly to Elizabeth Thomas, 5 Jan. and 14 Jan. 1938, 7 Oct. 1938.

77. Clark's resignation announced in Board Meeting Minutes, 8 June 1938; 1968–69 *Bryn Mawr School Bulletin*, 18, BMS Archives.

78. Undated notice from board announces Margaret Hamilton's and Elizabeth Thomas's respective responsibilities, BMS Archives. Beirne, *Let's Pick the Daisies*, 92.

79. Elizabeth Thomas (?) to Amy Kelly, 24 Oct. 1932, Correspondence, BMS Archives.

80. Elizabeth Thomas (?) to Amy Kelly, 7 Oct. 1932, 2 Mar. 1933.

81. Elizabeth Thomas to Amy Kelly, 15 Mar. 1933; Charles Barton to Amy Kelly, 10 June 1933.

82. Elizabeth Thomas (?) to Amy Kelly, 7 Oct. 1932.

83. BMS Board Meeting Minutes, 20 Oct. 1933. BMS's senior class lost thirteen members.

84. Elizabeth Thomas (?) to Amy Kelly, 24 Mar. 1933, Correspondence, BMS Archives. Beirne, *Let's Pick the Daisies*, 86, reported, e.g., that BMS bought a temporary Sunday school building and had it moved and reconstructed as a study hall on the new campus.

85. Thomas's announcements in BMS Board Meeting Minutes, 1 May 1928.

86. BMS Board Meeting Minutes, 11 Oct. and 19 Dec. 1932.

87. Elizabeth Thomas to Amy Kelly, 2 May 1933.

88. Elizabeth Thomas (?) to Amy Kelly, 26 Oct. 1932; Elsie [Elizabeth] Thomas to Kelly, 26 Nov. 1932; Elizabeth Thomas to Kelly, 15 Feb. 1933; Elsie [Elizabeth] Thomas to Kelly, 26 Nov. 1932; Elizabeth Thomas (?) to Kelly, 24 Mar. 1933.

89. See, e.g., BMS Board Meeting Minutes, special meeting between the board and faculty, 25 May 1933; letter from BMS staff to BMS Board of Managers, 26 Apr. 1933, BMS Archives.

90. Undated report discussing effect of the extended school day on teachers, BMS Archives.

91. Margaret Hamilton to Amy Kelly, 9 May 1933.

92. BMS Board Meeting Minutes, 18 Mar. 1938.

93. 1941 catalogue, BMS Archives.

94. 1936–37 and 1941 catalogues, BMS Archives.

FOUR: An Establishment Vision

1. Harvey Kantor and David B. Tyack, eds., *Work, Youth, and Schooling: Historical Perspectives on Vocationalism in American Education* (Stanford: Stanford University Press, 1982), 248.

2. Barbara Solomon, *In the Company of Educated Women: A History of Women and Higher Education in America* (New Haven: Yale University Press, 1985), 191.

3. Kantor and Tyack, *Work, Youth, and Schooling*, 261; Solomon, *In the Company of Educated Women*, 186–87, table 6 on p. 133.

4. Solomon, *In the Company of Educated Women*, 191; Mabel Newcomber, *A Century of Higher Education for American Women* (New York: Harper & Brothers, 1959), 241.

5. Solomon, *In the Company of Educated Women*, 188–89.

6. Betty Friedan, *The Feminine Mystique* (New York: W. W. Norton, reprint 2001).

7. For a concise overview of the period, see Sara Evans, "The Cold War and the 'Feminine Mystique,'" in *Born for Liberty: A History of Women in America* (New York: Free Press Paperbacks, 1997), ch. 11.

8. Kantor and Tyack, *Work, Youth, and Schooling*, 214.

9. Solomon, *In the Company of Educated Women*, 186–88, 261.

10. Evans, *Born for Liberty*, 254–55.

11. Ibid., 249.

12. Newcomber, *A Century of Higher Education*, 133–34, 67.

13. Ibid., 243, 234, 67.

14. Solomon, *In the Company of Educated Women*, 191–92, 195, 197.

15. Ibid., 192–93.

16. Millicent Carey McIntosh, quoted in ibid., 193.

17. On Thomas's reaction to women in general and her niece in particular combining careers and marriage, see Helen Lefkowitz Horowitz, *The Power and Passion of M. Carey Thomas* (New York: Alfred A. Knopf, 1994), 442.

18. BMS Board Meeting Minutes, 3 Dec. 1938, BMS Archives.

19. Ibid. Rosamund Randall Beirne, *Let's Pick the Daisies: The History of the Bryn Mawr School, 1884–1967* (Baltimore: Bryn Mawr School, 1970), 92, describes Van Bibber and her accomplishments.

20. E.g., Van Bibber and McIntosh believed it unnecessary to humiliate or exclude students with academic deficiencies. BMS Board Meeting Minutes, 17 Mar. 1939, 14 Dec. 1945; Katharine Van Bibber, "Presenting the Head Mistress," *Bryn Mawr School Bulletin* 1, no. 1 (Apr. 1941).

21. BMS Board Meeting Minutes, 9 Mar. 1938; "A Year of Decision at Bryn Mawr," *Alumnae Association Bulletin* (1948), 5–6; "Miss Howell Plans to Leave School," *Baltimore Evening Sun*, 19 Sept. 1972, all in BMS Archives.

22. BMS Board Meeting Minutes, 9 Mar. 1938.

23. Beirne, *Let's Pick the Daisies*, 99.

24. BMS Board Meeting Minutes, 17 Oct. 1941; letter to BMS parents asking for money to help the school retire its debt and improve its campus, in BMS Board Meeting Minutes, 5 Dec. 1941; BMS Board Meeting Minutes, 27 Mar. 1943.

25. E.g., BMS launched a new fund-raising drive in 1949 (special meeting of board, in BMS Board Meeting Minutes, 15 Feb. 1949). In 1954, the BMS Alumnae Association began organizing alumnae classes to appeal for donations (Alumnae Association report, in BMS Board Meeting Minutes, 12 May 1954). That year, the board also formed a Long Range Planning Committee to identify the school's most pressing needs and work with fund-raising committees (BMS Board Meeting Minutes, 22 Oct. 1954). BMS identified these building priorities in 1955 (BMS Board Meeting Minutes, 25 Mar. 1955).

26. M. Carey Thomas to "Fellow Members of the Board and Dear Caroline and Helen," 2 Jan. 1928, box 2, Correspondence, BMS Archives.

27. Special meeting of the board, BMS Board Meeting Minutes, 15 Feb. 1949; report in BMS Board Meeting Minutes, 19 Oct. 1956; BMS Board Meeting Minutes, 18 Jan.

1957; President of the Alumnae Association to Alumnae, "Suggested Letter to Friends of the School and Business Men," 1953.

28. Proposal by Mrs. King in BMS Board Meeting Minutes, 28 Mar. 1941; BMS Board Meeting Minutes, 4 Apr. 1952; "Meet the Board," *Bulletin* 14, no. 1 (1957): 4.

29. "Meet the Board" (1957).

30. BMS Board Meeting Minutes, 17 Oct. 1952, 21 Oct. 1953, 14 Jan. 1955.

31. BMS 1930–31 catalogue, BMS Archives.

32. BMS late 1940s catalogue (no year specified in catalogue), 31.

33. BMS 1936–37 catalogue.

34. This statement first appeared in BMS catalogues of the late 1940s. It was still being used in the BMS 1958–59 catalogue, p. 11.

35. BMS Board Meeting Minutes, 18 Oct. 1940, 22 Oct. 1943, 21 Oct. 1949.

36. Millicent Carey McIntosh to Board, in BMS Board Meeting Minutes, 17 May 1946; Van Bibber's arguments and the board's resolutions in BMS Board Meeting Minutes, 20 May 1955.

37. *Bulletin* (Fall 1935); BMS Board Meeting Minutes, 19 May 1950.

38. BMS Board Meeting Minutes, 22 Oct. 1948, 21 Oct. 1949, 30 May 1951, 17 Jan. 1957.

39. BMS 1958–59 catalogue.

40. BMS Board Meeting Minutes, 19 May 1944, 18 Oct. 1957, 18 Jan. 1957.

41. Katharine Van Bibber, typed article or speech, "Notes on the Philosophy of an Independent College Preparatory School for Girls," hand-dated "around 1960," p. 2, in Van Bibber's file, BMS Archives.

42. Van Bibber, "Presenting the Head Mistress," 1.

43. BMS Board Meeting Minutes, 17 Mar. 1939, 14 Dec. 1945.

44. Van Bibber, "Presenting the Head Mistress," 1; Katharine Van Bibber, "A Year of Decision at Bryn Mawr," *Bulletin* (1948): 5–6. BMS Archives.

45. BMS Board Meeting Minutes, 21 Oct. 1953, 26 Mar. 1954. According to BMS Board Meeting Minutes, 12 Oct. 1955, the Bible class proved so popular that two sections were needed. Music Appreciation also proved popular (BMS Board Meeting Minutes, 18 Oct. 1957).

46. BMS Board Meeting Minutes, 17 May 1946.

47. BMS 1936–37 catalogue; *Bryn Mawrtyr*, 1938 Yearbook; BMS Board Meeting Minutes, 19 May 1944, 17 Oct. 1952.

48. BMS Board Meeting Minutes, 19 May 1944, 17 Oct. 1952, 18 Oct. 1957, 12 Dec. 1952; *Bryn Mawrtyr*, 1938 Yearbook.

49. BMS Board Meeting Minutes, 18 Jan. 1957.

50. Katharine Van Bibber, "Preparedness in the Bryn Mawr School," *Bryn Mawr School Bulletin* (May 1942).

51. BMS Board Meeting Minutes, 30 Mar. 1951; Parent–Teacher Association report, BMS Board Meeting Minutes, 4 Apr. 1952.

52. BMS Board Meeting Minutes, 12 June 1941, 17 Oct. 1941; Van Bibber, "Preparedness in the Bryn Mawr School."

53. Miss Johnson, BMS Board Meeting Minutes, 17 May 1957. Headmistress Van Bibber frequently reflected on the relationship between education and the world far beyond the schoolroom, setting a clear tone for BMS in the 1940s and 1950s. Individuals had to assume responsibility for maintaining democracy and freedom—and for destroy-

ing all encroachments upon it—and schools were critical in giving their students the tools for that task, she argued. In 1941, she urged BMS graduates to use their training "to think independently and critically," to value "intellectual honesty," and to tolerate and respect individuals with different ideals—all critical elements of democracy that Hitler's youth disregarded. In 1944, decrying her generation of the 1920s for ignoring society's problems in favor of pursuing personal pleasure, she again urged her students to use their education to solve society's problems. Van Bibber's addresses to BMS graduating classes, 1941 and 8 June 1944, both in Van Bibber file, BMS Archives.

54. BMS Board Meeting Minutes, 13 Dec. 1940; *Bryn Mawrtyr*, 1964 Yearbook. During the 1950s, BMS publications repeatedly reported the association's charitable activities. As late as 1964, the Christian Association described itself as committed to "attempting to see the Christians' responsibility in all phases of community life and to society as a whole" and "believing that we have a definite responsibility to the community."

55. Van Bibber, "The Aims and Purposes of the Bryn Mawr School," in Van Bibber's file, BMS Archives.

56. Alumnae Association to Alumnae, "Suggested Letter to Friends of the School," 1953.

57. BMS Alumna, Address to Alumnae Association at their meeting of 26 Apr. 1949, BMS Archives.

58. Ibid.

59. Francis F. Beirne, *The Amiable Baltimoreans* (New York: E. P. Dutton, 1951), 284, 285. It was Francis Beirne's wife, Rosalind Randall Beirne, who chronicled BMS's history in *Let's Pick the Daisies*.

60. "The New Preps: They're Changing Our WASPy Private Schools (and Our Power Elite)," *Baltimore* (Nov. 1989): 38.

61. Ibid.

62. Beirne, *The Amiable Baltimoreans*, 286; full-page feature in the "Smart Set Magazine," *Baltimore American*, 16 May 1943. BMS archives contain numerous newspaper clippings from the 1940s and 1950s, many from the "Smart Set Magazine" of the *Baltimore American*. Undated newspaper clipping, BMS Archives.

63. *Bryn Mawrtyr*, 1956 Yearbook, BMS Archives.

64. *Bryn Mawrtyr*, 1948 and 1956 Yearbooks.

F I V E : Challenging the Vision

1. Sara Evans, *Born for Liberty: A History of Women in America* (New York: Free Press Paperbacks, 1997). Ch. 11, "The Cold War and the 'Feminine Mystique'," and ch. 12, "Decade of Discovery: 'The Personal Is Political'," provide an excellent overview.

2. Otto Kraushaar, *American Nonpublic Schools: Patterns of Diversity* (Baltimore: Johns Hopkins University Press, 1972), 14; George H. Callcott, *Maryland and America: 1940 to 1980* (Baltimore: Johns Hopkins University Press, 1985), 247.

3. BMS Board Meeting Minutes, 18 May 1939, 23 May 1940, BMS Archives.

4. Admissions Policy Committee meeting, 10 Mar. 1958, box 3, BMS Archives. This meeting, attended by Katharine Van Bibber and seven other board members, addressed the concerns raised by the Alumnae Association on 17 Jan. 1958.

5. Admissions Policy Committee meeting, 10 Mar. 1958.

6. BMS Board Meeting Minutes, 17 May 1946; Katharine Van Bibber, untitled arti-

cle or speech, hand-dated "probably c. 1959?," in her file in BMS Archives; McIntosh quotation in BMS Board Meeting Minutes, 17 May 1946.

7. BMS Board Meeting Minutes, 13 May 1946, 17 May 1946, 13 Mar. 1959.

8. BMS Board Meeting Minutes, 17 May 1957, 3 Mar. 1959; Van Bibber, untitled speech, "probably c. 1959?"

9. Van Bibber, untitled speech, "probably c. 1959?"

10. Admissions Policy Committee meeting, 10 Mar. 1958.

11. BMS Board Meeting Minutes, 13 June 1977, 29 Sept. 1977.

12. David B. Tyack, *The One Best System: A History of American Urban Education* (Cambridge: Harvard University Press, 1974), 279; *Brown v. Board of Education*, 347 U.S. 483 (1954).

13. Joel Spring, *The Sorting Machine Revisited: National Educational Policy since 1945*, updated ed. (New York: Longman, 1989).

14. *Desegregation in the Baltimore City Schools* (Baltimore: Maryland Commission on Interracial Problems and Relations and Baltimore Commission on Human Relations, 1955), 17.

15. *Desegregation in the Baltimore City Schools*, 17; Callcott, *Maryland and America*, 245.

16. *Desegregation in the Baltimore City Schools*, 17.

17. Special BMS board meeting called in response to a Parent-Teacher Association resolution passed at their meeting, Nov. 1956, BMS Archives.

18. BMS Board Meeting Minutes, 14 Jan. 1955, contain the first recorded mention of the school integration issue in BMS records. Letter of denial in BMS Board Meeting Minutes, Nov. 1955.

19. BMS Board Meeting Minutes, 20 Jan. 1956.

20. BMS Board Meeting Minutes, 20 June 1955.

21. The sentiment that isolating BMS students from different kinds of people might have negative effects was first expressed in debates over integration recorded in BMS Board Meeting Minutes, 20 June 1955. Also, "The Board and Its Admission Policy," three-page report from "E.D.Y. to KVB, President of the Board Williamson, & Mrs. Levering" in BMS Board Meeting Minutes, 18 Oct. 1957.

22. BMS Board Meeting Minutes, 20 June 1955.

23. BMS Board Meeting Minutes, 12 Nov. 1956.

24. Discussions about integration were extensive. The following examples are all from BMS Board Meeting Minutes. The board formed committees to assess how BMS could best introduce the integration process (20 June 1955, 14 Jan. 1955, 16 Mar. 1956, 19 Oct. 1956, 12 Nov. 1956, Jan. 1962).

25. BMS Board Meeting Minutes, Jan. 1962; notification of this new policy in undated letter to "Parents, Alumnae and Friends."

26. BMS Board Meeting Minutes, 12 and 15 Jan. 1962. The school was still debating its admissions policy: Should African American students be admitted on exactly the same basis as white students? Should African American students with scholarships from African American community groups be admitted? Should the BMS board review and approve applicants? Should BMS begin the integration process with any particular grades or age groups?

27. "Excerpts from Statement Made by Miss Katharine Van Bibber on Admissions Policy of the Bryn Mawr School, 31 Jan. 1962, When Integration Was Announced," in Katharine Van Bibber's file; Diane Howell to Mrs. Millspaugh, 10 Feb. 1962.

28. "Miss Van Bibber on Admissions Policy, 31 Jan. 1962."

29. Diane Howell to Mrs. Millspaugh, 10 Feb. 1962.

30. Special board meeting in response to Parent-Teacher Association resolution, 1956.

31. Ibid.

32. Articles on Diane Howell in BMS archives include "At Bryn Mawr: New Headmistress Speaks" from the Women's Pages (paper unknown), Jan. 1962; "New Head Named for Bryn Mawr," *Baltimore Sun*, 26 Dec. 1961; "Miss Howell Plans to Leave School," *Baltimore Evening Sun*, 19 Sept. 1972.

33. "E.D.Y. to KVB, President of Board Williamson, & Mrs. Levering"; "The Board and Its Admission Policy," three-page report attached to BMS Board Meeting Minutes, 18 Oct. 1957, BMS Archives.

34. Articles about the relationship of the independent school and the greater society appeared frequently during Howell's years at Bryn Mawr. See Diane Howell, "The Freedom of the Independent School: A Report to the Board of Managers, 18 Nov. 1964, by Diane Howell, on Her 'Philosophy of Education,'" in Howell's file, BMS Archives.

35. Ibid.

36. For one expression of this perspective, see interview with Diane Howell on "The Women's Page," *Baltimore Evening Sun*, 10 Jan. 1962, in Howell's file, BMS Archives.

37. Diane Howell, "Let's Unplug Them and Wire Them into the World," *Bulletin* (1968): 2–3, in BMS Archives.

38. "Aims and Purposes," BMS 1966–67 catalogue, 6; "BMS: A Tradition in Service," *Bulletin* (Summer 1968): 1; *Bryn Mawrtyr*, 1968 Yearbook; Linda Lee (president of Bryn Mawr Self-government Association), "Students Look Outward," *Bulletin* (Summer 1968). These themes are also explored in *Communique* (1968), BMS Archives.

39. "BMS: A Tradition in Service," 1.

40. Profile of school dated 1976, BMS Archives.

41. BMS catalogue, no specific date but from the 1970s; "A Farewell to Bryn Mawr's Sixth Headmistress," *Bulletin* (c. Fall 1980): 5.

42. BMS Board Meeting Minutes, 27 Sept. 1978, 5 May 1983.

43. "Academic Program for the Junior and Senior Years," memo dated Feb. 1966; course requirements and descriptions in BMS catalogue from 1970s (no specific date). BMS Archives.

44. BMS catalogue from 1970s (no exact date—BMS apparently used one catalogue for several school years and thus did not date it).

45. For a discussion of federal policy, see "Career Education and Equality of Educational Opportunity," in Spring, *The Sorting Machine Revisited*, ch. 6.

46. Callcott, *Maryland and America*, 246–47.

47. National Association of Independent Schools (NAIS) goals discussed in BMS Board Meeting Minutes, 5 May 1983.

48. Isaac Rehert, "She Got a Better Job: Family Moved for Bryn Mawr Headmistress's Career," unreferenced newspaper article, BMS Archives.

49. Elizabeth Eck, "Barbara Chase: A Decade of Dedication to Bryn Mawr," *Baltimore Messenger*, 28 Mar. 1990.

50. BMS Board Meeting Minutes, 9 May 1978.

51. "Evenings at the Bryn Mawr School," flyer (Spring 1981), BMS Archives. "Say-

ing Goodbye to Barbara Chase," *Communique* (1994): 4, describes "Summertech" and "Readers' Camp" programs.

52. "Introducing Bryn Mawr's Seventh Headmistress: Barbara Landis Chase," *Bulletin* (c. Fall 1980), 1–2; BMS Board Meeting Minutes, 21 Sept. 1980. The lecture series was named the "Carey Seminars."

53. BMS Board Meeting Minutes, 24 Sept. 1981. The board set the exploration of "pilot projects in community service" for the entire school as a priority in the upcoming school year. "Saying Goodbye to Barbara Chase," 4.

54. "The New Preps: They're Changing Our WASPy Private Schools (and Our Power Elite)," *Baltimore* (Nov. 1989): 3; Diane Howell, "Why the Independent School? Why Bryn Mawr?" 1 Feb. 1966, in her file, BMS Archives. In BMS Board Meeting Minutes, 5 May 1983, there is a discussion of BMS's commitment to this NAIS goal.

55. According to a 1989 analysis, BMS's ethnic makeup in 1989 was 80.3% white, 10.6% black, 6.3% Asian, and 2.9% "other." Enrollment Management Consultants Ransome/Maguire, *Image Analysis and Strategies for Action: Presented to the Bryn Mawr School—Draft of Final Report*, 12 Apr. 1989, copy provided by BMS. "The New Preps," 40.

56. Barbara Chase, "Pride and Prejudice: The Founding of the Bryn Mawr School and the Education of Girls," Carey Seminar Lecture, 11 Apr. 1985, in BMS Archives. Chase outlined two other major "areas of concern and challenge": the crisis in the teaching profession and the "issue of gender in education" (a subject discussed at length in this volume's ch. 6).

57. BMS 1970s catalogue; BMS 1981–82 catalogue.

58. Headmistress's report, BMS Board Meeting Minutes, 18 Nov. 1982. The new emphasis in BMS's curriculum was also to encompass science and technology and foreign languages.

59. BMS 1994–95 Viewbook, BMS Archives.

60. "The New Preps," e.g., noted how the curriculum of private schools like BMS reflected "an updated social awareness."

61. One of many examples is BMS Board Meeting Minutes, 5 May 1983.

62. Headmistress's reports, BMS Board Meeting Minutes, 9 Mar. 1983, 18 Nov. 1982.

63. BMS Board Meeting Minutes, 5 May 1983; "Saying Goodbye to Barbara Chase," 5; BMS 1994–95 Viewbook, BMS Archives. Headmistress Chase herself taught the senior seminar on "Ethics and Contemporary Issues."

64. *Bryn Mawrtyr*, 1981 Yearbook.

65. "The New Preps," 66, 70.

66. Ransome/Maguire, *Image Analysis and Strategies*.

67. "The New Preps," 42.

68. The NAIS website (www.nais.org) presents a wide variety of statistical information about member independent schools. Especially helpful is the "Facts at a Glance" section.

s i x : Reinventing the Vision

1. Diane Howell, "Why the Independent School? Why Bryn Mawr?" (article or speech launching a new building campaign), 1 Feb. 1966, in Howell's file, BMS Archives.

2. *Baltimore Evening Sun*, 10 Jan. 1962, in Howell's file, BMS Archives.

3. Barbara Miller Solomon, *In the Company of Educated Women: A History of Women and Higher Education in America* (New Haven: Yale University Press, 1985), 204–5; table 5 on p. 127.

4. Solomon, *In the Company of Educated Women*, table 1 on p. 44. Solomon based her information on Mabel Newcomer's *A Century of Higher Education for American Women* (New York: Harper, 1959), 37, and the U.S. Department of Health, Education, and Welfare, National Center for Education Statistics, *Digest of Education Statistics*, 1976 and 1982.

5. Solomon, *In the Company of Educated Women*, table 1 on p. 44, 203.

6. Mary K. McPherson (Assistant Headmistress and College Advisor), "Choosing a College: Single-Sex or Coed?" *Bulletin* (Spring 1980): 26–27.

7. Martha Brant, "Far beyond White Gloves and Teas. Education: Women's Colleges Enjoy a Revival," *Newsweek*, 25 Apr. 1994, reprinted in "In the News," National Coalition of Girls' Schools (NCGS) pamphlet (Concord, Mass.: early 1990s).

8. Solomon, *In the Company of Educated Women*, 203; Maria Newman, "Women's Colleges Find a New Popularity," *New York Times*, 15 Jan. 1994, reprinted in "In the News," NCGS pamphlet; David Tyack and Elizabeth Hansot, *Learning Together: A History of Coeducation in American Public Schools* (New York: Russell Sage Foundation, 1992), 280; Daryl G. Smith, Lisa E. Wolf, and Diane E. Morrison, "Paths to Success: Factors Related to the Impact of Women's Colleges," *Journal of Higher Education* 66, no. 3 (1 May 1995): 245.

9. Tyack and Hansot, *Learning Together*, 280.

10. "It's Out of the Doldrums for Private Schools," *US News & World Report*, 31 May 1976, 51–52. Statistics from Tyack and Hansot, *Learning Together*, 280–81. For BMS headmistress's discussion of these trends, see Barbara Chase, "From the Headmistress: A Mission Reaffirmed," *Communique* (1985): 1–2, BMS Archives.

11. "Bryn Mawr–Gilman Coordination," *Communique* (1985): 4–8.

12. Sherry H. Olson, *Baltimore: The Building of an American City* (Baltimore: Johns Hopkins University Press, 1980), 37.

13. "It's Out of the Doldrums," 51–52.

14. National Association of Independent Schools web page (www.nais.org), Jan. 2003.

15. Sara Evans, *Born for Liberty: A History of Women in America* (New York: Free Press, 1989), 301.

16. Mary Field Belenky, Blythe McVicker Clinchy, Nancy Goldberger, and Jill Mattuck Tarule, *Women's Ways of Knowing* (New York: Harper Collins, 1986).

17. Carol Gilligan, *In a Different Voice: Psychological Theory and Women's Development* (Cambridge: Harvard University Press, 1982).

18. Girls' schools seemed particularly drawn to the work of David and Myra Sadker, *Failing at Fairness: How Our Schools Cheat Girls* (New York: Touchstone, 1995); Mary Pipher, *Reviving Ophelia: Saving the Selves of Adolescent Girls* (New York: Putnam, 1994); and Peggy Orenstein, *Schoolgirls: Young Women, Self-esteem, and the Confidence Gap* (New York: Doubleday, 1994).

19. Linda K. Kerber, Catherine G. Greeno, Eleanor E. Maccoby, Zella Luria, Carol B. Stack, and Carol Gilligan, "On *In a Different Voice*: An Interdisciplinary Forum," *Signs: Journal of Women in Culture and Society* (Winter 1986): 304–32: Catherine G. Greeno and Eleanor E. Maccoby, "How Different Is the 'Different Voice'?" 310–16, acknowledge

that, while Gilligan's theories are compelling to many women, they are not supported by concrete research. In the same forum, Zella Luria, "A Methodological Critique," 316–21 (esp. 317–18), concurs on Gilligan's questionable method and evidence.

20. Linda Kerber, "Some Cautionary Words for Historians," 304–10, esp. 309, in Kerber et al., "On *In a Different Voice*," 304–32.

21. Christopher Lasch, "Gilligan's Island," *New Republic* (7 Dec. 1992): 38; Carol Tavris, *The Mismeasure of Woman: Why Women Are Not the Better Sex, the Inferior Sex, or the Opposite Sex* (New York: Simon & Schuster, 1992); Martha T. Mednick, "On the Politics of Psychological Constructs: Stop the Bandwagon, I Want to Get Off," *American Psychologist* (Aug. 1989): 1120.

22. Headmistress's Report, BMS Board Meeting Minutes, 9 Mar. 1983, BMS Archives. BMS Headmistress Barbara Chase reported on Gilligan's discussions of moral development and the ethic of care at the meeting of the National Association of Principals of Schools for Girls.

23. Announcement in 1977 BMS Board Meeting Minutes; *Communique*, Apr. 1989, highlighted the history of BMS's career days.

24. Isaac Rehert, "She Got a Better Job: Family Moved for Bryn Mawr Headmistress's Career," unreferenced newspaper article, BMS Archives.

25. Barbara Chase,"Pride and Prejudice: The Founding of the Bryn Mawr School and the Education of Girls," Carey Seminar Lecture, 11 Apr. 1985, in Centennial Celebration file, BMS Archives.

26. Chase quoted in "Holding on to Confidence," *Communique*, Fall 1991, 6–7, in BMS Archives. Chase discussed the negative influences of advertising and obsession with physical appearance on adolescent girls.

27. BMS's Fall 1991 *Communique* magazine reprinted parts of an interview with Carol Gilligan (which had appeared in the *Baltimore Sun*, 1 May 1991) in "Holding on to Confidence: Parents and Schools Can Help Young Women Build Self-esteem, Beginning in the 'Confidence-Crumbling' Middle School Years." BMS Archives.

28. BMS Board Meeting Minutes, 27 Oct. 1961.

29. "History of the Coalition" outlines the formation and development of the organization (NCGS website: www.ncgs.org, 2003).

30. Founding date from graph in "In the News," NCGS pamphlet. Also NCGS's pamphlet "Choosing a Girls' School: 1995 Guide to Member Schools," 22.

31. "What Every Girl in School Needs to Know," NCGS pamphlet from the early 1990s, 15; Carol Gilligan, David Riesman, and Rachel Belash (head of Branksome Hall, part of the Canadian Association of Girls' Schools and an affiliate of NCGS), quoted: 5, 9. Belash also noted that, at girls' schools, there is "instant friendliness" and "a sense of respect and affection from students to teachers and vice versa."

32. "AAUW's History: How Far We Have Come," from American Association of University Women website (www.aauw.org); Helen Lefkowitz Horowitz, *The Power and Passion of M. Carey Thomas* (New York: Alfred A. Knopf, 1994), 392, 395–96.

33. Alice Ann Leidel, 1995 foreword to *How Schools Shortchange Girls—the AAUW Report: A Study of Major Findings on Girls and Education*, commissioned by the AAUW Educational Foundation and researched by the Wellesley College Center for Research on Women (New York: Marlowe, 1992), x, 3.

34. Sadker and Sadker, *Failing at Fairness*, 1.

35. AAUW Educational Foundation, *How Schools Shortchange Girls*, 19, acknowledges that generalizations about loss of girls' self-confidence in adolescence hold true "at least among the white-middle class girls most often studied." See A. Rogers and C. Gilligan, "Translating Girls' Voices: Two Languages of Development," Harvard University Graduate School of Education, Harvard Project on the Psychology of Women and the Development of Girls, 1988, 42–43, quoted in *How Schools Shortchange Girls*, 20–21. Also, *How Schools Shortchange Girls*, 18, 19, 22.

36. Meg Milne Moulton and Whitney Ransome, "Women and Minorities Must Be Encouraged in Math and Science," *Boston Globe*, 5 Dec. 1993, quoted in "In the News," NCGS pamphlet; AAUW Educational Foundation, *How Schools Shortchange Girls*, 50, 40–41, 25. "High school girls, even those with exceptional academic preparation in math and science, are choosing math/science careers in disproportionately low numbers" (ibid., 44–45).

37. Office of Educational Research and Improvement, U.S. Department of Education, *Single-Sex Schooling: Perspectives from Practice and Research* (1992 draft), quoted in "What Every Girl in School Needs to Know," 7.

38. "What Every Girl in School Needs to Know," 1; "Choosing a Girls' School: 1995 Guide," 1.

39. "Choosing a Girls' School: 1995 Guide," 1.

40. Moulton and Ransome, "Women and Minorities Must Be Encouraged"; "What Every Girl in School Needs to Know," 19.

41. "Choosing a Girls' School: 1995 Guide," 2; "What Every Girl in School Needs to Know," 19. NCGS's "Choosing a Girls' School: 1995 Guide" reported the same information in a different context: "four times as many graduates of girls' schools intend to pursue careers in math, science, and technology."

42. 1995 BMS Viewbook, BMS Archives.

43. Copies of papers from these symposia on girls in math and sciences are available in "The National Coalition of Girls' Schools Publication Series." BMS Board Meeting Minutes, 18 Oct. 1978: Sheila Tobias, a "nationally recognized math expert," spoke at BMS. Education Committee Report, Board Meeting Minutes, 20 May 1981. Headmistress's Report, Board Meeting Minutes, 18 Nov. 1982. Both BMS's headmistress and the Education Committee emphasized the school's need to strengthen its science programs, retain better faculty in mathematics and the sciences, expand its computer studies, and explore the influence that expanding technology should have on its curriculum.

44. "Mathematics at Bryn Mawr," *Communique* (1982): 2–4. A 1985 article by Headmistress Barbara Chase emphasized the need for close attention to the different ways in which girls and boys learn—again with particular reference to the fields of mathematics and science, which, whether because of inherent tendencies or social factors, have traditionally been male-dominated subjects and careers (Chase, "From the Headmistress: A Mission Reaffirmed," 1–2). The mentoring program with women from Goucher College is discussed in "Mathematics at Bryn Mawr." Summertech flyer, 1988; "Saying Goodbye to Barbara Chase," *Communique* (1994): 4. Summertech was initiated in 1984. BMS Archives.

45. BMS Board Meeting Minutes, 17 May 1957, 13 Mar. 1957; Howell, "Why the Independent School?" 3.

46. Mrs. Anthony Byrk and Valerie Lee, quoted in "What Every Girl in School Needs to Know," 5, 19; "Choosing a Girls' School: 1995 Guide," 2.

47. M. Carey Thomas, quoted in Solomon, *In the Company of Educated Women*, 84.

48. Evans, *Born for Liberty*, 291. Law school enrollment statistics are available at the American Bar Association's Legal Education website: www.abanet.org/legaled/statistics/femstats.html.

49. Rehert, "She Got a Better Job"; Halaine Silberg, undated article at the time of Barbara Chase's appointment, both in BMS Archives.

50. BMS pamphlet, 1983–84, in BMS Archives.

51. *Newsweek* and *New York Times* articles—Brant, "Far beyond White Gloves and Teas," and Newman, "Women's Colleges Find a New Popularity"—reprinted in "In the News." Statistics on increases in girls' school applications for admission and enrollment in Brant, "Far beyond White Gloves and Teas" and "Choosing a Girls' School: 1995 Guide," 5. Earlier NCGS literature reported smaller yet still significant increases. According to "In the News," "Member schools have enjoyed a 4.5% increase in enrollments since 1989." "Saying Goodbye to Barbara Chase," 3–4, reported enrollment trends at BMS. BMS's Little School also expanded greatly, from 48 students in 1980 to 218 in 1993.

52. "Choosing a Girls' School: 1995 Guide"; "Saying Goodbye to Barbara Chase," 3–4; BMS 1994–95 *Annual Report*, 3. All in BMS Archives. Comparative statistics from *Private Secondary Schools: The Ultimate Resource for Private School Education* (Lawrenceville, N.J.: Peterson's, 2001), 183, 267, 437–38.

53. "What Every Girl in School Needs to Know," 1; "Choosing a Girls' School: 1995 Guide," 1; Nanette M. Holden, "Women and Philanthropy: Women Give Because They Care about the Values of the Institutions They Believe In," *Communique* (1994): 16. BMS Archives.

54. "The Education of Girls: An Agenda for the Future," Centennial Conference program, 2 Mar. 1985, BMS Archives. Papers presented at this conference included "Sexist Educations—Math Anxiety and Girls: An Update" by Sheila Tobias, "Women and Science: Casting a Critical Eye on Objectivity" by Bonnie Spanier, "New Insights in Adolescent Development: Implications for Schools" by Edith Phelps and Nona Lyons, and "Conceptualizing a Curriculum for Women of the Future" by Nannerl Keohane. Chase, "Pride and Prejudice."

55. The NCGS pamphlet, "What Every Girl in School Needs to Know," 15, asserted that each of its member schools "welcomes boys into selected academic, artistic, extracurricular, or social events." Enrollment Management Consultants Ransome/Maguire, *Image Analysis and Strategies for Action: Presented to the Bryn Mawr School—Draft of Final Report*, 12 Apr. 1989, 59, 146. Copy provided by BMS.

56. Christina Hoff Sommers, *Who Stole Feminism? How Women Have Betrayed Women* (New York: Simon & Schuster, 1994), 144, 149–50. See esp. ch. 7, "The Self-esteem Study," and ch. 8, "The Wellesley Report: A Gender at Risk."

57. Ibid., 166. For Sommers's discussion of the Sadkers and their research, see 162–73.

58. Ibid., 174–75, 179–81.

59. American Association of University Women Educational Foundation, *Separated by Sex: A Critical Look at Single-Sex Education for Girls* (Washington, D.C.: American Association of University Women Educational Foundation, 1998), 2.

Conclusion

1. BMS Web page: www.brynmawr.pvt.k12.md.us; 1996 BMS Annual Report, BMS Archives; *Private Secondary Schools: The Ultimate Resource for Private School Education* (Lawrenceville, N.J.: Peterson's, 2001), 183.

2. NAIS Web page: www.nais.org; Valerie Strauss and Jay Mathews, "Area Private School Rates Endanger Diversity," *Washington Post,* 11 Apr. 2002.

3. Terry Moe, professor of political science at Stanford University, and Josiah Brunting, president of the Virginia Military Institute and former head of the Lawrenceville School in New Jersey, quoted in Amanda Paulson, "More Knock at the Doors of Private Schools," *Christan Science Monitor,* 8 May 2001.

4. Paulson, "More Knock at the Doors."

5. Mark Mitchell of NAIS, quoted in Strauss and Mathews, "Area Private School Rates."

6. See "Statement on Public Purpose of Private Education," by NAIS Board of Trustees, June 2002, available at www.nais.org.

7. M. Carey Thomas to "Fellow Members of the Board and Dear Caroline and Helen," 2 Jan. 1928, box 2; Mary Garrett to Mamie Gwinn, unreferenced, Correspondence, BMS Archives.

Index

academic achievement of girls: detrimental to physical health, 32–34; disproportionate, 10, 88, 183–86; establishment vision, 132–40, 142; lack, 52–53, 59; measurement, 28–29, 147; new dialogue, 182–92, 194; standards, 2–3, 12, 15, 21, 27, 100, 113; statistical criticisms, 192–96
academy model: female schools, 3, 6–7; influential figures, 7–9
access: to extracurricular courses, 90, 164; to private schools, 198–99
accreditation, 146–48
activism on college campuses, 143–44, 148
Addams, Jane, 64–65
administration. *See* Board of Managers
administrator(s): Elizabeth Thomas, 115–17, 119; founders' standards, 48, 55; Margaret Hamilton, 56, 61, 74, 81, 100, 106–7, 115–17, 120. *See also* headmistress(es)
admissions to Bryn Mawr School: "by certificate," 99–100; Committee screening, 24, 26, 29, 41; denying, 59; difficulty attracting, 24–25, 49–50; rising, 191–93; social change affecting, 145–46; standards, 21, 29, 39–40, 59, 192. *See also* college admissions
adolescence as critical female stage, 180–81, 183–85
Advanced Placement, 188
advertising as student recruitment, 24–25, 50, 106, 133, 145–46
aesthetic education, 104–5
African Americans, 39–40, 96, 148–49, 152–53, 160, 176, 194
afternoon school, 104–5

alumnae: financial support, 130–31, 191–92; Hamilton's rapport, 63–68; school reconfiguration role, 78–84, 108, 139; Thomas's transformation conflict, 112–15
Alumnae Association/League, 63, 65–67, 94, 138–39, 155–56, 158
American Association of University Women (AAUW), 182–84, 194–96; report on women's education, 183
Andrews, Eleanor, 36, 40
anti-Semitism, 40–41, 44
antiwar protests, Vietnam, 144, 161
architecture: country campus, 109–11, 114, 130; reflection of ideals, 36–39
art: curriculum value, 14–15, 28, 57, 104, 110, 121, 134, 136, 160, 166; European, 28, 38, 111
Association of Collegiate Alumna (ACA), 183
athletic programs, 88, 102–3, 105, 108, 136, 160
attendance: disproportionately female in high school, 10; early students, 53; founders' promotion of, 29–30

Baby Class, 61
background checks on potential faculty, 43
Baltimore: enhancement of cultural life, 14–15, 18; founders of school from, 1–2, 13, 15; nineteenth-century urban problems, 13–14; shifting residential patterns, 61–62, 95–97, 101–2; urbanization and social reform, 93–95, 149–50, 162, 175–76

school, 185–92; Bryn Mawr as, 127–28, 139–42; coeducation, 11–12, 20–25, 90, 159–60, 172–77; desegregation, 146, 148–50, 176; disadvantages of all-girls school, 192–96; external validation, 147–48; first for females, 3, 6–7, 11, 20; mission, 12, 21, 26–27, 53, 127, 198; recent applications rise, 190–92, 198; redefining after 1960s, 160–69; social responsibility, 124, 146, 154–58; tuition increases, 198; urbanization affecting, 96–98, 118, 144–46, 175–76
professions and professionals. *See* careers
Progressive Era: social reform, 64–65, 87–88, 92, 94; women alumnae and, 63–68
pscyhological development, gender differences, 180–81, 183–85, 194
public education: coeducation model, 9–10, 20; declining quality, 94–95, 197–98; early-twentieth-century reform, 88–89, 118, 144; modern crisis, 175–77; post–World War II, 144–46
public opinion/relations: alumnae, 63–68, 76–78; candidate selection, 42–43, 49; influence on model school, 3, 23, 25–26, 57–58, 60, 84, 106
public speaking by women, 8

Quakers, 15–17, 40

racial mixing, 162
racism, 39–40, 44, 143, 148
recruitment: preschool children, 61–62; students, 4, 24–25, 49–50, 106, 145, 164
Reid, Doris, 80–82
Reid family, 78–80
relationships of school founders: during difficult transitions, 47–50; with Hamilton, 71–80; as intimate, 18–19; as supportive, 36, 47
religion: founders' prejudices, 40–41; influence on curriculum, 137–38; influence on women's education, 6, 9, 14–16, 144, 155; racial desegration and, 149–53
Republican Motherhood, 5–7

research advocating female higher education, 182–83, 186, 190–91
residential patterns, shifting in Baltimore, 61–62, 95–97, 101–2
Rogers, Julia Rebecca, 15, 18, 37, 40
Roland Park Country School, 124, 152, 175, 193; as competitor, 95, 97, 101, 106–7, 110–11, 118

Sadker, David, 182, 194
Sadker, Myra, 182, 194
salary of faculty, 49, 70–71, 129; during Depression, 116–17, 119–20
scholarship programs, 30, 50, 53, 66, 119, 164
science: curriculum value, 27–28, 34, 37, 56, 121, 134, 159–60, 186, 197; gender-based differences, 92, 183–84, 187–88; new dialogue for achievement, 164, 182–92
second class educational citizenship, 183, 185
secondary education: coeducation model, 9–10, 20; twentieth-century reform, 88–89, 144–46
secretarial profession, 92–93
secretaries: founders' standards, 31, 36, 42; implementation role, 40–41, 48, 207n. 5
segregation, racial, 141, 143, 148
self-confidence in adolescence, 178, 180–81, 183–86, 194
self-esteem: development, 178, 180–81, 184; new dialogue for, 182–92, 194
self-support, 21, 31, 51–52, 64, 113, 119–20
seminary model of female schools, 3, 6–7, 9
Settlement movement, 64–65, 89
Seven Sister colleges, 11, 37, 69, 99, 133, 173
Sex in Education (Clarke), 33
sexism in modern schools, 183–85
single-sex education: advantages of all-girls school, 185–92; coordination of opposite gender programs, 159–60, 174–75, 193–94; disadvantages of all-girls schools, 192–96; origins, 9–10, 20, 97–98; recent understanding, 4, 173–76, 179–82; socially favored, 4, 25–26, 89, 171–72, 187